# Postcolonial Liberalism

CW01096099

*Postcolonial Liberalism* presents a compelling account of the challenges to liberal political theory by claims for cultural and political autonomy and land rights made by indigenous peoples today. It also confronts the sensitive issue of how liberalism has been used to justify and legitimate colonialism. Ivison argues that there is a pressing need to re-shape liberal thought to become more receptive to indigenous aspirations and modes of being. What is distinctive about the book is the middle way it charts between separatism, on the one hand, and assimilation, on the other. These two options present a false dichotomy as to what might constitute a genuinely postcolonial liberal society. In defending this ideal, the book addresses important recent debates over the nature of public reason, justice in multicultural and multinational societies, collective responsibility for the past, and clashes between individual and group rights.

**Duncan Ivison** teaches in the Department of Philosophy, University of Sydney. He is the author of *The Self at Liberty* (1997), and co-editor of *Political Theory and the Rights of Indigenous Peoples* (Cambridge University Press, 2000).

Out of the earth house I inherited
A stack of singular, cold memory weights
To load me, hand and foot, in the scale of things.

Seamus Heaney
'Squarings xl', *Seeing Things* (1991)

To Hamish and Isobel

# Postcolonial Liberalism

Duncan Ivison

*University of Sydney*

CAMBRIDGE
UNIVERSITY PRESS

PUBLISHED BY THE PRESS SYNDICATE OF THE UNIVERSITY OF CAMBRIDGE
The Pitt Building, Trumpington Street, Cambridge, United Kingdom

CAMBRIDGE UNIVERSITY PRESS
The Edinburgh Building, Cambridge CB2 2RU, UK
40 West 20th Street, New York, NY 10011–4211, USA
477 Williamstown Road, Port Melbourne, VIC 3207, Australia
Ruiz de Alarcón 13, 28014 Madrid, Spain
Dock House, The Waterfront, Cape Town 8001, South Africa

http://www.cambridge.org

First published 2002

Printed in China by Everbest Printing Co.

*Typeface* Plantin (Adobe) 10/12 pt.    *System* QuarkXPress®  [MAPG]

*A catalogue record for this book is available from the British Library*

*National Library of Australia Cataloguing in Publication data*
Ivison, Duncan, 1965–
Postcolonial liberalism.
Bibliography.
Includes index.
ISBN 0 521 82064 2.
ISBN 0 521 52751 1 (pbk.).
1. Liberalism. 2. Indigenous peoples. I. Title.
320.51

ISBN 0 521 82064 2 hardback
ISBN 0 521 52751 1 paperback

# Contents

*Preface and Acknowledgments*                                    viii

**Introduction: Why postcolonial liberalism?**                      1

**1  The liberal justificatory ideal**                             14

**2  The postcolonial challenge**                                  30

**3  Reason and community**                                        49

**4  Disagreement and public reason**                              72

**5  Historical injustice**                                        95

**6  The postcolonial state**                                     112

**7  Land, law and governance**                                   140

*Conclusion*                                                      163
*Notes*                                                           167
*Index*                                                           206

# Preface and Acknowledgments

When I was growing up in Montreal and was taught Canadian history for the first time at school, our teacher was a fluently bilingual Irish-Catholic Quebecois separatist. But what I remember most clearly from his lessons at the time was not so much the quintessentially Canadian juxtaposition of competing allegiances and cultural traditions he embodied – teaching as he was in an English-language Protestant school on the West Island – but the way he ruthlessly applied the logic of self-determination appealed to by Quebec nationalists to the situation of the Aboriginal peoples in Quebec. He suggested that Quebecois nationalism would be morally suspect if it did not find some way of accommodating the aspirations of those whose claims, in fact, pre-dated their own. It made a big impression on me. History all of a sudden became not simply a series of dates and names to remember, but also a series of complex moral arguments and concepts competing and changing across time and space (most of which then I barely understood). But later on, as I thought more about it, I became perplexed, because the problems of reconciling not just two, but now a whole array of distinct peoples and ways of life sharing the same territory seemed almost insurmountable. If Quebecois nationalism could be accommodated within a revamped Canadian state only with great difficulty (as it seemed at the time), what would it take to accommodate the claims of indigenous peoples?

I would like to think that the origins of this book lie in that classroom, and perhaps they do. I began to think about these problems again, this time in a very different academic setting, when I moved to Australia to take up my first academic appointment. It was soon after the High Court's groundbreaking *Mabo* decision, and questions about not just Aboriginal land rights, but about the moral character of the nation, and especially the moral relation between the past and the present were being hotly debated. In wrestling with these questions, and trying to join in the debates, I found myself constantly driven back to my residual liberal intuitions about the nature of distributive justice, moral responsibility, and political obligation and my increasing sense that they seemed ill-suited to addressing the claims Aboriginal people were making. Once again I was perplexed. If you were committed to roughly liberal egalitarian principles, was it possible to do justice to these claims? My unfamiliarity with Australian history, and the unique circumstances of Australian colonization, forced me to read up on it. In so doing I found myself revisiting the Canadian history I thought I knew well, which, as it turned out, I did not. And thus I found myself venturing into different disciplines and literatures, in search of alternative arguments and conceptual frameworks that might provide some new insight or angle that seemed to be missing from the existing philosophical literature.

Around this time I had also begun to become interested in the history of international political thought, in part out of a frustration with the existing theoretical material on globalization. The more I learned about the intellectual history of the justification of colonial expansion, as well as the complex forms of interaction that occurred between indigenous peoples and the early settlers in North American and Australasia, the more I became convinced that liberal political thought had deep and tangled roots in these histories. But what were the consequences of these histories for contemporary liberalism? I began to think it would take a book to properly address such a question, and what follows is the result. Some argue that we are entering a new era in which sub-state and trans-national political movements and institutions will redraw the geographic and intellectual map of world politics. I am excited by the prospect, but wary about just how it will work. Perhaps in studying the history of liberalism's entanglement with empire, the way indigenous difference has persisted in the face of colonialism, as well as how indigenous peoples have resisted, yet also co-opted and turned around aspects of liberal-democratic thought towards their own ends, we may just catch a glimpse of the possibilities of globalization from the bottom up.

I was very fortunate to have had the opportunity to present versions of the chapters below in many different settings, both academic and non-academic. I am particularly grateful to the many people at the various public forums I addressed in Australia, whose comments and questions pushed me to be much clearer about what I was trying to say. These forums were invaluable to me. My academic debts are also many and overwhelming. I am particularly grateful to Sue Mendus, Paul Patton, Matt Matravers, James Tully, Tim Rayner, Patrick Macklem and two other reviewers for Cambridge University Press, for reading portions of the manuscript, or indeed the entire thing (in some cases, more than once). I have failed to respond adequately to all the points and criticisms they raised, but the struggle to address at least some of them has, I hope, made the book far better than it might otherwise have been. I am especially grateful to Paul Patton, James Tully and William Connolly for the innumerable discussions and the help they have offered me as I have been working on this project.

I am also very grateful for the many invitations I have received over the past few years to speak at various universities in Australia, Canada, the United Kingdom and the United States. I am particularly grateful for the comments and help I have received in these instances from Mick Dodson, Charles Fox, Tim Rowse, Brian Barry, Simon Caney, Peter Jones, David Campbell, Melissa Lane, Annabel Brett, David Owen, Russell Bentley, Chris Brown, John Charvet, Janet Colemen, David Miller, John Horton, Jeremy Moss, Tony Coady, Robert Fullwinder, Philip Pettit, Robert Goodin, Will Kymlicka, William Connolly, Joseph Carens, Alan Patten, Paul Redding, Moira Gatens, Sue Dodds, Ian Hunter, Conal Condren, Jeff Minson, Chris Colegate, Matt Butt, Tim Rayner, John Maynor, Monica Mookherjee, Alex Callinicos, Audra Simpson, Andrew Fitzmaurice, Jeremy Webber and Tom Baldwin. Fiona Jenkins was a valuable interlocutor about some of the themes discussed in Chapters 2 and 4, and Tim Rowse put his encyclopedic knowledge of the history of Aboriginal politics in Australia at my disposal (which I plundered), as well as his razor-sharp analytical approach to these issues in general. I would also like to thank Barry Hindess for encouraging me – at an early stage – to pursue these questions and for providing the practical and moral support to do so. More recently, Moira Gatens has been a remarkable source of support as Head of Deparment at Sydney, as well as a valued colleague and friend. I am also extremely grateful to Quentin Skinner, both for his unstinting support and encouragement, and for the example of his work.

The University of Sydney Sesqui Research and Development Scheme provided crucial financial support over 2000–1, which enabled me to complete the penultimate draft of the book.

At CUP, Sharon Mullins and Phillipa McGuinness showed great enthusiasm for the original proposal and since then Peter Debus has been a helpful and supportive editor. I am also grateful to Paul Watt and Roger Bourke for their help in preparing the manuscript for publication.

Finally, to Di, Hamish and Isobel, I owe most of all. Their love and support sustains me, as always, and I would be lost without them.

Parts of Chapters 4, 5 and 7 draw on material which first appeared in 'Modus vivendi citizenship', in Iain Hampsher-Monk and Catriona Mackinnon (eds), *The demands of citizenship* (London, Continuum, 2000), pp. 123–143; 'Political Community and Historical Injustice', *Australasian Journal of Philosophy*, 78, 3 (2000) 360–373; and 'Decolonizing the rule of law: *Mabo*'s case and postcolonial constitutionalism', *Oxford Journal of Legal Studies*, 17,2 (1997). I am grateful to the publishers for allowing some of this material to be used here. The extract from Seamus Heaney's poem 'Squarings x 1' is reprinted from *Seeing Things*, copyright and permission from Faber and Faber.

# Introduction: Why postcolonial liberalism?

Why postcolonial liberalism? In Australia, where this has been written, public debate between indigenous and non-indigenous peoples has been mired, more often than not, in mutual recrimination and misunderstanding.[1] Perhaps this is to be expected, and the experience is not unique to Australia. The matters are complex, explosive and rub up against deep political and cultural issues, both symbolic and material. They involve, for example, questions about the moral character of the nation, the nature of justice and the struggle against poverty and social and cultural alienation. People of good faith will disagree and argue about these things. The answers are not easy to come by.

This book attempts to present a larger picture within which to consider these questions, beyond the technicalities of legal doctrine and the bureaucratic imperatives of public policy. The idea is to craft a conceptual and discursive framework within which the argument between indigenous and non-indigenous peoples can be carried out on a more satisfactory footing than has hitherto been the case. It is presented from a non-indigenous perspective, building on mainly non-indigenous intellectual resources and tools. There will be, and increasingly are, important indigenous perspectives on these issues making their way into public debate. Aboriginal law and politics in Australasia and North America involve a sophisticated and overlapping set of practices, discourses and bodies of knowledge, drawing on indigenous and non-indigenous sources, both domestic and international. What postcolonial liberalism aspires to is articulating a space within liberal democracies and liberal thought in which these Aboriginal perspectives and philosophies can not only be heard, but given equal opportunity to shape (and reshape) the forms of power and government acting on them. But to do this, liberals can not simply prescribe *a priori* a place within their existing conceptual schemes and political structures into which to slot indigenous people's claims but rather grasp the ways in which they challenge fundamental liberal notions of public reason, citizenship and justice. 'Both ways' learning is required if mutually acceptable arrangements are to be arrived at. We do not live, as yet, in a postcolonial world, and perhaps never will, and this is especially true of the situation of indigenous people around the world today. So the ideal sketched here remains just that – an ideal – and is offered from only one side of the table.

The book is intended, then, as a hopefully positive and constructive contribution to public debate about these issues in Australasia and North America in particular. But it has another aim too. This is to contribute to an important debate in contemporary political philosophy about the best way of conceiving of the fit between liberal institutions and the social, cultural, and political diversity of modern societies. The situation of and demands made by Aboriginal peoples in contemporary liberal democracies present an acute challenge for these broader philosophical debates. I shall consider, in particular, the demand it presents to an important strand of contemporary liberal political theory – John Rawls's conception of 'political liberalism'. I do this, in part, to show how contemporary political philosophy – despite the often arid ways in which it is presented and discussed – is importantly related to some of the biggest public issues of the day. But I also think doing so sheds light on the kinds of values and issues at stake in our public arguments about not just Aboriginal rights, but about what our political communities look like and should aspire to be in these late-modern times.

The basic argument of the book is that the values and practices appealed to by both indigenous and non-indigenous peoples are best realized in a particular kind of liberal political order. This political order is one characterized by an ideal of complex mutual coexistence; *complex* because the legitimacy of such an order depends upon mutual engagement and cooperation between the parties, rather than hostility or studied indifference. And that means discovering modes of interacting and communicating that are acceptable to and effective for the parties involved, especially given the extent to which they are also internally differentiated. My claim will be that liberal practices and institutions have the greatest chance of being endorsed and supported, and resulting in political arrangements which are just, when they emerge out of and combine with the complexity of local environments and frameworks, and most importantly, with the dynamic forces therein. This is in part a general point about how complex social systems and networks actually work, but also a political one, as I hope to show.[2]

One of the most striking examples of this notion is the way that indigenous activists and theorists have taken up, used and reshaped the language(s) of rights. This has occurred within countries such as Australia, Canada and the United States, but also at the international level, in the attempt to draft an international 'Declaration of the Rights of Indigenous Peoples'. But what are 'Aboriginal rights'? Philosophers understand rights, generally speaking, as expressions of a particular kind of a justification or demand that certain important or urgent interests be protected or promoted in particular (especially institutional) ways.[3] There can be legal and moral rights. Human rights seem to fall somewhere in between. Legal rights presuppose some kind of legal system, both formal and informal. A statute or constitution, as long as it is itself definite about this, gives rise to rights, connected as they are to a visible system of enforcement. Moral rights involve more general assertions, of the kind when we say everyone within some specified set should have 'equal rights', that is, everyone should be treated equally or given equal consideration.[4] But specific assertions of rights are always particular demands of some kind, a claim that people *ought* to have X, not something that in itself *justifies* that claim. To do that, some argument will have to be given, and then some way of translating that argument into an effective mechanism for implementation and enforcement. So: to say A has a right to X against Y means that some interest of A is important enough to hold Y under some kind of obligation to provide A with X, if X furthers that interest.[5] Precisely because rights ultimately rest on moral beliefs and claims of this kind they are subject to disagreement. The extension of the abstract concept is subject to change over time and space according to historical and contextual circumstances.

On the one hand, it is clear that the discourse of rights has been imposed on indigenous peoples, and often with terrible consequences: 'these intellectual traditions have created discourses on property, ethics, political sovereignty, and justice that have subjugated, distorted, and marginalized Aboriginal ways of thinking'.[6] Taiaiake Alfred has argued that

'Aboriginal rights' are in fact the benefits accrued by indigenous peoples who have agreed to abandon their autonomy in order to enter the legal and political framework of the state. After a while, indigenous freedoms become circumscribed and indigenous rights get defined not with respect to what exists in the minds and cultures of Native people, but in relation to the demands, interests, and opinions of the millions of other peoples who are also members of that single-sovereign community ... .[7]

This is an extremely plausible, if depressing, hypothesis. Because we do not discover rights out there, pre-existing us, but create and evaluate them in light of our existing moral beliefs and our practical and historical situation, the intrusion of relations of power here is no less likely then in any other aspect of our social and political lives.

On the other hand, precisely because rights are not foundational to political evaluation and justification, and that proposing any particular set of rights is always in some sense a strategic decision, it does not follow that rights discourse is therefore inherently corrupt.[8] There may be times when, in fact, it is a very effective course of action to pursue. Thus some Aboriginal theorists and activists have begun developing and articulating their own understandings of what follows from asserting Aboriginal claims as rights. As Dale Turner has argued, in Canada (and, I would argue, in Australia and New Zealand too), 'Native Law' has become the subject of not only growing interest and sophistication on the part of non-Aboriginal scholars, but increasingly Aboriginal ones too, and their re-articulation of Aboriginal rights from within these distinctive frameworks and idioms could begin to reshape all of our – meaning both indigenous and non-indigenous – understandings of them as well. Thus the 'common law doctrine of Aboriginal rights', is *common* law, it is argued, in the sense that it does not originate from the Crown or Parliament, but is based upon the rights of Aboriginal nations as these were recognized 'in the custom generated by relations between these nations and [European settlers] since the seventeenth century'. What distinguishes them is that they are neither entirely Aboriginal nor European in origin; '[t]he doctrine not only forms a bridge between the different societies, it is a bridge constructed from both sides'.[9]

Thus postcolonial liberalism fails if 'Aboriginal rights' do, in fact, come to embody only the reality of *extant* relations of power so vividly described by Alfred. I am committed to arguing that the ideal of complex mutual existence does not result in Aboriginal ways of life, and the concepts developed in public reason to express the values and practices that make up those ways of life, being liberalized in the wrong way. That is, of being converted or translated in ways that undermine or distort indigenous people's own best understanding of those ways of life. Michael Sandel once asked what marriage would be like if it became 'liberalized', that is, if spontaneous affection and generosity between partners gave way to demands of fairness and the observance of rights.[10] There is a good response to Sandel's argument, but the general drift of the question is penetrating, at least for anyone defending liberal political arrangements. The worry is that although liberal public reason is meant to be compatible with different ethical and cultural ways of being in the world, and is not *intended* to supplant them, what if in fact it does? How should we conceive of the impact of liberal public arrangements on these (as liberals think of them) 'non-public' domains?

This aspect of the book is important because sometimes the discussion of these issues by liberals implies that claims made by groups like indigenous peoples are always presumptively suspect. Assuming, for example, that all of these claims boil down to the demand that these groups 'should be able to discriminate with impunity'[11] against their own members, completely ignores the complex ways in which indigenous peoples have struggled to combine, reshape and at the same time, hang on to their own values and practices in the face of the dominant institutions and values of liberal democracies.

For some, the idea of liberalism 'going local', as I have suggested it should, is an insidious one, representing a sophisticated form of liberal imperialism or 'governmentality'. For others, it is an unnecessary one: an unpalatable pact with particularism and a forsaking of genuine liberal cosmopolitanism. These objections are understandable, but ultimately misplaced. The aim of my argument is not to provide a justification for soft or benign liberal imperialism, if there is such a thing. I am not seeking to provide an account of when it is reasonable or just to impose liberal institutions on non-liberal cultures or states. For one reason, I think that way of characterizing the problem is fundamentally mistaken. The world is not easily divided up between liberal and non-liberal cultures or peoples. Instead, I am seeking to provide an account of liberal institutions and norms that might gain the reasoned support of those subject to them, and in this particular case, on the part of peoples who have experienced a long history of injustice at the hands of liberal-democratic states. This history of unjust interaction is a complicating feature of the kind of cultural pluralism faced by liberal states. Since we are never in a position to choose social and political norms, practices or institutions *de novo*, but instead work with the imperfect and unjust arrangements we have, sometimes the very institutions we assume to be pluralism-friendly have been experienced by others in a radically different way.

In a nutshell, then, postcolonial liberalism aims to draw on liberal political thought in order to offer a different framework for relations between indigenous and non-indigenous peoples, from a non-indigenous perspective. The search for reasons that *both* indigenous and non-indigenous peoples can share is on-going, and will not be settled here; there are no 'neutral reasons' out there waiting to be discovered or unwrapped. I want to try and persuade liberals and indigenous peoples, as well as critics of liberalism, that such a project is not only important but viable; that there really is enough room within the liberal tradition for such possibilities. In so doing, postcolonial liberalism must address a whole series of arguments that suggest this is not possible; that it means relativizing liberalism and thus gutting it, or that liberalism is so tainted by its colonial past that any such project is doomed from the beginning.

In the end, postcolonial liberalism builds on three distinctive liberal values: that individuals and peoples are fundamentally equal; that they are free; and that social and political arrangements should be such as to promote the well-being of individuals and groups in the manner, generally speaking, that they conceive of it. Of course each leaves tremendous

scope for interpretation. Liberalism admits of a wide range of variations
and combinations of all three. Again, this is important to emphasize.
Sometimes in debates about multiculturalism and group rights, it is
presumed that liberalism is always opposed, in principle, to any kinds of
intermediary bodies or local forms of autonomy, for fear of the threat to
individual freedom they might pose. But there is a long debate *within*
liberal political thought between those who are suspicious about inter-
mediaries between the citizen and the state (such as radical republicans
and democrats), and those who think that intermediary bodies perform
a crucial task in promoting and preserving freedom, rather than undermining it (such as Montesquieu, Burke or Madison).

Note an immediate tension in postcolonial liberalism: the acceptance
of the centrality of disagreement about political values such as justice,
and yet an appeal to substantive values to do with democracy, equality,
freedom and well-being. There is no avoiding this tension. For there is
no way of arguing about the best way to proceed in light of our disagreements about justice which does not appeal to potentially controversial
ethical premises. My argument will be that the values of postcolonial
liberalism condition, but do not necessarily determine, the way people
live their lives according to their own lights.[12] There is no avoiding
conditioning goods in our social and political lives whether explicit or
implicit, constraining or enabling. We are all subject to direct and indirect actions on our actions as individuals and as members of groups and
associations. From basic norms of coordination to thicker and more
complex cultural, social and political norms, we are all governed, in the
broadest sense of the term, in a multitude of ways. Relations of power
are ubiquitous. Reconciling this fact with our familiar notions of freedom, both personal and collective, is a complicated task, and although
not the exclusive focus of this book, an important aspect of postcolonial
liberalism. One of the deep questions the book is wrestling with, and
with political liberalism in general, is this: Where should the most
important work of social construction or reshaping be done in a free
society, and how?[13]

It is sometimes argued that a theory of justice should aim to provide
the capacities that enable a citizen to feel 'at home in the world', by
which is meant that a person not be alienated from the central institutions and practices of her society. More positively, to be at home in the
world is to be able to identify with those institutions and practices, to
see the norms and ends as expressed in the public life of her community as ones that are connected to her flourishing. And it is not just
about feelings. These institutions and practices should actually help
make her life go better; 'being at home' is not only about a warrantable
attitude to the world, but standing in a particular concrete relation to it.

One's subjective attitude to the arrangements of one's social and political world is crucial, but is also shaped and affected by those very arrangements.[14] Hence these arrangements must also be justifiable in some such way that being at home in the world is not simply a way of resigning or accommodating oneself to injustice.

There are stronger and weaker accounts of the need to be at home in the world. Hegel provides perhaps the most comprehensive and powerful account of this need, putting what he refers to as 'reconciliation' at the very centre of not only his political philosophy, but arguably of political philosophy in general.[15] For Hegel, I am at home in the world when it is no longer alien to me; when I grasp how it makes possible the actualization of *both* my true individuality and social membership (or 'expressive unity').[16] As Charles Taylor puts it, an unalienated life is one in which 'the institutional matrix in which [I] cannot help [live] in is not felt to be foreign [but] is the essence, the "substance" of the self'.[17]

On a weaker reading, I am at home in the world if and only if I am not alienated from the central institutions and practices of my society; when I can identify with them and see the norms and values expressed therein as valuable and relevant to my flourishing, but not necessarily on the grounds of a shared evaluation of the good or the unfolding of Reason (in the Hegelian sense[18]). In other words, my sense of being at home in the world comes from not being alienated from the 'basic structure' (in John Rawls's phrase) of society, and in having my individuality and social membership actualized through the provision of 'basic liberties' and 'primary goods' compatible with a wide range of different conceptions of the good. To use Rawlsian language, this is a 'political' conception of being at home in the world as opposed to a more comprehensive one.[19]

Interestingly, Rawls himself sometimes conceives of the project of political philosophy in a Hegelian vein. 'Our exercise of political power', he writes, 'is … justifiable only when it is exercised in accordance with a constitution the essentials of which all citizens may reasonably be expected to endorse in light of principles and ideals acceptable to them as reasonable and rational'.[20] The aim, Rawls argues, is 'free agreement, reconciliation through public reason'; of people being able to endorse the institutions and practices amongst which they live, rather than merely tolerate them.[21]

The idea of reconciliation through public reason provides an important undercurrent to this book, and especially the relation between normative claims about public reason and the historical, cultural and practical contexts in which they are made. For it is a further claim of Rawls's that convergence on principles of justice embodied in a liberal constitutional regime and informing an ideal of public reason, can reconcile us to conflicts deriving from citizens' 'different status, class position, and occupation or from their ethnicity, gender and race'.[22] In fact, Rawls argues, political philosophy can help 'calm our frustration and rage against the social world by showing us the way in which its institutions, when properly understood from a philosophical point of view, are rational, and developed over time as they did to attain their present, rational form'.[23]

There are a number of objections that can be made to such a claim. Most fundamentally, it could be argued that to even think of the social world as a home in any other sense than the trivial one that there is nowhere else for us to be, is to presuppose what is precisely, philosophically speaking at least, what is at issue (i.e. why think of the world as a home in the first place?).[24] It might be, for example, that feeling at home in the world is simply not feasible; it just is a metaphysical fact that the social world is not and cannot be a home for people like us.[25] Indeed, many contemporary social and political theorists emphasize the radical disjointedness of late-modernity, and the need to face up to it without hope of reconciliation. This has been emphasized with particular force by many postcolonial writers, who form a special focus of this book. The postcolonial subject, on this rendering, is characterized precisely by the in-betweenness or hybridity of the relations she has with the world. She is, it seems, inescapably homeless.

These are powerful objections, and to a certain extent, well taken. One problem they raise, however, is the extent to which the logic of an objection based on the affirmation of difference or disjointedness undermines the possibilities for *any* legitimate sense of belonging. If the claim is not simply that liberals get it wrong, but that there is a form of affirmation or belonging that does not misconstrue the nature of our social world, or illegitimately homogenize otherness, then the onus is on those critics to produce such an account.

Recent liberal discussions have argued that cultural or national belonging, other things being equal, is valuable and deserving of political and institutional support insofar as it helps individuals overcome alienation from their social world (e.g. by providing a 'context for choice'), and contributes to fostering the intersubjective trust and mutual identification required for re-distributive justice to be realized.[26] But everything hangs on the 'other things being equal' proviso. When is the value of cultural membership, for example, outweighed by other more general considerations? When is the demand for feeling at home in the world, cashed out as the right or capacity to live according to culturally specific norms or practices, unreasonable? Why should the state subsidize any particular cultural structure (or choices), rather than simply ensure everyone has reasonable access to some kind of cultural goods?

## The plan of the book

The run of chapters will proceed as follows. In the next chapter, I outline the liberal justificatory ideal and some of the more general challenges that the claims of indigenous peoples present to it. In Chapter 2, I get more specific, and identify *four* key arguments that constitute the postcolonial challenge to liberalism: claims about liberalism's individualism, its 'abstract rationalism', the narrowness of its conception of justice, and the need for 'complex identification'. In Chapter 3, I begin to canvass possible liberal answers to these challenges. First, it is important to get a sense of the kind of pluralism at issue. It is not always a conflict of fundamentally incommensurable values (although at the limit, it can be), as between different weightings and trade-offs of values based on different perspectives.[27] The same ends, in other words, might be shared by different communities but the trade-offs between them (e.g. freedom vs social order) might be radically different. Two broad themes which the postcolonial challenge touch upon here are (1) the relation between reason and community, and (2) what David Copp has called the 'problem of political division'. The postcolonial critique of liberalism raises serious questions about liberalism's individualism and abstract rationalism, both of which feature in the story of its historical complicity with colonialism. I attempt to show that, at least with regard to the charge of individualism, the matter is much more complex. Connecting the debate between liberalism and communitarianism to 'the problem of political division', I attempt to show how liberalism has the resources to accommodate the value of communal goods in any number of ways, although there are important questions about the limits according to which these goods can be pursued. The determination of these limits requires paying attention not only to the principles and large-scale normative questions involved, but also the historical, cultural and practical contexts in which the goods are appealed to.

The rest of the book takes up this challenge. The charge of abstract rationalism is a strong one, I believe, and requires careful consideration. For it is often the case that normative political theorists do underplay the extent to which public deliberation is shot through with historical and practical features difficult to transcend or set to one side. Hence, in Chapter 4, I explore *five* dimensions of public reason (power, procedure, practice, *modus vivendi* and affect), paying particular attention to the way presumptions about the transparency and accessibility of political communication are connected to the legitimacy of political institutions. Each dimension features in different combinations and emphases in various arguments addressing the claims of ethnic and cultural minorities, and each has advantages and disadvantages that I shall seek to highlight. In the end, I shall defend a mode of public reason geared more to an ideal of what I shall call a *discursive modus vivendi*, as opposed to a Rawlsian 'overlapping consensus', or the Habermasian strategy of trying to derive principles of equal and universal participation in the practices of public reason from the logic of communicative action. Rather, I ask: can the justificatory project of egalitarian liberalism be redeemed *given* the history of relations between indigenous peoples and the liberal state over the past five centuries?

Chapter 5 develops this alternative ideal of public reason by considering one of the most important features of the discourse around Aboriginal rights, namely, questions over the consequences of historical injustice. Conflicting attitudes to historical time produce intense and often divisive public disagreements. Thus a crucial feature of postcolonial societies is disagreement over the legacy of colonial domination with regard to matters of justice. I shall attempt to do two things in this chapter. First, to use consideration of what is at stake in disagreements about historical time as a means of elaborating on the idea of public reason sketched in Chapter 4. And second, to begin laying the groundwork for the discussion of the postcolonial state in Chapter 6. If postcolonial liberalism appeals to the values of equality, freedom and well-being as conditioning goods – as goods which condition but do not determine the way people live according to their own values – then there will be an important and distinctive role for the state (as well as for transnational authorities) to play. This is particularly true in the case of relations between the liberal state and groups such as indigenous peoples. But the only way the state can play a justice-enhancing role in this context is if the legacy of domination and injustice that has characterized those relations is addressed. As Chapter 5 attempts to show, this has proved to be a very difficult challenge for many liberal theories of justice.

So what is the nature of the postcolonial state? The danger is always that the politics of recognition, if conceived of too literally, can promote the telescoping and hardening of cultural and political identities that are, in fact, always internally differentiated and inherently dynamic. Identities are dynamic in the sense that they are constituted as much by our response to others and to the context we find ourselves in, as they are the product of processes of self-identification and determination. The opportunity to express dissent, to try and reshape and rework the norms and practices amongst which one lives can only be preserved in a state where the capacities for doing so are promoted and secured. Hence the need to say something about the nature of these capacities, and how a postcolonial state (in a postcolonial international system of states) can help promote them.

If disagreement is central to postcolonial liberalism then the individuals and groups that make up postcolonial states must be able to live with the decisions and policies that emerge from politics, and the only way this is possible is if they are able to feel that they can effectively participate in the formation and shaping of public debate and policy making, as well as live with the 'losses' that will inevitably result. This means that the postcolonial state will obviously be a democratic one, but the question then is, to what extent do democratic norms provide a reasonable standard for evaluating local decision procedures and social practices, given our acceptance of the persistence of disagreement about justice?

A large part of the discussion in Chapter 6 will therefore be taken up with asking what the conditions must be, in the case of relations between indigenous and non-indigenous peoples, such that the outcomes of politics could be acceptable to both parties, building on the earlier discussion of public reason. The main aim of the postcolonial state is to minimize domination, and pursuing equal recognition for indigenous peoples in the public sphere is a means to that end.[28] But at the same time, the postcolonial state must ensure that its citizens, whatever their background, have the capacities to contest and modify the norms, practices, and rules that govern them. In developing this ideal I shall draw, in part, on some of the recent work on a 'capabilities' approach to distributive justice. This offers an interesting way, I think, of coping with the objection that liberal theories of justice tend to underestimate or ignore the relation between the social, cultural and political location of citizens and their access to 'primary goods' (as well as the apparent abstractness and cultural particularity of such goods). It also offers a way of defending Aboriginal rights in a way other than relying on the securing of 'culture' as the be all and end all of different forms of collective rights. Thus, I will elaborate and defend what I shall call a *normative thesis* underlying Aboriginal rights, which attempts to connect the specific rights of indigenous peoples as they understand them, to general principles in the public sphere. It is crucial to see how these rights are not only about culture, but also about interests in land and self-government. One way of grasping these interests, I shall argue, is that they constitute a distinctive kind of 'capability set' that helps indigenous peoples secure their effective freedom.

The key, however – and this is where we depart from some of the capabilities literature – is to see the determination of basic 'capabilities' or 'functionings' as *itself* wrapped up in a dynamic and ultimately political set of processes oriented by local practices. This will require paying attention to the way democracy can be linked to the project of liberalism going local, and especially to the notion that the currency of liberal justice is 'irreducibly heterogeneous'. Postcolonial liberalism aims to ensure that it is the members of various groups themselves who are in a position to modify and reshape, as much as is possible, the norms, practices and rules that act on them. The twin aims of the postcolonial state – that is, minimizing domination whilst also promoting the capacities of individuals and groups to modify and contest the norms and practices that govern them – are difficult to conjoin.

Finally, in Chapter 7, I shall attempt to put postcolonial liberalism to work. What difference does it make in considering some of the pressing problems faced by indigenous communities today? What happens if indigenous understandings of the interests protected and promoted by Aboriginal rights conflict with liberal understandings of basic rights? I shall consider three models for dealing with these conflicts – the core-periphery, deliberative and institutional design models – and evaluate each with regard to the values of postcolonial liberalism. The discussion of these concrete examples will draw on mainly Australian, Canadian and, to a lesser extent, American contexts. But I hope it will give a sense of how the conceptual work done in earlier chapters might work *in situ*. The importance of a 'problem-driven' or contextual approach to political theory has been promoted by a number of political theorists in recent years, especially with regard to multiculturalism and the claims of national groups, and this book follows in that spirit.[29]

Some of the issues addressed by postcolonial liberalism involve matters of high moral and political principle. But perhaps we get closest to its essence when we turn to the more everyday and micro-political level, where matters of historical and cultural interpretation, openness to institutional (re)innovation, and the building of cross-cultural norms of trust and cooperation at the most basic levels of social interaction loom large. In many ways, the real test of postcolonial liberalism is not so much finding the right set of principles to orient social and political practice, but the manner in which already existing liberal institutions and norms remain open to the variety of ways indigenous peoples have attempted to sustain, adapt, and change their ways of life from the ground up over centuries. To be oriented according to local knowledges and practices in this way, I think, is to come closest to what postcolonial liberalism ultimately involves. This aspect is difficult to theorize about, let alone promote through institutional design. We are born into a complex of norms, practices and institutions with which we must work and try to reshape as best we can. Although the prospects for the apparently far-reaching nature of indigenous claims in contemporary liberal democracies might seem, on the surface, to be very dim, it would be a mistake to become too pessimistic. In fact, there have already been tremendous changes in the way contemporary liberal democratic states and their citizens have conceived of relations with indigenous populations compared to even twenty years ago, let alone over a century ago. The bulk of changes for the good have come as a result of indigenous people's everyday practical struggles to assert and sustain their identities, interests, cultures, practices – their forms of life – through cultural, political and legal activism, against huge odds. What can we learn from these struggles and changes? In what ways do they prefigure new visions or possibilities for the way we think about liberal societies and the nature of justice and political belonging? This is one of the deep questions motivating much of the discussion in this book.

# 1    The liberal justificatory ideal

*Q*: Do you think that liberalism is, in this sense, essentially European, then? Or Western?

*Berlin*: Yes. I suspect that there may not be much liberalism in Korea. I doubt if there is much liberalism even in Latin America. I think liberalism is essentially the belief of people who have lived on the same soil for a long time in comparative peace with each other. An English invention. The English have not been invaded for a very, very long time. That's why they can afford to praise these virtues. I see that if you were exposed to constant pogroms you might be a little more suspicious of the possibility of liberalism.[1]

## The ideal

Contemporary liberals, as I understand them, have a special commitment to public justification.[2] Liberalism aims to justify the political arrangements of a state, and arguably the world, to each and every person subject to those arrangements. And yet almost every state, and by implication the international order of states, is the product of a combination of historical contingency, force, fraud and injustice. Even more to the point, we are born into a complex of norms, practices and institutions that are imperfect and unjust which we reproduce even in the midst of trying to reshape and reform them. So what is the point of the justificatory ideal? It seems impossible to begin with. How is it relevant to a consideration of the claims of indigenous peoples in liberal democracies today?

But first, to put it bluntly; why care so much about indigenous people's claims? Such people usually constitute a very small proportion of the general population of the states in which they live.[3] One answer is that there is a sense in which, as Ross Poole has put it, the expropriation of Aboriginal lands and the forced assimilation or outright elimination of Aboriginal peoples represents the 'original sin' of liberal democracies such as Australia, Canada, New Zealand, and the United States, and to a different extent, those in Central and South America.[4] The historical injustices committed against them in the process of settler nation-building seem to persist into the present in ways that affect internal as well as external perceptions of the moral character and national identity of these societies. Secondly, the situation of most indigenous peoples poses an acute and urgent challenge to any liberal-democrat committed to social justice. They are consistently amongst the most disadvantaged people on earth according to any number of different socio-economic indicators; suffering from poorer health, education, life-expectancy, employment prospects, as well as being more likely to end up in jail, than most of their fellow citizens. Anyone concerned about justice should be concerned about these facts.

But also, in a world full of ethnic, religious and cultural conflict (ones in which indigenous peoples often feature[5]), how liberal-democratic states cope with the claims of cultural minorities such as indigenous peoples has potentially far-reaching consequences for how other states cope with minority groups within their borders. The history of relations between settler states and indigenous peoples is one of violence and historical injustice; current relations are often characterized by mistrust and misunderstanding; the socio-economic situation of indigenous peoples is too often one of terrible disadvantage; and popular perceptions as to what needs to be done about the situation are often indifferent, and at worst, actively hostile. These historical, social and economic features recur, in their own distinctive ways and contexts, in relation to other 'stateless nations' in many parts of the world. Developing peaceful and effective ways of addressing these claims is thus of critical importance for many states today, as well as for the emerging architecture of global political institutions and international law.

Indigenous claims are also beginning to attract some very close theoretical attention on the part of contemporary political theorists. Not because, as some have suggested, they are the easy option when it comes to considering cultural difference;[6] or because of some new-age inspired attraction middle-class academics have for supposedly pre-modern cultures; or because the consequences of recognizing indigenous claims are essentially benign. Rather, indigenous claims have attracted attention because they strike at the heart of liberal conceptions of political community and justice. In particular, I shall argue, they present a considerable challenge to the *justificatory* ambitions of egalitarian liberalism.

Before going any further I should be more explicit about what I mean by liberalism. Liberalism is a complex of evolving discourses, beliefs and ideals, as opposed to a static tradition. In fact, it is such a 'vital, politi-cally, morally, and ideologically engaged movement' – that it probably 'has no definition'.[7] But that does not prevent us from trying to identify certain particular features or problems that remain central to it. There have been at least two basic problems that have fed into the development of much liberal political thought since the early modern period.[8] First, the attempt to fix some moral limits to the powers of government. And second, the struggle to cope with the consequences of what Rawls has called 'the fact of reasonable pluralism': the fact that people disagree pro-foundly, and often violently, about a great many aspects of what consti-tutes a good life. Liberalism thus asks, amongst other things; under what terms and conditions can people nonetheless live together peacefully in political association? Deep social and political diversity complicates attempts to answer the first problem. If power is to be fixed by moral limits then citizens will have to agree as to what these moral grounds are, and such agreement is elusive. Hence the emergence of the idea of the *neutrality* of the liberal state. A liberal political order is said to be neutral with regard to controversial conceptions of the good. Note that it remains a moral ideal. It aims to justify political principles that do not rely on controversial conceptions of the good, but which can still pro-vide grounds for regulating the exercise of the coercive power of the state that citizens holding diverse worldviews could accept.

Neutrality has come under withering attack in recent years, from both within and outside of liberalism.[9] The very word 'neutrality' leads to misunderstanding. As a procedural ideal, it is intended to mean that political norms governing the exercise of power should not discriminate against any reasonable conception of the good or way of life. But of course, since the procedural ideal is itself based upon particular inter-pretations of moral conceptions of freedom and equality, the effects of these norms will entail that some communal or cultural practices will, in fact, be ruled out in liberal societies, and others will fare less well than liberal ones over the long run. Neutrality of aim is not the same as neu-trality of effect.[10]

For our purposes, however, there is something still misleading about describing even the reasons offered for state action as 'neutral'. For it risks a kind of false impartiality not only because states cannot, practically, remain neutral with regard to many public matters cultural, historical and political, but because the whole idea of 'neutral reasons' seems problem-atic. There may, in fact, be such reasons – and the whole idea of public reason, as we shall see, trades off this possibility – but in the end they are only 'neutral' because they are grounded in explicitly liberal kinds of reasoning processes. It is not clear why someone who is inclined to reject liberal grounds would be moved to change his mind if they were presented to him as 'neutral' reasons. He needs to be persuaded of the reasonableness of liberalism, not brought to see the neutrality of the reasons he is offered. Thus, given the history of relations between indigenous people and the state, it is not only pragmatically wrong-headed but morally misplaced to ask indigenous people to imagine the state as 'neutral' in any such way. It has never been so and probably never will be, as far as indigenous peoples are concerned. Norms of fairness and impartiality are crucial for intercultural political interaction, as we shall see, but they depend for their emergence on an acknowledgment of the inescapably imperfect and partial nature of existing institutions and practices, and the substantive moral views upon which theories of justice as fairness or impartiality are based.

If it is difficult to imagine state action and the character of public reason as neutral, does this mean the state is justified in actively promoting a particular conception of the good? There is a difference between thinking the state cannot help but influence the character of civil society, and thus the kinds of beliefs individuals will ultimately hold and the lives they lead, and that it should actively promote a particular set of beliefs about what is the right or most valuable way to live.[11] But there is a further difference as to how even these kinds of values can best be promoted by the state, setting aside for now which particular set of values the postcolonial state should appeal to. And this is the idea that the state is justified in securing or promoting the conditions in which people will best be able to decide for themselves the justifiability and legitimacy of the norms that govern them – the processes through which people come to grasp and express their common status and interest as moral equals. Even the belief that all people are of equal moral worth can be promoted or acted upon by the state in ways that end up treating people unequally. (In fact, this is a feature of the history between liberalism and colonialism.) So if the state cannot be neutral, that is not to say it is justified in promoting whatever particular conception of the good it wants.

The state is said to be justified when it is deemed to be good in some way and thus deserving of our support or endorsement. A state is legitimate when it possesses the warrant to direct and coerce us in *specific* ways: for example, to force us to pay our taxes, put out the garbage on Mondays, or to punish us (for not paying our taxes, or putting the garbage out on Wednesday). The relation between legitimacy and justice is therefore complex. No state is perfectly just, but that hardly means it is illegitimate. The gap between legitimacy and justice is, obviously, a permanent feature of contemporary liberal democracies (thus there is hardly an *impending* 'legitimation crisis').[12] What changes is the sense of how much injustice we are prepared to live with, and how we draw and justify the relevant boundaries around that very 'we'.

The gold standard of legitimacy for liberals has traditionally been consent, and more specifically, informed voluntary consent. But taken in its strongest form, the implication is that no state is legitimate. No one has 'transacted' with the state in the morally relevant ways set as the benchmark by Lockeans. The standard goes wrong in two ways. First, societies that are impeccably voluntarist may also be illiberal. Individualism is insufficient as a value upon which to ground liberal institutions, however important it may be generally, since individuals might consent to all kinds of things that are harmful to themselves and more likely, to others. Second, our conduct is shaped and governed in such a way by the basic social, political and economic institutions of society as to influence not only the options we have, but also what interests, desires and capabilities we may have in the first place. In other words, to speak of our consenting to the main political institutions of society has to be heavily qualified to take into account the manner in which we are born into a whole complex of norms, practices and institutions we had no hand in choosing.

Moreover, the interactions between individuals and institutions in market societies breed complex networks of interdependence and causation that render a straightforward 'interactionist' approach to institutional evaluation itself somewhat incomplete, to put it mildly.[13]

The alternative ideal is that coercive political power should be justifiable on public grounds; on grounds that we *could* endorse, or at least not reasonably reject. How this commitment is spelled out varies greatly between different components of the liberal tradition. The danger of this approach, of course, is the worry about how my hypothetical consent – something I give only in highly structured thought experiments – *actually* bind me to anything, let alone to a modern state, especially given the kinds of things states do and ask of me?

Another way the commitment to public justification has manifested itself in recent years is an increasing emphasis on promoting more genuinely deliberative democracy. Deliberative democracy presents an ideal of a political community in which decisions about important public matters are reached through an open and un-coerced discussion that aims for an agreement that either all (in principle) can accept, or which at least minimizes disagreement. As Amy Gutmann and Dennis Thompson argue, 'deliberative democracy asks citizens and officials to justify public policy by giving reasons that can be accepted by those who are bound by it'.[14] 'Reciprocity' regulates public reason; '[t]he "good received" is that you make your claims on terms that I can accept in principle. The "proportionate return" is that I make may claims on terms that you can accept in principle'.[15]

Although there are real differences between these various ways of articulating a commitment to public justification, one thing they all express is a belief in the idea that 'reason is the tool by which the liberal state governs'. Indeed Jean Hampton calls this the 'common faith' of liberalism. Whatever the differences over the various conceptions of freedom, equality, democracy or modes of public justification, they all express a general commitment to 'rational argument and reasonable attitudes' aimed at procuring the general agreement of individuals through reason and persuasion rather than force.[16] Hampton accepts that there are different views on the nature of reason – for example between utilitarian and Kantian notions of practical reason, and furthermore between differing accounts of how morality is actually 'based on' reason. However the underlying point is crucial; human beings share a common faculty for reasoning, and it is upon this that a liberal polity must build its foundations. For Hampton, reason is capable of revealing the truth about matters that are central to our political life: 'The liberal reliance on reason to produce order is … not based on the idea that reason can hand us the moral truth any time soon, but on the idea that it can provide us with a political process and structure enabling us to work out what each of us believes, and to deal with the inevitable differences in our beliefs civilly, and peacefully'.[17]

There are stronger and weaker versions of this liberal faith in reason. Rawls famously argues that his theory is 'political' and not metaphysical, and thus is ultimately agnostic about the truth status of its claims. He thinks reasonable people will disagree over metaphysical questions (reason is indeterminate about these matters, though not about everything), but that it is nevertheless possible for them to converge on a more limited set of views about a 'political conception' of justice.[18] Some think such agnosticism lamentable and ultimately incoherent, others that it could be taken further,[19] and still others that Rawls is not actually as agnostic as he claims.[20] But whatever the ultimate metaphysical status of the theory, Rawls is still committed to the idea of citizens, reasoning together, establishing the common ground upon which to determine fair and reasonable terms of social cooperation. His theory still aims to 'formulate a coherent view of the very great (moral) values applying to the political relationship and to set out a public basis for justification for free institutions in a manner accessible to free public reason'.[21]

How could such a commitment to public justification be hostile to indigenous claims? Would not a commitment to justifying the exercise of political power and the distribution of benefits and burdens in ways that no one can reasonably reject be an essential component of meeting them? To be sure, as much as it has been a common faith of liberalism to realize a transparent and ultimately acceptable social and political order for all, it remains – like most faiths – still to be redeemed. But to criticize a political ideal for being idealistic is hardly a devastating objection.

The nature of reasonableness is important to consider, especially in light of the critiques of liberalism made by postcolonial theory (which we shall be exploring in chapter 2). How we come to understand what constitutes a reasonable conception of the good, or a reasonable conception of harm or individual responsibility will have important consequences for adjudging the overall reasonableness of indigenous claims. One thing that does not follow from such considerations is that – 'Reason' or 'Reasonableness' needs to be rejected altogether. Rather, I agree with something Michel Foucault once said: the crucial question is 'What is this Reason that we use? What are its historical effects? What are its limits and what are its dangers?'[22] Consider, for a moment, the point about the role of truth in political argument. If what is 'right' about political arrangements is right simply because of what people happen to believe, given their experience and the available evidence, then this seems a justification of the status quo, which is worrying, especially if it happens to include a great deal of social and economic inequality. If, on the other hand, what is 'right' about political arrangements is right in virtue of the 'commonly accepted standards of rational belief formation'[23] in that society, then everything will depend on how those 'commonly accepted' ways of forming beliefs are understood. If the beliefs according to which political arrangements are legitimated are reasonable in virtue of standards provided by the particular culture and history of a political society, then what about those societies or cultures with the wrong kinds of practices? If the standards of reasonableness are meant to be objective, in the sense of independent of cultural practices and history, then how are these standards actually accessible to citizens with regard to highly contestable and often ambiguous political questions?[24] By virtue of the fact that reasoning is a basic capacity or ability common to all human beings?

Remember that the advantage of the Lockean account of legitimacy was that it showed very clearly the relation between the actual historical choices of a person or community and their relation to the state. The legitimacy of the state, and my obligation to obey its directives, does not derive from the *attitude* I have towards it, but the manner in which I have actually transacted with it. But this means relying upon an impossibly strong condition of consent. However, if we reject the 'transactional' account of legitimacy, where does it leave that historical legacy? If we are to evaluate institutions on the basis of what citizens *ought* to have chosen, as Rawlsians and others ask us to do, then where does that leave the habits, dispositions, norms, practices, and institutions that we have not chosen (and never could), but which continue to govern and shape our conduct in so many ways?

So the liberal justificatory ideal is a powerful one, but it faces some acute challenges, especially when married to a further ideal of deliberative democracy. Behind it lies the belief that a liberal social order is one not shrouded in mystery, but where 'people should know and understand the reasons for the basic distribution of wealth, power, authority and freedom'.[25] Postcolonial liberalism builds on the justificatory ambitions of liberalism, but also departs from it in a number of ways. I shall argue that the ideal needs to be placed in the context of a very different account of the nature of power than is usually associated with liberal discussions. I shall also argue that the kinds of agreement or mutual acceptability aimed at by postcolonial liberalism will be closer to a *modus vivendi* than an 'overlapping consensus' on constitutional essentials, and none the worse for it. Moreover, unlike much contemporary liberal political thought, postcolonial liberalism does not subscribe to a strong 'asymmetry thesis' between the right and the good. For one thing, the distinction between the right and the good – if the liberal-communitarian debate has shown anything – is almost impossible to maintain. But more importantly, I see no reason to think convergence on principles of right is any less vulnerable to the forms of disagreement and deep diversity said to characterize people's beliefs about the good.

### Liberal registers

The conceptual and practical scheme within which indigenous claims have been taken up in liberal discourse has been one constructed out of a particular family of conceptions to do with land, culture and justice. And this conceptual scheme, in turn, operates according to a particular discourse or 'register', made up of assumptions concerning power, history and the nature of public reason.[26] Invoking the metaphor of a 'register' or discourse in this way is to make a general point about the structure of moral experience. There is no such thing as a 'view from nowhere'; we are always coming to understanding and interpreting morality from somewhere, from within a particular context, moral language, and set of affective and practical relations. But that is not to say we are subsumed in these relations, nor does it follow that universality or impartiality is necessarily a sham. But it does have consequences for how we think about the boundaries of the reasonable and the unreasonable. So I will be arguing that a particular liberal account of the relation between land, culture and justice is partly held in place by a particular set of presumptions about power, the relevance of history and the nature of public reason. This conceptual scheme is in the process of being re-thought by a number of theorists today. My aim will be to try and link some of these developments to a distinctive account of postcolonial liberalism.

Now it might seem that I am doomed before I even begin. For, on the one hand, it could be argued that there cannot be a postcolonial liberalism because the very terms of liberal discourse and practices are too deeply compromised through their complicity with colonialism. This is sometimes connected to a more general thesis about the self-undermining nature of the Enlightenment project (defined as the attempt to provide an independent rational justification of morality).[27] Hence some kind of post-liberal conceptual scheme is needed. Or, on the other hand, I have completely misunderstood what is valuable about liberal political thought, and especially contemporary liberal theories of justice. The currency of liberal theories of justice – the equal distribution of liberties, resources, and income – is intended precisely to allow individuals, whatever their cultural, ethnic or religious background, to realize their effective freedom and live lives of dignity and self-respect. Hence the question should not be so much changing the conceptual scheme within which liberalism operates, but *sticking to it* with even greater fidelity than ever before.

Both of these answers miss something important, I believe, about what is at stake in the encounter between liberalism and the claims of indigenous peoples. Those who advocate abandoning liberal values and institutions on the basis of the radical incommensurability of cultures and traditions usually still cleave to the need for critique and reform of existing practices and institutions, and presume that pluralism will somehow work out to peaceful co-existence.[28] On the other hand, simply reiterating the value of individual rights independently of the context and historical circumstances of colonialism misses the conceptual and practical challenge presented by indigenous peoples' claims. The demands for the return and securing of Aboriginal lands and rights of self-government touch on fundamental issues of justice, and broader questions about the relation between ethical liberalism and deep cultural diversity.

The challenge for postcolonial liberalism is thus to be oriented according to the local, and yet also provide an account of the conditions and institutions that distinguish this from merely deferring to existing relations of power. My answer, roughly speaking, will be that post-colonial liberalism aims for a state of affairs in which the legitimacy of the norms, practices and institutions upon which people's well-being depends inheres in a form of social and political conversation – or embodied argument – about what is legitimate and illegitimate; an argument that is ultimately 'without any guarantor and without any end'.[29] And one of the crucial conditions contributing to the legitimacy of a postcolonial state will be to reorient itself around a model of complex coexistence, rather than the usual choice between 'toleration' or 'autonomy'.[30]

Thus the tension between substance and procedures is central to postcolonial liberalism, as is disagreement over justice. The legitimacy of any set of democratic procedures is dependent on substantive claims about justice, not only in terms of the actual results of the processes, but of the norms and values promoted by the procedures themselves.[31] But since we disagree about justice and hence about the evaluative standards to judge the outcomes of the procedures, we must aim to promote the conditions in which the collective decisions that have to be made can achieve, if not the consensus of all concerned, then at least a kind of loyal opposition on the part of those who disagree.[32] The decision-procedures, in other words, have to be ones the parties can live with.[33] But living with disagreement in this way requires a belief in the effectiveness and general trustworthiness of the main political institutions; that political decisions will be enforced, citizens' rights protected, and thus future opportunities for reconsideration of contestable policies ensured. And this in turn also depends on citizens being capable of making demands for equitable treatment on these institutions and on each other; demands and forms of contestation which might bring to light forms of injustice or domination hitherto unnoticed or unrecognized.

My point here is that moral and political reasoning is practice-dependent. It occurs within historically and culturally specific contexts and frameworks. It is not *determined* by these frameworks, but shaped by them. Liberal proceduralism, as a normative argument for dealing with reasonable pluralism, runs up against these often-less-than rationalistic foundations and frameworks. This descriptive fact does not, in itself, undermine the normative project. But it does have serious consequences for it, as I hope to show. Liberal proceduralists face something of a paradox here. In order for proceduralism to work, it has to promote the right kind of sociability amongst those subject to it; i.e. the willingness on the side of the parties to offer the right kind of mutual justifications to each other, and to uphold institutions and practices that might undermine their valued ways of life. But since it is an ideal inspired by neutrality, and thus a strict separation between enforcing public and non-public virtue – upon which its legitimacy is said to rest – it seems limited in terms of what it can hope to promote or encourage in the non-public sphere.

## Colonial reasoning

Here the debate with postcolonial critics of liberalism is joined, since the ways in which conceptions of liberal reasonableness and sociability are elaborated provides a set of crucial background conditions against which indigenous claims are understood and judged. Consider two objections: the *false objectivism thesis* and the *false community thesis*. Both feature prominently in postcolonial discussions of liberalism's claims to universalism and impartiality, as well as liberal and communitarian ideas of political community. The former sees claims about the discovery of moral facts in the public sphere through rational discourse as masking, or sometimes rationalizing, a set of culturally specific (and thus unwarrantedly exclusionary) beliefs about what counts as a rational argument, or who counts as a rational person. The latter appeals either to notions of community that are merely collective extensions of the liberal concept of the person, or over-romanticize social and political relations and endorse existing and often unjust relations of power.

Charles Mills, for example, argues that a *racial* contract – political, moral, epistemological and economic – underlies the historical ideal of the liberal social contract, wherein '[b]y virtue of their complete non-recognition, or at best inadequate, myopic recognition, of the duties of natural law, nonwhites are appropriately relegated to a lower rung on the moral ladder ...'.[34] These and other racialized assumptions informed the justifications of early modern conquests of indigenous lands and societies. In fact, as Robert Williams argues, the doctrine of 'discovery' which granted European nations absolute dominion over indigenous territories and peoples in virtue of their presumed moral and civilizational superiority, 'was *the* paradigmatic tenet informing and determining contemporary European legal discourse respecting relations with Western tribal societies'.[35] If such a doctrine was as important to colonial relations as Williams argues, then the justification of colonialism is not peripheral to liberal political thought, but close to the very heart of its intellectual foundations. Can liberal political thought overcome such a legacy? Are remnants of the colonial edifice built upon the doctrine of discovery still operative in liberal discussions of indigenous peoples' claims?

Furthermore, it has been argued that liberalism continues to be complicit in the maintenance of colonial relations not only by mis-recognizing indigenous claims, but more generally by upholding and legitimating a global economic order that results in the subjugation and domination of millions of 'third' and 'fourth' world people. Gayatri Spivak refers to this as economic rather than territorial neocolonialism, part of the relentless 'financialization' of the planet by powerful multinational economic and political actors.[36] This is a considerable challenge, and the constraints that global capitalism place on the effective capacity of individuals and groups to act collectively to govern themselves should be at the centre of any contemporary democratic political theory. However Spivak's concerns are shared by a number of contemporary liberals.[37] So a critical approach to global capitalism is not incompatible with contemporary liberalism.

But how have liberal democracies typically responded to minority nationalism, and more specifically, to indigenous claims?[38] The historical record is not pretty. In many cases, liberal democracies tried to suppress various 'nations within', including indigenous peoples, by banning minority political associations, forbidding the use of their languages in schools and public institutions, or redrawing political boundaries to minimize the potential for cultural enclaves. In the case of indigenous peoples, not only did all of this happen, but their lands were forcibly expropriated and massively settled, they were often massacred, forced to live in appalling squalor, and, in some cases, had their children removed without permission.

As bad as this history is, recent historical work has been at pains to complicate this picture by emphasizing the extensive networks of political and economic relations that often existed, and more importantly, were valued by both communities.[39] These revisionist histories of interaction and interdependency are important. For they challenge the usual stories of cultural contact and change – of 'absorption by the other or resistance to the other' – and encourage a more complex and overlapping account of these relations, and especially the capacity of indigenous peoples to adapt and make use of the resources and space available to them, however diminishing and increasingly contested that was.[40] The historian Richard White has written of the emergence (in seventeenth and eighteenth century North America) of a 'middle ground' – 'a place in-between; in between cultures, peoples and in between empires and the non-state world of villages … [an] area between the historical foreground of European invasion and occupation and the background of Indian defeat and retreat'.[41] It was a ground constructed more often than not out of cultural *mis*understanding, but it was fertile enough to provide *some* means of accommodating divergent values and ways of life. Settlers and indigenous peoples lived, as Nicholas Thomas has put it, in a kind of 'strange proximity'; often interdependent out of necessity but always uneasily so.[42] Such anxiety sometimes manifested itself – in light of ideals of classical ideals of civic virtue – as an anxiety about corruption and the ultimate compatibility of empire and liberty, but usually in renewed appeals to the language of moral and civilizational superiority to justify on-going colonial expansion and thus dispossession of indigenous lands.[43] Later on, as Thomas points out, the very peoples and lands settlers sought to appropriate were re-inscribed and redisplayed – but now de-politicized and literally de-moralized – as distinctive cultural icons of the new emergent settler nation.

The 'strange proximity' of colonial encounters and the accompanying anxiety about its effects persists, I think, in many ostensibly postcolonial states today. It persists, as Thomas and others have shown, in the appropriation of indigenous images and works of art as national symbols, as well as in the emphasis upon the land and the links drawn between geography and national identity (especially in countries such as Canada, New Zealand and Australia). But it also persists in the way indigenous claims for land and self-government are interpreted and evaluated in the public sphere. The origins of all states are stained by violence and deceit, but the colonial origins of the nation states of the New World have left a distinctive imprint on their modern descendants. Indigenous claims press on the relation between fundamental matters of justice and the politics of national identity. Are indigenous claims special kinds of claims? If so, why? Or should they be considered no differently – and no more or less urgently – alongside those of other disadvantaged groups such as the poor, other ethnic or cultural groups, or the physically handicapped? The intensity of debates over the nature of what justice or equality calls for in addressing indigenous claims attests to the moral and cultural force of their continuing presence in and around the lands that were taken from them. The move from the 'strange proximity' of colonialism to the 'strange multiplicity' of postcolonialism requires traversing some difficult conceptual and political terrain.

## Three arguments for Aboriginal rights

There are basically three arguments addressed to indigenous claims which resonate to varying degrees within liberal political thought in recent years. These are: (1) arguments based on equality; (2) on compensation for historical injustices, and (3) on difference. Each has various complex elaborations. The tendency amongst most of the leading liberal discussants of these issues has been to plump either for (1) independent of (2) and (3), or to plump for (2) or (3) as a means of realizing the value of some conception of (1). Still others have argued on the basis of (3) to the apparent exclusion of (1) and (2), but usually end up appealing to some variation of (1). I shall try to clarify these arguments, and the relations between them, in the chapters to come.

In general, most discussions which are not simply dismissive of indigenous claims rely on *some* account of equality to address them. Some arguments reject the value of equality altogether and claim that freedom (and particularly the freedom of association) is what matters. But then they have to make clear what conception of liberty they are appealing to and have to rely anyway (often implicitly) on an account of the equal distribution of these liberties. Another set of arguments see 'special' measures taken to secure indigenous cultural frameworks (such as collective land rights or self-government rights) as compatible with and indeed required by the moral demand of treating others with equal respect, or securing the value of equal citizenship. Others insist that given the dangers such measures present to individual welfare – indigenous or otherwise – a commitment to equality requires ensuring the fair value of *individual* rather than group rights, which provide more than adequate scope for people to form cultural and other kinds of associations with whomever they wish.[44] Thus where indigenous peoples have been discriminated against or denied basic citizenship rights, the answer lies not in remedial collective rights, but in addressing the reasons why the effective realization of their individual rights has been blocked.

There are also important arguments focusing on historical injustice and difference. Liberals have remained wary of some of these arguments, however, for a number of reasons. First, if indigenous claims are to be understood as demands for compensation for past injustices, then they are vulnerable to a number of powerful objections that have been made against historical entitlement theories of justice in general.[45] But it is also unclear that if indigenous people are owed certain rights or resources on the basis of a particular historical pattern of discrimination, why those privileges should continue once those specific forms of discrimination have ceased. Hence, as much as historical injustices are recognized as at least somehow connected to the recognition of indigenous claims, liberals have tended to appeal less to the compensatory logic of historical entitlements and more to the value of equality in the present to do the real work. And yet, as we have seen, the connection between the history of relations between Europeans and indigenous peoples (and non-Europeans in general) and the background conditions of the properly 'rational' or 'reasonable' individual has been a prominent feature of postcolonial writings.

The relevance of 'difference' has been interpreted in many different ways.[46] If indigenous peoples are owed special rights or privileges on the grounds of their radical 'otherness' from Europeans, and of their having suffered grievous harm as a result of this otherness, then it is not clear if that means that if they choose to adapt or borrow from Western cultures and practices they are somehow undermining the very grounds of their rights. Do they forfeit their 'difference' if they choose to abandon some of their 'traditional' or 'customary' ways? Most liberals are uncomfortable with the idea of rights protecting extant traditions from criticism or change. Also, given the way cultural difference was used within international law and the common law as a means of distinguishing between 'civilized' and 'barbarous' nations, and thus justifying the enslavement or dispossession of the latter, many liberals are wary of promoting cultural difference as a relevant category for distributive matters all. The state has got these things terribly wrong in the past and there is no reason to think it will not get them terribly wrong again in the future. Moreover, rights may be perceived as an inherently problematic way of institutionalizing or protecting social and cultural difference because they can freeze and even distort the conditions necessary for mutual accommodation and the working out of arrangements that stay close to the ground and promote 'goodness of fit'. Social cooperation in culturally diverse contexts needs some form of rights-based guarantees of individual interests, but they should not necessarily dominate the medium of political and cultural exchange.

There is another invocation of difference which has been prominent in recent debates. Here the emphasis is on an alternative ethical-political ontology; one in which a particular ethical disposition to the world – a radical receptiveness or openness to difference – orients political theorizing about the nature of public reason and cross-cultural interaction. For these theorists, the liberal emphasis on consensus and the cognitive gain associated with a dialogical engagement with others impedes rather than promotes the appropriate form of ethical response to difference. It is not clear what alternative form of public reason or political community this ethical as opposed to political approach to difference suggests. It seems, for the most part, to be focused on the critical limits of liberal assumptions concerning social and cultural difference, and especially the ethical grounds of responsiveness to the other. Liberalism, on this reading, offers a far too limited and cramped mode of ethical responsiveness to difference; possibly too narrow even for its own explicit ethical commitments (such as to the norm of equal respect for others).[47]

I shall try to show that the three arguments based on equality, historical injustice and difference are actually interdependent and complementary, as opposed to independent and contradictory. Each argument on its own is flawed in some way, but taken together the flaws are not fatal. Each provides a partial justification for relations between indigenous and non-indigenous peoples which, taken together, make a case for postcolonial liberalism. The partial, contestable, incomplete nature of this conceptual *modus vivendi* is analogous to the kinds of agreements postcolonial liberalism actually seeks. An advantage of this approach is that the three arguments form part of the way many people already think of these issues, and thus in an Aristotelian vein, postcolonial liberalism takes seriously (and connects with) the views of both the 'many and the wise' on these questions. Another reason for emphasizing the interdependence between the equality, historical injustice and difference arguments is because liberal political theorists have been quick to translate indigenous claims into the currency of egalitarian justice. But there is no such obviously agreed-upon currency. Moreover, the justificatory project at the heart of recent liberal theories entails that the grounds for the legitimate exercise of political power necessary to realize justice be, as we have seen, *reasonable*; i.e. accessible to each and every member of that society (accepting that what 'accessible' actually means is itself a complicated question). And it is clear that there are not easily established independent criteria for determining what is reasonable or unreasonable.

For postcolonial liberalism, the reasonable refers to not only moral frameworks but to cultural and historical ones as well. As Onora O'Neill has argued, if practical reason is actually to guide human conduct it must be accessible to the people whom it is meant to guide, and this means paying critical attention to the 'idealizations' about deliberative and cognitive capacities that inevitably creep into our theoretical abstractions concerning individual and collective agency.[48] (Identifying unwarranted idealizations in the history of political thought is a crucial aspect of postcolonial studies.) To be oriented by local reasoning about the right and the good, as postcolonial liberalism is, is not to be locked into it. For the ideal of public reason it embraces is one of *arguing* about justice, and this presupposes, as O'Neill puts it, that '[n]othing is more central to human reasoning than shifting between different possible descriptions of situations'.[49] The very possibility of such shifting descriptions rests on the fact that political questions always turn on controversial empirical claims and contestable ethical premises. What postcolonial liberalism seeks to exploit, therefore, is that the currency of liberal justice is, in the end, 'irreducibly heterogeneous'.[50]

# 2 The postcolonial challenge

Foreignness does not start at the water's edge but at the skin's.[1]

## Introduction

Liberalism has come under withering attack in recent years, and especially from those whom we might think of as being at the sharp end of social, economic and political disadvantage: cultural and ethnic groups, indigenous peoples and other 'stateless nations', migrants and refugees. Members of these groups often invoke the language of freedom and human dignity in relation to their plight, and the need to respect and foster difference, but just as often in *opposition* to liberalism, rather than in appealing to it. The simultaneous invocation of the inadequacy and yet the indispensability of liberal values and concepts such as justice, equality and freedom seems to lie at the heart of the postcolonial project. So it is not a matter of simply discarding European thought but seeing how it can be taken hold of, translated and renewed 'from and for the margins'.[2] As I argued above, this is an attractive project, and indeed one that liberals can and should embrace. But for it to work, there is also a need from *within* the liberal tradition to try and identify possible points of contact and exchange; to see what conceptual resources exist for creating the space in which such mutual translations and conceptual reshapings can take place. Even if the ultimate aim of postcolonial liberalism is a form of mutually acceptable coexistence between indigenous and non-indigenous peoples, such arrangements require a set of transitive concepts and norms to guide these interactions. They will have to be the product of both indigenous and liberal democratic traditions.

In this chapter the focus will be on the postcolonial challenge to liberalism. It is a complicated challenge because the most interesting postcolonial theorists accept that European thought is both inadequate and yet indispensable to the project of developing a genuinely postcolonial political theory. In this chapter we concentrate on the criticism of liberalism. The chapters to follow will attempt to craft a response to these challenges.

To begin with it might be fair to ask: how could a philosophical and political creed of individual rights and human dignity *not* find favour with those suffering from racial or cultural discrimination and economic and political marginalization? There are a number of possible answers. The first is that liberalism is often equated with support for the unbridled supremacy of the market, and especially for what Gayatri Chakravorty Spivak has called the 'financialization of the planet'.[3] In so far as liberals support the expansion of free and unfettered markets and minimal government on a global scale, they support the means through which the poorest and worst off are dominated and discriminated against. But not all liberals do support the coercive imposition of unfettered markets and minimal governments on a global scale. Just as many liberals, especially egalitarian liberals, are ardent critics of unregulated global capital, and argue for a considerable redistribution of wealth both domestically and globally.[4] Economic liberalism and egalitarian political liberalism are not synonymous, and the latter can be seen as offering a plausible critique of the former.[5]

Another reason often alluded to is liberalism's deep commitment to individualism; the belief that only individuals, and hence individual goods, are morally relevant.[6] There is some truth to this claim, as we shall see, but it isn't the whole answer (or even the best answer). For it is clear that liberalism has often made room for the claims of groups and collective goods – even, arguably, irreducibly social goods – in its conceptual landscape. Moreover, individualism is insufficient to ground many liberal outcomes, since individuals are often prone to do all kinds of illiberal things to each other if unconstrained in various ways.

One general problem is the very ambiguity of what liberalism actually entails these days. It seems spread between left, right and centre. The ambiguity of its political commitments stems in part from the very pluralism it accepts as a fact of political life. Hence liberalism may be a creed that promotes freedom and equality for all, but there is no neutral account of free action upon which everyone agrees. Nor is there a neutral account of what it is to treat someone with equal respect, or what constitutes genuine as opposed to spurious or self-serving claims about harm. Nor does there seem to be a neutral way of identifying what constitutes the basic 'primary goods' individuals need in order to live a decent life, or in what a decent life actually consists. It's not that liberalism ignores these difficult questions, but that the answers are prone to deep 'reasonable disagreement', as Rawls puts it.

Ever since Locke's *Letter Concerning Toleration*, for example, liberals have tried to isolate the kind of harm a liberal state should seek to prevent, or at least to minimize the harm it can do. The formula has tended to be something like this: Harm equals the violation of individual rights, or at least, the 'basic interests' of individuals. But what *are* the 'basic interests' of individuals? Do they include membership in groups? If so, can group interests ever take priority over individual ones? What kind of harm counts? Is pornography a kind of harm? Or hate speech? Or the violation of a group's 'sacred site'? It does not follow that relativism is a consequence of reasonable disagreement, but it does mean the project of justifying the exercise of political power is considerably complicated by such diversity.

Thomas Nagel has referred to this evaluative pluralism as involving the 'fragmentation of value'; diverse sources of moral value incapable of being arranged into a final comprehensive ranking or order.[7] Thus the values liberals cherish – whether they be freedom, equality, autonomy or equal respect – are inevitably thickened out when applied in particular cultural and practical contexts, and this generates not only conflicting principles but often conflicting interpretations of the principle itself.[8] No principle is self-interpreting. The social practices and modes of identification (political and otherwise) into which we are encultured shape our moral and political deliberation in numerous ways, including and especially our judgments about what constitutes 'reasonable' conduct, whether moral, legal or political.

More often than not, as we shall see, the disagreement or conflict is one to do with different trade-offs between often universally valued ends.[9] The values of individual freedom and social order, for example, are prized by many communities. But some might value more social order over a greater degree of individual freedom, and others vice versa. Liberal states have to contend with these different weightings and trade-offs within their borders as well as outside of them. It is a difficult task, to be sure, but that degree of difficulty is overestimated, I think, in presuming the differences are fundamentally incommensurable. Difference conceptions of freedom and social order, for example, are at least comparable if not always neatly commensurable, precisely because as values they leave so much underdetermined.

Political deliberation, it is true, operates more often than not in the absence of a common measure or standard of value, rather than in light of one.[10] But the conclusion to be drawn from this is not that value pluralism means accepting the impossibility of rational deliberation or judgment. Rather, it is that a rationale or justification has to be found for the way we go about balancing and making the tradeoffs we do, and that the rationale be as mutually acceptable as possible to those affected by the political arrangements thereby established.

Another serious challenge to liberalism which is prominent in the postcolonial literature is one tied to a critique of 'liberal governmentality'. The notion of governmentality is borrowed from the work of Michel Foucault, and has been put to work in a wide variety of contexts in the social sciences and humanities today.[11] The gist of it has to do with the way liberal norms and modes of governance – including but not reducible to the state and its agencies – shape the conduct of its population. Liberal governance presupposes that individuals are free, but free in the right way; free to exercise choice, to act rationally and reasonably and to subject themselves to certain kinds of social and political obligation. Applied to the politics of multiculturalism, non-liberal cultures or peoples are seen as subject to the practices of liberal governmentality. They may be granted various forms of collective rights, or rights of 'self-determination', but only if they are exercised in an appropriate manner, the content of which is given in terms of seemingly pre-loaded and unquestionable liberal values and norms. This criticism strikes home, especially with regard to the situation of indigenous peoples living in liberal democracies today.

Postcolonial critiques of liberal political thought work away at the difficult juncture in which pluralism is simultaneously embraced and delimited. The history of liberal political thought is littered with contradictory moments of official egalitarianism and universalism combined with unofficial cultural parochialism and discrimination. But how deep does this collusion go? To begin with, we need to have a sense of the relation between liberalism and various notions of culture.

## A short discourse on culture

Edward Said has written of the 'schizophrenic habit' of nineteenth-century liberals to justify rights and obligations respecting national independence, whilst at the same time – almost in the same breath – allowing for their abrogation in distant imperial realms.[12] For Said, a complex series of presumptions about culture made such a disjunction possible. He goes on to suggest how an awareness of these historical relations has consequences for interpreting eighteenth and nineteenth century literature. 'We should try to discern … a counterpoint', he argues, '[that] is not temporal but spatial. How do writers … situate and see themselves and their work in the larger world? We shall find them … using careful strategies … positive ideas of home, of a nation, and its language, of proper order, good behaviour and moral values'.[13] In doing so, Said claims, they tend to devalue other worlds and this renders colonialism more palatable and less susceptible to critical scrutiny.

The call by Said to seek out such 'spatial counterpoints' is in part a call for literary theorists and cultural historians to see the connections between literature and the history of empire. But something similar is going on in political philosophy and the history of political thought. For it is clear that liberalism, empire and colonialism are historically entwined. The Age of Enlightenment was also the age of colonial expansion and domination.[14] As David Armitage has put it, 'Empires gave birth to states, and states stood at the heart of empires'.[15] Moreover such states themselves, whether 'composite monarchies' (such as England and France) or 'multiple kingdoms' (like Britain and Spain) were not only compounded in ways similar to empires (by force, annexation, secession and inheritance) but faced some of the same problems (governing at a distance, clashes between metropolitan and provincial legislatures and cultures, and imposing common laws and norms over diverse and often resistant populations).[16] Imperialism is thus consistent with state formation, not distinct from it, and the ideologies that were generated to justify one were crucial to the justification of the other.

The mere fact that liberalism is implicated in the justification of colonialism is evidence enough for some that it is thus tainted beyond redemption. It is a fact that many liberal political thinkers have supported and justified colonialism, and often with explicit reference to liberal values (one of the most notorious being John Stuart Mill).[17] But one response might be: so what? All this might seem like water under the bridge. Were not these liberal thinkers simply mistaken to believe what they did about 'backward civilizations' or 'barbarous' peoples not being eligible for individual and collective rights of self-determination? Contemporary liberal political theory has no truck with such assumptions. The history of liberalism's complicity with colonialism is thus of no normative relevance save to remind us of the fact that human beings are fallible.

This short answer is too short, I think, to make sense of some of the questions raised by postcolonial theory. That it is too short can be checked by thinking about liberalism's relationship to the situation of indigenous peoples. A moment's reflection should make us realize that evaluating the claims for Aboriginal rights – to land or self-government, for example – involves more than simply stripping liberal political theory of the biases of nineteenth- and twentieth-century social and anthropological theory. Dropping the assumption that Aboriginal peoples are 'barbarous' or 'uncivilized' still leaves us with the task of developing a response to their claims. Postcolonial liberalism thus aims to develop not just a 'liberal theory of rights for liberal minorities',[18] but an account of liberal political order in which indigenous people can, as far as it is possible, find a home, on terms mutually acceptable between them and the liberal state (and the international legal and political order as well).

But first, what do we mean by culture? Much hangs on what role we think culture plays in relation to what (and how) people value the things they do. This is difficult given the elusiveness of the concept of culture in general. But it is important to try and be as clear as possible as to what we mean by it. Within philosophical, political, legal, and anthropological argument two senses of culture were prominent in the early modern and modern eras: the first, tied to human development (both individual and collective), and the second tied to the notion of a distinct way of life of a particular people. The relation between these two meanings has a complicated historical and conceptual lineage. Early modern conceptions of culture were often linked to a four-stage theory of human development which placed 'hunter-gatherer' societies at a primitive stage along the way to the emergence of properly civil and commercial society.[19] Differences of cultural behaviour were accounted for in terms of differences in rates of historical growth.[20] With the rise of biological and evolutionary theory by the end of the eighteenth century, a tight connection was in place between the superiority of European culture, and the cultural (and racial) inferiority of other peoples. Tying human development to an evaluation of the relative worth of different cultures – or to the related but different sense of 'civilization'[21] – was a presumption shared by some of the leading liberal thinkers of the nineteenth and early twentieth centuries. Even when the emphasis on the proper development of mankind was modified in favour of some form of comparative relativism, there was still a tendency to see primitive or non-western cultures as existing in a kind of exotic cultural aspic, either to be preserved or 'helped' into modernity.[22]

More recently, culture has tended to be conceived of in two further ways. Both have moral and political consequences, as we shall see. The first is to see culture as a 'total body of behaviour', or a kind of 'individuable whole'.[23] Thus it is conceived of as a coherent body of beliefs and practices that lives and dies: 'culture is enduring, traditional, structural (rather than contingent, syncretic, historical). Culture is a process of ordering, not of disruption. It changes and develops like a living organism. It does not normally "survive" abrupt alterations'.[24] It may accommodate internal diversity and change, for it must if it is to survive, but not too much. Thus along with it come 'expectations of roots, of a stable, territorialized existence', and a sense of historical continuity, or at least of non-radical discontinuity.[25] Culture is thus associated with a continuous and integrated set of practices and beliefs held by a particular people occupying a distinct territory.

The second more contemporary sense of culture is very different, and somewhat harder to fix. It has emerged in part because of the dissatisfaction with thinking of culture as a coherent and 'articulable whole'. Philosophers and political theorists have been unhappy with the consequences of such a conception. Arguments about relativism, or for the radical incommensurability between world views, have drawn on anthropological work infused with this thick sense of cultural wholeness.[26] Morally and politically speaking, the worry is that this standpoint can be used to justify, or at least disallow criticism of, the unequal distribution of power and other goods within culturally distant and distinctive societies from ours. So if the first sense of culture involved thinking of it as a more-or-less coherent body of values and beliefs, then the second sense is more open-textured and amorphous. Here, culture is conceived of as a permeable and (ultimately) contingent framework within which both individual and collective agents act. Thus it is no longer thought of as a seamless or fully integrated web of beliefs. Taking culture seriously entails taking its internal complexity seriously. If on the first understanding, an 'authentic' culture is one belonging to a territorially distinct people who share a 'seamless web' of beliefs, values and practices, then on the second, culture is de-territorialized and detached from 'shared values' as well as quasi-biological notions of race or ethnicity.[27] Cultures are thus made up of negotiable, replaceable stuff, more patched-together and reassembled than woven of the same cloth. Understanding culture is more akin to interpreting or translating an assemblage of not necessarily coherent texts, as opposed to observing and 'reading off' human conduct on the basis of underlying shared values and beliefs. Cultural difference then should not be thought of as establishing a boundary marking the authentic off from the inauthentic, or the traditional from the modern, but rather a 'nexus of relations and transactions actively engaging a subject'.[28] This means accepting a certain amount of displacement and estrangement built into the very idea of culture, 'irremovable strangeness we can't keep clear of'.[29] Cultural difference is real, especially in the case of clashes between liberal institutions and indigenous societies for example, but it doesn't follow from this that the differences are therefore radically incommensurable.

Note that the idea of culture as providing a specific framework that enables an agent to act meaningfully in the world has not completely vanished. Conceiving of culture as providing frameworks for meaningful thought and action is still there, it is just that these frameworks are much more permeable and eclectic than previously thought. If not, then the idea of culture would be empty.[30] But then how are we to characterize culture without falling back into presumptions about coherence and authenticity that mask its internal complexity? Clifford Geertz's influential argument still resonates, I think, when he talks about culture as providing a 'set of control mechanisms – plans, recipes, rules, instructions (what computer engineers call "programs") – for the governing of behaviour … [M]an is precisely the animal most desperately dependent upon such extragenetic, outside-the-skin control mechanisms, such cultural programs, for ordering his behaviour'.[31] These mechanisms – or software, keeping with Geertz's prescient metaphor (the article was published in 1973) – are 'already current in the community where he is born, and they remain, with some additions, subtractions, and partial alterations he may or may not have had a hand in, in circulation after he dies'. Man orients himself in the world, comes to grasp the nature and meaning of his life, through these mechanisms with a view to putting 'a construction upon the events through which he lives'.[32]

So culture is a kind of software that orients human conduct, albeit one that is inherently dynamic and context-sensitive. Human beings act in relation to it, but in the process they act on it and thus cause it, and themselves, to change and evolve in unpredictable ways (just the kind of software computer scientists still dream of developing). Culture, in this sense, has a performative and mediatory function, not just a repository of values or choices for the autonomous subject to draw on, but (in Bhabha's phrase) an 'enunciative space' in which subjects move between 'groupishness and individuation, between having and doing'.[33] Cultural frameworks represent dense 'webs of complex actions and interactions … the density of their details defy[ing] explicit learning or comprehensive articulation'.[34] Hence there can be no simple equation, on the one hand, between culture and oppression, and on the other, between culture and freedom. Instead we need to ask what culture means or involves in this or that specific context, and how it relates to this or that particular agent or group. Human beings, as Geertz argues, are culture-dependent animals. The capacities required for the development of critical self-reflection and moral concern are connected to our upbringing and orientation in particular ways of life, and especially our acquisition of a particular language with which to explain and interpret our experiences therein.[35] Moreover, to be able to understand and contribute to public debate requires being able to grasp the common political medium and mode(s) of political communication and competition. To lack such capacities is to be seriously disadvantaged.[36] Jeremy Waldron argues that we should therefore see cultural practices and norms as tied to a context of reasoning and deliberation. Human beings value the cultural norms and practices they identify with because they see them as responding to and embodying goods and practices they value, and not only because of the fact that they are *theirs*. But as much as culture is tied to practices of reasoning it is also embodied in concrete ways of life, which complicates the implied commensurability and potential hybridity (see below) between cultural practices appealed to by

Waldron.[37] Identifying the fact that we have good reasons to value the norm or practices we do is not the same thing as identifying reasons we can share with others. (We shall return to this problem in Chapter 4.)

The two views of culture I have been discussing have important consequences in political and legal spheres, especially with regard to the claims of indigenous peoples. For as we shall see, significant legal decisions affecting their basic interests have often tied recognition of their rights to the continuing presence or continuity of 'traditional' or 'customary' ways of life, even where the lands upon which these practices depend have long been expropriated from them. The racist presumptions informing earlier decisions may have been dropped, but assumptions about culture still play an important role. What constitutes a 'continuing connection' with the land and who decides how 'traditional' or 'customary' those connections are, or must be? The complications cut both ways. If cultural membership is valuable and thus recognizable legally and politically only where the culture in question is coherent and 'continuing', then, given the effects of colonisation, very few indigenous groups will benefit from such a description. But if, in turn, culture is understood to be dynamic, permeable, and ever-changing, then just what is it that is being recognized and accommodated? Do people need access to simply *a* culture – any culture – as opposed to a specific one? How do we reconcile the idea of a distinct culture with the permeable, dynamic and hybrid conception of culture popular in anthropological and postcolonial thinking today?

We will examine some of the main arguments for doing so in the next chapter. My answer, in short, will be that precisely because cultures and the modes of identification associated with them are dynamic and subject to constant modification from within and without, any form of public accommodation of them will have to be guided by these facts as well. Thus political and legal recognition and accommodation of culture, premised on assumptions about the holistic or seamless nature of a cultural group, is presumptively suspect. First, because there are no such cultures. But secondly, it increases the risk of domination both internally and externally. Internally, the risk is increased for more vulnerable members of the group. Externally, the risk is increased for the group as a whole, given the way such assumptions tend to justify legal and political intervention into their practices. Postcolonial liberalism seeks to minimize domination by acknowledging the value of cultural membership, among other important interests, but also the ways in which the identities, norms and practices associated with culture are modified in the course of being contested and challenged. Relations of power are ubiquitous and no one can question everything about themselves or their situation at once, but the always limited capacity to contest the norms and practices that govern you is central to the ideal of citizenship postcolonial liberalism seeks to promote.

Let me summarize the discussion at this point. Culture should not be thought of as providing a set of coherent and shared values to individuals who identify with it, but rather a framework of beliefs, norms and practices (including a language or set of languages) within which they can orient themselves in the world. Second, culture is Janus-faced.[38] This is a crucial point. Various cultural practices can be open-textured, dynamic and freedom-enhancing. But they can also be exclusionary, discriminatory and oppressive.[39] In liberal political thought, as we shall see, the most interesting work on cultural rights rejects the bounded and static view of culture and accepts the more open-ended and dynamic notion familiar to the student of the best recent work in anthropology and cultural studies.

But to think that a genuinely intercultural liberalism is possible requires addressing a number of recent powerful criticisms of liberalism. Many of these theorists suggest that there are deep conceptual barriers or contradictions within liberalism that make it unreceptive to not only minority cultural and ethnic groups in general, but to 'third world' and indigenous peoples in particular. I want to set out this postcolonial critique of liberalism as clearly as I can, and then try to systematically address it in the chapters that follow.

## The postcolonial critique

I shall try and isolate from within postcolonial theory a number of methodological, philosophical and political themes relevant to liberalism's relation to colonialism, and especially with regard to the claims of indigenous peoples.[40] One reason for doing so is that often grand philosophical and political claims are made by postcolonial theorists (especially in literary and cultural studies) on the back of rather slender philosophical argument. As a result, many philosophers and political theorists can be dismissive of postcolonial theory. Some of this is to do with the often impenetrable prose of some of postcolonial theory's brightest lights. But debates over literary style are a distraction from what is philosophically and politically at stake. So I shall try to focus on what I take to be the substantive philosophical issues raised by postcolonial theory in general, and especially for liberalism in particular.

First, how to characterize postcolonial theory? Like many recent theoretical trends, it is difficult to generalize about. For one thing, the subject matter is vast and complex. There is a huge variation in the historical patterns and consequences of imperialism and colonialism in different parts of the world. Most importantly, perhaps, much of the theoretically inclined and more influential postcolonial writing has focused on South Asia and especially India. There are, needless to say, significant historical and ideological differences between the settler colonialism of the early British Empire stemming from the sixteenth and seventeenth centuries, and the later, originating in the latter half of the eighteenth century and associated especially with India. It is beyond my competence to evaluate the historical linkages and discontinuities between these two periods. My aim, rather, is to evaluate the philosophical consequences of various postcolonial arguments. The historical differences matter though, and I shall return to them at various points.

Philosophically speaking, much postcolonial theory has been avowedly anti-foundationalist.[41] Gyan Prakash, for example, has suggested that postcolonial theory, in general, seeks to answer a particular question, namely, how does the 'third world' write its own history?[42] For Prakash (and others) it can only do so in an anti-foundationalist and anti-essentialist manner, given the complicity, they claim, of 'essentialist' and universal concepts of the person or community with justifications of colonialism. Hence postcolonial theory entails 'the rejection of those modes of thinking which configure the third world in such irreducible essences as religiosity, underdevelopment, poverty, nationhood, [or] non-Westernness'.[43] Thus postcolonial criticism seeks to:

undo the Eurocentrism produced by the institution of the west's trajectory, its appropriation of the other as History. It does so, however, with the acute realization that postcoloniality is not born and nurtured in a panoptic distance from history. The postcolonial exists as an aftermath, as an after – after being worked over by colonialism. Criticism formed in this process of the enunciation of discourses of domination occupies a space that is neither inside nor outside the history of western domination but in a tangential relation to it.[44]

I take this to mean that the 'postcolonial condition' is one in which the legacy of colonialism – practically, historically and theoretically – is everpresent, even in the attempt to think beyond it. As Dipesh Chakrabarty has put it, '[European thought] is at once both indispensable and inadequate in helping us to think through the experiences of political modernity in non-Western nations'.[45] The postcolonial subject always starts from within a set of relations of power, in this case, including the discursive, normative and institutional practices of western domination. The presumption of the ubiquity of relations of power is a crucial tenet of postcolonial theory, as it is in other domains, and one that postcolonial liberalism embraces as well. However, postcolonial theorists develop the consequences of this claim in very strong terms. For

Prakash, it suggests that the 'meta-narratives' told by nationalist, Marxist and liberal histories and theories are tainted not only by Eurocentrism, but assume wrongly that history is founded upon and 'representable through some identity – individual, class, or structure – which resists further decomposition into heterogeneity'.[46] For the post-colonial theorist it is precisely this radical heterogeneity that must, somehow, be theorized.

Postcolonial writing often focuses on the particular forms of agency, subjectivity and modes of sociality governed by colonial and imperialist institutions, as well as the historiography and political theory that accompanied them. Dipesh Chakrabarty, for example, has argued that the public/private distinction at the heart of liberal conceptions of citizenship, deployed in nationalist interpretations of Indian politics and history, displaces and suppresses the distinctive ways in which various Indian subaltern communities challenged and contested such a distinc-tion. He claims these 'voices' and communities were denied their appro-priate place in histories driven by European models of nation building, including histories written by various Indian nationalists as well.[47] Similarly, Bikhu Parekh has emphasized the extent to which the methodological individualism at the heart of much of normative liberal political theory often precludes proper consideration of non-western communities' collective understandings and experience of culture, especially where they are minorities living within liberal democracies.[48]

Another important theme of recent postcolonial writing is an empha-sis on what we might call 'complex identification'; the diverse ways in which individuals and groups identify themselves culturally, socially and politically. Some theorists claim that liberal political theory is incapable of capturing the complex, overlapping and ambivalent mode of subaltern agency. Homi Bhabha has made famous what he refers to as the 'hybridity' of postcolonial identity: of identities and practices constituted by 'in-betweenness' and movement – 'the overlap and displacement of domains of difference'.[49] The positing of hybridity at the centre of the postcolonial experience by writers such as Bhabha is not intended only as a descriptive claim, but also a normative one as well. Bhabha, for example, accuses liberals of too often conceiving of minorities as 'abject "subjects" of their cultures of origin huddled in the gazebo of group rights, preserving the orthodoxy of their distinctive cultures in the midst of the great storm of Western progress'.[50] When this becomes the common view of minorities in liberal societies they become only 'virtual citizens', never quite considered 'here and now … relegated to a distanced sense of belonging elsewhere, to a there and then'.[51] Thus hybridity seems to entail an ethical claim on behalf of a particular conception of the self and society, one that operates in the 'interstitial passage between fixed identifications [and which] opens up the possibility of a cultural hybridity that entertains difference without an assumed or imposed hierarchy'.[52] The idea of a genuine flourishing of difference is another crucial tenet of postcolonial theory. Liberal political thought is accused of cramping the space for difference, by not only imposing Eurocentric conditions on the legitimate political accommodation and expression of difference, but in missing the way liberalism itself might be – needs to be – transformed in its encounter with these 'new minorities'.

A set of distinctive political commitments follows from these postcolonial themes. Bhabha, for example, argues that the 'postcolonial perspective [in resisting both holistic and methodological individualist forms of social explanation] forces a recognition of the more complex cultural and political boundaries that exist on the cusp of these often opposed political spheres' (i.e. between first, third and fourth worlds).

[It] forces us to rethink the profound limitations of a consensual and collusive 'liberal' sense of cultural community. It insists that cultural and political identity are constructed through a process of alterity ... The time for 'assimilating' minorities to holistic and organic notions of cultural value has dramatically passed. The very language of cultural community needs to be rethought from the postcolonial perspective, in a move similar to the language of sexuality, the self and cultural community, effected by feminists in the 1970's and the gay community in the 1980s.[53]

This is true at both the domestic and international level. There is, claims Bhabha, a new public sphere which is emerging 'in-between the state and non-state, in-between individual rights and group needs ... an analytic and ethical borderland of "hybridization" '.[54] The 'new minorities' emerging from this borderland, argues Bhabha, do not fit comfortably into liberal theories of rights, including recent theories advocating collective rights. These theories tend to focus on 'national cultures', he argues, the definition of which either privileges a certain kind of cultural identity conveniently amenable to liberal norms, or if not, demonises them as ripe for legitimate liberal intervention. As applied to the situation of cultural minorities in the world today, Bhabha's notion of the hybridization of cultural and national identities seems to entail a radical rethinking of how we conceive of cultural minorities in the first place, which in turn should force a rethinking of the nature of the idea of 'minority rights' themselves:

[I]ndividual and group, singularity and solidarity, need not be opposed or aligned against each other. They are part of the movement of transition or translation that emerges within and between minority milieux. For an international community of rights cannot be based on an abstract inherent 'value' of humanness: it requires a process of cultural translation that, each time, historically and poetically inquires into the conflictual namings of 'humanity'.[55]

Dipesh Chakrabarty calls for a 'radical critique and transcendence of liberalism', that is, 'of the bureaucratic construction of citizenship, the modern state and bourgeois privacy that classical political philosophy has produced'.[56] Some of liberalism's main concepts – of civil society, equal citizenship and negative freedom – are categories 'whose global currency' can no longer be taken for granted, since they have been deployed in the 'colonial theatre' in aid of dubious projects aimed at 'civilizing' or developing the natives. Thus for Chakrabarty, liberal political thought has played a part in assimilating 'all other possibilities of human solidarity'.[57] What needs to be mapped instead is what 'resists and escapes the best human effort at translation across cultural and other semiotic system, so that the world may ... be imagined as radically heterogeneous'. This means exploring other 'narratives of human connection' which are defined neither by the 'rituals of liberal citizenship' nor the 'nightmare of "tradition" that "modernity" creates'.[58] But again, this does not mean simply rejecting out-of-hand, 'liberal values, universals, science, reason, grand narratives, totalizing explanations and so on'.[59] Rather, Chakrabarty suggests, it means trying to critique European 'historicism' without completely abandoning European theory. By analogy, it means criticizing liberalism without abandoning a commitment to justice, freedom or human well-being.

Thus one of the central claims of postcolonial critics, in light of this focus on the historical character of philosophical argument, has been that the universalizing ethos of 'Enlightenment liberalism' included a justification of imperialism and colonialism.[60] There are two variations on this critique which are relevant to the themes of this book. First, that even when liberal rights were extended to previously disenfrachised peoples, there were usually special conditions attached. Liberal thinkers were constantly concerned that liberal citizens exercise their freedoms in the right way.[61] Postcolonial theorists have been concerned with what we might call the 'governmentalization' of minority rights.[62] Gaining political or legal recognition from the state, or from an international system of states, entails organizing yourself in light of certain regulative norms enforceable by the state.[63] The paradox is that in order to reduce the presence of the state in one sphere of social or political life requires that it be increased in others, acting at a distance. To a certain extent there is no avoiding this. All social and political relations are mediated relations. But what postcolonial theorists have pointed out are the particular ways in which regulative conceptions of freedom, sovereignty, self-determination and reason, for example, have been deployed in colonial contexts – as forms of control and domination as much as anything else.

Elizabeth Povinelli, for example, argues that liberal multiculturalism is essentially continuous with the racist and colonial policies it succeeded. Since power, not moral argument, shapes social and political interaction, moral argument without a transformation of the relations of power is simply vacuous moralizing. Worse, liberal attempts at recognizing cultural difference, especially indigenous alterity, are merely more sophisticated ways of constraining and controlling it. Thus liberal respect for Aboriginal 'traditional' or 'customary' practices represents, in fact, 'the political cunning and calculus of cultural recognition in settler modernity'. In 'postcolonial multicultural societies', argues Povinelli, a new form of liberal power is at work, whereby recognition is 'at once a formal acknowledgement of a subaltern group's being and of its being worthy of national recognition and, at the same time, a formal moment of being inspected, examined and investigated.'[64] The inevitable failure of the indigenous subject to match the liberal state's pre-conceived notion of what constitutes a *valid* 'traditional culture' then justifies the legal curtailment of the expression of this alterity, and sets them apart from dominant social values. Liberalism is incapable of recognizing alterity except as 'otherness' which is already 'deeply recognizable [and] does not violate core subjective or social values'.[65] (I return to this argument in Chapter 4.)

Similarly, consider two of the most important tools in international law for the protection of minority rights – Article 1 of the *United Nations Charter*, and Article 27 of the *International Covenant on Civil and Political Rights*. Article 1 states that 'all peoples' have a right to self-determination. Article 27 protects the 'right of minorities, in community with the other members of their group, to enjoy their own culture, to profess and practise their own religion, or to use their own language'. Existing states tend to interpret Article 1 as entailing a right to form a state, which of course they reject as applicable to the case of indigenous peoples.[66] But the protection afforded by Article 27 is too weak, since the 'right to enjoy one's culture' is compatible with and has been interpreted as entailing only negative rights of non-interference, as opposed to more robust forms of self-government or public recognition.[67] In fact, some states worked hard to try and block the extension of even this relatively weak form of protection to various national groups, claiming that it provided incentives for 'new minority groups' to threaten the unity of the state.[68] So indigenous peoples are offered, on the one hand, self determination as peoples but only if they fit a narrow and arbitrary definition of what constitutes a colonized people, which – unsurprisingly – they do not. On the other hand, they are offered a 'right' to exercise their culture through freedom of association and expression, but one that is compatible with policies that undermine their very capacities to do so, since a right to freedom of association or expression is compatible with a state abolishing special language rights, or encouraging settlers to swamp minority homelands.[69] Hence an apparently 'liberal' form of international law is either unable to accommodate the distinctive nature of indigenous peoples' assertion of autonomy because it miscontrues it, or is simply unwilling to.

The second variation of the criticism tying liberalism to colonialism has been dramatized by turning to the work of two of liberalism's greatest historical icons – John Locke and John Stuart Mill.[70] Locke, for example, is said to have thickened out the anthropological minimalism grounding man's natural freedom with socio-cultural conceptions of rational competency and 'reasonableness' that ruled out taking the claims of indigenous peoples seriously. His conception of property, and of what constituted a proper 'political society', are elaborated with reference to a specific set of European assumptions which conveniently delegitimated Native American sovereignty and landholding practices.[71] Mill, on the other hand, tied his claims about human development to the worth of particular cultures and 'civilizations', managing to justify the universal value of individual liberty alongside the acceptability and necessity of imperial tutelage over 'backward' peoples.[72] Gyan Prakash, has argued, for example, that there was a distinctive form of colonial governmentality that emerged in India in the nineteenth century, built on the assumptions of liberals like Mill, about the need for despotic rule over backward peoples in order to create the conditions for good government in the future. Hence for Prakash, the attempt to develop an Indian liberalism was born in imperialism. Thus Locke and Mill exemplify, on these postcolonial readings, the way liberalism presupposes all manner of specific cultural assumptions which are built into the conditions for the articulation of its supposedly universal principles. The universal, in other words, gains its meaning through conditions which are less than universal.

But this does not entail the rejection of universality per se. The fact that arguments originate in a particular culture hardly constitutes a demolition of the notion of universality. In fact, the debate between liberals and postcolonial theorists (and other critics of liberalism) is not actually between 'universalists' and 'particularists', but, it seems, between different conceptions of the universal. For postcolonial critics of liberal universalism, the demand is more often than not for a more expansive and open-ended reformulation of the universal, especially one unhinged from neo-liberal economic policy, and forged from a genuine engagement with the multiple and complex array of 'locations of culture' in the world today. As Judith Butler has put it, moral universalism should not be about 'looking for a Kant in every culture'.[73] Instead the universal becomes redefined as the project of exposing the parochial limits of the concept of universality itself. For postcolonial theorists, the task is more like one of cultural translation; the analogy suggests that settling on an appropriate universal is more akin to the partial, imperfect and painstaking work of translation than it is to philosophical argument.[74] Translation involves the persistence of difference – of the inability to fully represent the particular – even when settling on the equivalents necessary for communication. Translation does not necessarily entail transparency or reconciliation. In the case of indigenous peoples and the law, for example, it has meant conflict, coercion and above all, mediation through non-indigenous idioms and discourses.[75] We shall return to these issues in Chapters 6 and 7.

Finally, there is another way of framing some of these postcolonial concerns with the cultural limits of liberalism's universalism. William Connolly has argued that the priority assigned to distributive justice in liberal political discourse itself overlooks the ways in which particularistic limits insinuate their way into apparently universalistic premises.[76] Doing justice on this contractual model, according to Connolly, involves obligations and responsibilities towards and between those deemed 'rational' and 'responsible' parties to the social contract. Moreover, the conversation of justice, the framework within which claims of justice are made, and more importantly, recognized and understood by others, is carried out in a particular idiom (or 'register' as he writes elsewhere) of rights and resources (what Connolly calls 'justice as code').[77] Certain things are eligible for consideration as claims about justice and others are not; certain harms are considered genuine injuries and others not. Connolly's point is that the way questions are settled about the status of those persons and claims considered eligible for justice are skated over far too quickly in liberal discussions.[78] Instead, attention needs to be paid to the surface just beneath justice, to the way new claims and social movements are propelled (or not) 'upwards' into the conversation of justice and injustice. Connolly refers to this as a form of 'critical responsiveness':

In the politics of becoming, a movement hovers for a time in that paradoxical gap where it is not yet stabilized into something new even while its movement of the old configuration of persons, justice and diversity already jangles the sense of naturalness or self-assurance among established identities. Critical responsiveness is situated in precisely this space. It exceeds tolerance in a way that points to the insufficiency of justice, rights and code morality to democratic politics. For it is brought into play before a new identity has been consolidated and, hence, before the issues it poses are placed on the established register of justice, rights and legitimacy.[79]

Liberal conceptions of justice, in other words, presuppose a set of conditions that affect what shows up on – what gets propelled up into – the register of justice/injustice in the first place. These social, cultural, political and affective conditions often act as unacknowledged guardians of public reason, Connolly suggests, and new social movements and 'new minorities' must struggle to break through them.

## Conclusion

I hope I have shown that the postcolonial challenge to liberalism is a considerable one. It can be broken down and summarized into four general areas.

*1. Liberalism's abstract rationalism.* Liberalism's commitment to identifying norms or principles that can transcend particular social, cultural historical and political contexts and form the basis of a well-ordered society is based on a radical mischaracterization of the nature of social, cultural and political difference. Liberalism tends to obscure the ways in which apparently universal claims about justice or reasonableness in fact harbour particular presumptions about the relative worth of different cultures and ways of life. For some postcolonial critics, this means there is no such thing as universalism; all such claims are, in fact, particular cultural claims of one kind or another. For others, it means a much more critical and careful approach to making universal claims. The philosophical project of identifying and justifying universal moral principles capable of gaining a cross cultural rational assent should be replaced by something more akin to the imperfect and less imperious practices of mutual translation. Finally, liberalism obscures the affective dimensions of its own thought; of how processes of identification and judgment-making arise in the context of complex 'affective frameworks' of emotion circulating through systems of social relations.[80]

*2. Liberalism's moral individualism.* Given a commitment to moral individualism, liberalism is incapable of doing justice to the claims of groups seeking protection for or support for collective goods. By translating all claims about collective goods or interests into individual ones, liberals misconstrue the fundamental nature of claims made by various minority groups such as indigenous peoples. More generally, in clinging to methodological individualism, liberalism is unable to grasp the way contemporary cultural and political developments are increasingly difficult to analyse in either strictly individualist or communalist terms.

*3. The narrowness or insufficiency of liberal distributive justice.* Can liberalism address the injustices appealed to by indigenous communities and 'new minorities' when they are expressed in idioms other than the liberal currency of individual rights and 'primary' goods? What about claims based on historical injustice, or for recognition of distinctive conceptions of rights? Liberal public reason is thus said to be either too narrow or too parochial: too narrow because it admits only those claims that can be put into the language of primary goods and individual rights; and too parochial because it purports to be neutral when in fact it favours particular (and potentially controversial) sets of beliefs about the nature of social and political organization. Also, liberal theories of justice typically underestimate the effects of the structural features of society that contribute to inequality, such as the legacies of colonialism or slavery, or the social division of labour.

*4. The need for complex identification.* Liberal pluralism is not pluralistic enough. It often underestimates the kinds of differences it encounters, especially with regard to indigenous forms of life, and it slides over the extent to which the political identities it presupposes fix institutional arrangements and distributive outcomes in particular ways, and the need for these presuppositions to be open to contestation and re-negotiation. More complex and multilayered forms of political identification and association need to be developed in order to cope with the real complexity of multiculturalism within nation-states, the great movement of peoples, cultures and capital between them, the rise of transnational legal, political and economic processes and institutions, and the changing understandings of selfhood and community in light of these developments. Hybrid political institutions and associations – both domestic and international – are needed to accommodate increasingly hybrid people.

# 3 Reason and community

Après tout, nous sommes tous des gouvernés, et, à ce titre,
solidaires.[1]

## Introduction

The postcolonial critique of liberalism I have argued, is focused on four
key areas: liberalism's universalism, its 'abstract rationalism' and moral
individualism, the nature of liberal theories of justice, and liberal modes
of political identification. In this chapter I want to focus on the second
of these key areas, although critiques of liberalism's individualism and
abstract rationalism by postcolonial critics are ultimately connected to
worries about the ontological and political commitments of liberal universalism, hence it will touch on that issue as well.

In certain respects, the postcolonial critique crosses over to meet a
range of arguments launched against liberalism in recent years by so-
called 'communitarian' critics. But it also importantly departs from
these arguments as well. Postcolonial critics are as much critics of communitarian political thought as they are of liberal thought (or at least,
they should be). But I have no intention of revisiting the debate between
liberals and communitarians here. Of greater interest are the questions
raised under the guise of communitarianism, especially concerning the
relation between reason and community, which will be the focus of the
second section below.

In the third section, I turn to the problem of political division, which
I believe can best be seen as following on from how we answer questions
about the apparent individualism and rationalism of liberal political
thought. Why? Because the way in which we answer the question of
political division will be deeply connected to our beliefs about whether
only individuals count, morally speaking, or whether groups or peoples
should feature in our moral evaluation of political and social arrangements. What is the problem of political division? It consists in trying to
determine the moral constraints on the division of the world into

distinct territories under the exclusive control of one group rather than another.[2] Why should we take the political units as they exist in the world today as given? We should not. And nor do hundreds of millions of others, sometimes with disastrous consequences. Claims for secession and self-government, 'recognition' and self-determination are ubiquitous in modern politics. To dismiss all such phenomena as the effect of strategic machinations on the part of ethnic and cultural 'tribal entrepreneurs' seems far too quick. Some of these claims are undoubtedly fig leaves for just this kind of behaviour, but many others are not, and should be (and are) taken seriously by liberals.

What is it that states are made up from anyway? A people (or peoples)? A nation (or nations)? Individuals or groups? All of the above? If only individuals count, and cultural or associational commonalities are irrelevant, then why divide the world up into states or peoples in the first place?[3] How then could any political boundaries be justified, save for entirely pragmatic reasons?[4] But almost nobody thinks the communal dimensions of human experience are irrelevant, including in the case of the moral justification of political boundaries, or the recognition of political rights of self-government. The real question is the extent to which the interests individuals have as members of distinct associations and groups (including cultural and national groups) clash with other important interests, and what the best way of settling the inevitable clashes between these interests might be.


## Mediated individualism


Consider two claims:
(i)  That our identity is shaped by our situatedness or embeddedness in the world, by the particular cultural and historical contexts we inhabit; and,
(ii) that what we know, including what we know to be right or good, is also given by this situatedness.

How far do these claims go? That individuals are members of different communities and come to understand and value different practices and goods in virtue of their situatedness should not, on the face of it, be a controversial claim. For some, communities and their cultural frameworks literally constitute us; they define who we are and what we want. For others, we are always capable of standing back from and reflecting upon such 'constitutive attachments', and thus potentially rejecting them and crafting a different identity or set of goods to value. Liberalism is often thought of as a necessarily individualistic moral doctrine, but this is not the case. One can arrive at liberal conclusions from non-individualist premises, just as one can arrive at non-liberal conclusions from individualist premises.[5] But it is safe to say that contemporary liberal thought, in general, is clearly morally individualistic in tone. But even here there is great variation as to the kind of individualism appealed to.

A narrow conception of 'liberal individualism' is one associated with a particular conception of liberal rights; individuals possess rights that entitle them to a wide sphere of non-interference and free action, which in turn is thought to warrant minimal obligations to others (save for the duty to respect their basic rights), and thus minimal governmental regulation of and interference in civil society.

A broader account of moral individualism involves the belief that social and political arrangements ought to be judged primarily by how they affect the interests of individuals, as opposed to groups or other collective agents. In other words, that the importance of one's membership of a nation or culture is ultimately valuable only to the extent that they contribute to your individual well-being. But note that this is logically distinct from the vision associated with narrow individualism. Individual well-being might well require the presence of collective goods (such as a tolerant or cultured society), or a political system that does not take individuals' preferences at face value (i.e. 'deliberative' as opposed to 'aggregative' democracy). When Rawls, for example, talks of society as being a 'system of cooperation designed to advance the good of those taking part in it', he certainly is not equating individual good with unlaundered preferences, or ruling out a connection between collective goods and individual well-being. In fact, quite the opposite. For Rawls, the good of a well-ordered society is a good for citizens individually, but it is also a collective good. Citizens share the end of supporting and maintaining just institutions, which is only possible through their joint activity based on that shared general end. Thus living in a well-ordered society is not just instrumentally valuable, in so far as it enables you to realize your private ends – ends which could just as well be realizable under some other set of arrangements – it also represents a genuine collective good, one that you realize only in common with others and thus come to think of as good only by being a member of that society.[6]

Now for Rawls, of course, the crucial issue is that the state not become sectarian in its promotion of a well-ordered society. And he believes that he can provide what he calls a 'non-comprehensive' grounding for the good of a well-ordered society which diverse but reasonable citizens can assent to. Whatever the ultimate success of this move, note how far we are from the more narrow form of moral individualism. In fact, we have arrived at a form of 'holistic individualism',

in which the 'ontological bedding' of man is acknowledged at the same
time as the value of liberty and difference is also prized.[7] For Charles
Taylor this is a crucial, often occluded, strand of liberal thinking that
needs to be brought to the surface of contemporary debates. For only
when liberals acknowledge the good(s) upon which their commitment
to equality or liberty draw can they actually realize the conditions
required for societies to be organized around these values. Namely, the
willingness of people to live up to those values by identifying with and
acting so as to maintain and preserve the good of that community (i.e.
the free institutions and practices that underpin the procedural ideal, or
the free institutions and practices, including those related to a particular culture or language, associated with different kinds of liberal societies). Thus there is a real debate to be had about the best combination
of goods, as well as the best set of practical arrangements required to
realize them.

Holistic individualism implies mediated or variegated individualism.
Our relations between ourselves, our world and other individuals are
always mediated. This involves not only, as for Taylor, our relying on the
background of meaning provided through language, culture and our
membership in political communities, but also our being shaped by less
benign relations of power and force coursing through those very
processes. The mediated self is an inherently permeable self. As much as
the idea of the animating will of a 'sovereign artificer' is at best a metaphor
or at worst a myth for the scope of individual self-determination, it is, in
fact, the very inability of subjects to fix unmediated representations of self
or community under the unavoidable constraints of language (or
'discourse'), culture and relations of power that creates the conditions
for agency – for freedom.[8] As much as meaning is dependent, in other
words, upon a background social matrix, it does not follow that it is
wholly determined by it, even when those background conditions
include less than benign relations of power understood in a Foucauldian
sense (i.e. as ubiquitous and productive). Freedom, on this view, lies in
the creative capacity of agents to turn power against itself – wherever it
is found – rather than to secure a zone of non-interference or to restore
a more authentic or true representation of identity or community. In
this sense, as Foucault puts it, the only guarantee of liberty is liberty.[9]

Is this idea of the mediated or permeable self compatible with
liberalism? I believe that it is. One of the underlying aims of this book is
to argue for a vision of liberal political thought as a particularly
commodious and pliant set of family resemblances. There will be limits
to this commodiousness (as there is in any family, traditional or otherwise). But I do not think these limits are yet breached by complicating
conventional liberal ideas of individuality and selfhood; in fact, it seems

to me to that to rethink these conventional notions in light of new contexts and challenges is an impeccably liberal project itself.

Having argued for a form of mediated individualism, let us return to the postcolonial critique of liberalism. For I argued that the debate between communitarianism and liberalism (properly understood) can illuminate our understanding of what is at stake in that critique. It can do so in two ways.

First, it poses the question of community with some force. Granted that we are all situated within complex historical and cultural frameworks that condition our understanding of what is good and right, just how far does the writ of these 'maximal' moralities run? How embedded should we think of the self as being? To accept that the self is embedded in morally significant ways would go some way towards meeting the objections posed against the excessive individualism and 'atomism' of liberalism. And this many liberals are prepared to do. The debate is really over the extent and depth of cultural and historical encumbrance, not the fact of it. For it is clear that even the most autonomous of 'sovereign artificers', as Robert Goodin puts it, is constrained by the sociological, psychological and ontological truths of their origin and situatedness in particular communities.[10] As such, communities are manifestations of 'embedded rationality', the consequences of which matter morally, but not necessarily in the way that some communitarians suggest.

Here it might be useful to distinguish between two kinds of claims that could be made on behalf of the fact of embedded rationality. The first claim would be that in order to understand the moral and rational choices made by individuals, we need to understand what reasons people have to think something right. This usually entails knowing something about the position from where they start – the social, cultural and communal contexts within which they acquire knowledge and build their cognitions in the first place. Even rational choice theorists accept this. Hardin calls this 'communitarian residue' our cultural 'sunk costs'. He writes: 'Our sunk costs are us. [They] have been transmuted into information and putative knowledge that .... is a resource to us in our further actions ...'.[11] A danger, however, is that 'epistemological communitarianism' (or embedded rationality) can become transformed into a desire for the 'epistemological comforts of home'.[12] Thus from the claim that community matters for personal identity, and for what we take to be right or good, is derived a further claim that this particular community is right or good. This is the second kind of claim that can be made of the fact of embeddedness. And it is one liberals are usually keen to resist.[13] For it telescopes the kind of knowledge we can have about ourselves and our communities. If all knowledge is embedded and cannot be judged from some outside, then the risk of it being over-partial, blinkered or indeed contributing to relations of domination are increased. The epistemological liberal believes that 'exposure to more ideas ... is likely to give one a better chance at reaching correct conclusions about many factual and quasi-factual matters'.[14]

Thus the postcolonial critic of liberalism will have to be more specific about both the apparent individualism of liberalism and its abstract rationalism. For many liberals are only too willing to accept the fact of encumbered selves engaging in embedded practical reasoning. What differentiates them from certain communitarian views, however, is their willingness to distinguish morally between the different kinds of encumberances and embeddedness that individuals inhabit. Some forms of community deserve our censure rather than our allegiance, whatever their role in constituting our identity or knowledge of what is right and good. But there is room for disagreement and debate here, about the worthiness or value of one kind of community versus another, and what kind of support, protection, recognition or autonomy such communities deserve or could be granted by the liberal state. (It is precisely at this point that the communitarian engagement with liberalism crosses over into the problem of political division, which we shall examine below.)

The second way in which our discussion of community can illuminate the postcolonial critque of liberalism goes in a slightly different direction. The standard critique of someone like Walzer by liberals committed to more universal principles of justice is that he places too great an emphasis on the thick cultural meanings of particular communities, and too little on conceptions of practical public reason that might be applicable to any and every political community.[15] But in fact, he does think certain preconditions must hold for proper deliberation about the social goods and (complex) shared meanings that regulate their distribution. These deliberations – involving what he calls 'political knowledge' rather than 'philosophical knowledge' – must be conducted under the 'rule of reasons', and in conditions in which 'no one possesses or controls the means of domination'.[16] But how could we distinguish between reasonable and unreasonable claims in these deliberations? How could we identify the distortions caused by relations of power on public deliberation? By appeal to local narratives about those relations, or to the values implicit in those practices? By appeal to consent? We have already entertained the dangers of the first move, and the second invites all kinds of familiar objections. Simple agreement is not right making,[17] and to avoid this trap the most influential accounts of political contractarianism invoke standards of practical reason which must, by definition, transcend local narratives and contexts. (We shall explore these theories in greater detail in the next chapter.)

So Walzer seems caught between the desire to assert the moral relevance of thick cultural and historical encumbrances, and the apparently thin (though 'reiterated') preconditions for properly political speech. What the postcolonial critique of liberalism points out – accurately in my view – is the essential truth of the first claim; that moral and political debate in particular communities is shot through with cultural and historical factors that mark public debate in morally significant ways. And this truth is often under-appreciated by liberals (and others). It seems especially true for consideration of the claims of Aboriginal peoples in contemporary liberal democracies. Competing conceptions of property, harm, and historical injustice, for example, seem hard to detach from the thick cultural and historical contexts in which they are invoked. Such historical and cultural features are surely relevant to an evaluation of the micro-processes of consent, or to the analysis of the function of particular conventions or rules in a society.[18] They are certainly relevant to Aboriginal perspectives on liberal institutions. Walzer's perspective on moral discourse is highly sensitive to such features. Equally, however, it underplays the fact that such cultural and historical markers are the product of unequal and non-benign relations of power. Shared meanings are often coerced and manipulated meanings. Strangely then, *pace* Walzer, we might want a thicker account of public practical reason and a thinner account of extant shared meanings. That is, we might want to know more about how cultural and historical frameworks shape public reasoning; how it affects our judgments about the reasonable and the unreasonable, our conceptions of harm, of equal opportunity and where the line between public and private should be drawn. But we might want a much thinner account of shared meanings; that is, less presumption in favour of their being shared and more on the processes by which they come to be characterized as such. Rational choice theory meets Michel Foucault, as it were.

## Political division

How does the foregoing discussion of community cross over into the problem of political division? The latter is essentially the problem of justifying boundaries; how do we justify the external and internal boundaries of a political community? Answering this requires a normative theory of association, and for liberals, the tricky task of providing, potentially, a liberal theory of nationalism. I shall postpone that discussion until later. My hope is that in engaging with the claims of

Aboriginal peoples to some form of 'coordinate' or shared sovereignty, we might arrive at an attractive account of liberal association, of what I shall call the postcolonial state.

But first, what of the problem of political division within an already existing state? What are the moral constraints on the way a state is organized or divided internally? Note that in asking this question we are already accepting a rather more complex and 'layered' conception of sovereignty than is sometimes the case in the discipline of political science. For it might be assumed that if a state is recognized as sovereign by other sovereign states, the question of the moral constraints on how it organizes itself internally is moot.[19] The right to determine how a state governs itself (the right to self-determination) entails the right not to be interfered with in governing itself. However, this is deeply implausible for two reasons. First, such an exclusive conception of self-determination would seem to rule out any right of seccession on the part of other groups within that state. Sovereignty may give a state a right against other states interfering in the self-government of its territory, but it does not give that state a claim, as David Copp puts it, against 'populations internal to it that they not interfere with its governing them in their territory'.[20] In other words, there are legitimate issues concerning the interests of various groups within a state to exercising certain rights of self-determination. These may fall short of secession, but they might still entail a reconfiguration of the governance of that state, or indeed the collective identity underlying it. Secondly, although international law has always had a strong presumption in favour of the extant sovereignty and territorial integrity of existing states, this is increasingly restricted to those states that are not persistent and massive violators of basic human rights.[21]

For Michael Walzer, the commonality shared by humans everywhere is a kind of particularism. We are all culture-producing creatures, and we all participate in thick cultures of our own. We are equal in this regard. Thus each of us, and each of the cultures we inhabit, is owed a presumptive tolerance. Each nation has a right to self-determination to govern itself in accordance with its own political ideas. New nations should be held to recognize in 'the nation-that-comes-next the rights vindicated by their own independence'.[22] Boundaries should be drawn to enhance the 'cultural creativity' of particular communities, not repress them, and this might entail federal, confederal and international checks and balances on nation states. But at this point the problem of political division within a state touches on our discussion of Walzer's account of thick and thin forms of practical reason. For if public discourse is essentially a case of individuals working out, from within their shared maximal morality, the rights and duties they owe to each other and the benefits and burdens to be distributed, then it might follow that the boundaries of a state should match those of the shared (albeit complex) cultural traditions and practices. The political and the cultural-historical should coincide. This seems to be the presumption in *Spheres of Justice*.[23] (It raises issues for the external arrangement of states as well, but I shall leave those aside for now.) And this is a very problematic presumption, particularly for political communities in which different historical/cultural groups are – in O'Neill's apt phrase – 'uneasily intermingled'.[24] If political and historical communities do not coincide, argues Walzer, then each distributive decision as to the requirements of these communities 'must itself be worked out politically'. And how they are worked out will depend 'upon the understandings shared among the citizens about the value of cultural diversity, autonomy and so on ...'.[25] But this is precisely the problem where communities are deeply divided, or where minorities have persistent difficulties making their claims recognized or heard. Appeal to shared meanings becomes an appeal to the meanings held by a dominant majority.[26] The unequal bargaining positions of the parties are left as they are rather than subject to the 'rule of reason'. This is particularly true where the historical communities that make up a state disagree about the legitimacy of its very boundaries, as in Northern Ireland or Palestine/Israel. According to Walzer, in these contexts, minorities have essentially three options; they can assimilate, seek accommodation as best they can derived from the shared understandings of the community, or seek a divorce (but only where there is a plausible territorial claim, and the group has the numerical and political capacity to force the issue).[27] Majorities have no obligation to protect the survival of minority cultures; 'they have a claim to physical but not cultural security'. Though Walzer recognizes that there are many possibilities and permutations with regard to forms of accommodation, it is still the case that 'no minimalist account of justice can specify the precise form of these arrangements ... the forms are historically negotiated, and they depend upon the shared understandings of what such negotiations mean and how they work'.[28]

What seems clear from Walzer's discussion is that the viability of minority claims for protection of their cultural frameworks, or some form of self-government, will depend, in large measure, on the shared understandings concerning the value of cultural diversity or local autonomy, and even about how the negotiations premised on these values should proceed. As we shall see, this is a deeply problematic starting point for evaluating the claims of Aboriginal peoples in countries such as Canada and Australia. For it is clear that the shared understanding of the majority nation(s) was the source of great injustices committed against them, and often continues to be so. The histories of relations between the settler state and the Aboriginal peoples they encountered and sometimes cooperated with, but usually also tried to conquer and subjugate, provide a vivid record of how discriminatory attitudes and practices became embedded in the public institutions of liberal democracy.

But it is a complex story. As I mentioned in Chapter 1, one important difference between Canada and Australia is that in the former, there is an extensive history and practice of treaty-making between settlers and the diverse Aboriginal nations. And the re-invigoration and endorsement of the values implicit in these practices has recently been put at the centre of a Royal Commission on Aboriginal Peoples, set up to provide a new framework for relations between Aboriginal peoples and the state.[29] In Australia, on the other hand, there is very little history of treaty-making, and the model, despite repeated attempts to introduce it, has had little impact on the public debate over Aboriginal rights (although that may now be beginning to change).[30] Other resources have had to be drawn on, some borrowed from Canada and the United States, others drawn from the distinctive colonial experience of Australia. My point is that if one response to the abstract rationalism of liberalism is to go for cultural thickness – that moral discourse is nothing but cultural thickness reiterated in different times and places – then we must be prepared to investigate exactly what this commits us to. Postcolonial histories are invaluable in this regard. They cut against the congratulatory tone of so much of the myths of nation-building, and show the prejudices and exclusions built into the 'shared meanings' of complex political communities. It should not be the case that rejecting abstract rationalism entails rejecting anything other than a thick cultural account of the rights and duties we owe to others, or of the proper framework for the distribution of burdens and benefits. Postcolonial critics should have as much difficulty with Walzer's particularism as they do with liberalism's apparent abstract rationalism.

### Liberal collective rights

Does the postcolonial critique of liberalism entail thinking of liberalism as irredeemably tainted by a colonial past? Or can some of its central values, such as to do with liberty and equality, be put to work in genuinely postcolonial ways? And if they can, what are the limits that accompany them? Can they address the fundamental aspirations of the many different Aboriginal peoples residing in liberal-democratic states?

The fundamental obstacle to liberalism being capable of accommodating indigenous peoples' claims is said to be its presumption in favour
of individual rights. The primary purpose of the liberal state is to protect
civil and political rights, and insofar as it is, this prevents it from accommodating the just claims of Aboriginal groups. The issue is therefore a
face-off between individual and group rights. Or so it seems. In actual
fact, the concrete example of Aboriginal claims will allow us to see how
the distinction between group and individual rights as it is usually
wielded is too crude a measure of what is at stake. The good of community is, in many circumstances, a good for individuals. And in so far
as that is true, it might be the case that the good of community will
require group (or collective) rights. Some individual rights, like those of
freedom of association, expression and religion, are valued precisely
because they allow individuals to form groups. The value of membership in a group is a value for individuals.

But we might also think that there are goods which are irreducibly
social in nature.[31] A culture or community might be entitled to certain
group rights just in virtue of it being an 'impersonal good'.[32] Certain
cultures have value independent of the contributions they make to
individual lives. We value the survival of our culture, for example, not
simply because it plays an instrumental part in helping us live our lives,
or those of future generations, but because we believe such a culture
should survive even if it does not make the lives persons live more
valuable.[33] The good of a culture existing in this sense is thus not
reducible to the goods of individuals; it is not a means to a good, but
constitutes the good.[34] This is a controversial claim, and one that makes
most liberals uneasy. But since most claims for group or collective rights
made by Aboriginal peoples, at least, rarely depend exclusively on an
appeal to the intrinsic worth of their culture independent of its worth to
individual members, I shall leave it aside.

The basic point is that liberalism can affirm the good of community,
even whilst defending basic individual civil and political rights. For
some liberals, that is all it should do. The liberal right of freedom of
association, together with other basic rights of freedom of speech and
conscience, are powerful tools for forming a wide range of collective
associations. For liberals, churches, for example, should be free to
decide the terms of their association and the rules governing acceptable
and unacceptable behaviour within them. There might be times when
the costs imposed on an individual who chooses to leave a religious
association (or is forced to leave) are not inconsiderable, but which are
not, on liberal grounds, unreasonable – given the importance of freedom of association. If an individual's civil or political liberties were

being violated in the process, however, then things would be different. And even if civil liberties are not being violated, there may still be times when the costs imposed on individuals in these situations are ones that a liberal would think reasonable to seek some kind of legal relief for.[35] In the United States, for example, religious organizations are given lee-way to impose conditions on employees that, strictly speaking, seem to depart from anti-discrimination legislation. For liberals, however, there will be times when such leeway goes too far, in tying important secular benefits to a declaration of faith which conflicts with liberal beliefs about equal treatment and freedom of religion.[36]

In general, freedom of religion, and the freedom of association does not necessarily entail an exemption from generally applicable laws 'on the basis of the differential effect of those laws on people according to their beliefs, norms, compulsions or preferences'.[37] It does not follow, however, that a legislature might not go on and make certain exemptions in particular cases. I agree with Brian Barry that it should not be up to the courts, at least in every instance, to craft these exemptions where the more overtly political institutions have failed to do so. The public sphere, rather than the court room, is the more appropriate place for the airing and testing of these arguments. But it is also true, especially in the case of Aboriginal peoples, that political and legal institutions interact in complex ways. Extensive political activism, for example, preceded the landmark *Mabo* land rights case in Australia (to be discussed in Chapter 7). But equally, it took a decision of the High Court to motivate Parliament, large rural landowners and mining interests to begin to negotiate seriously with Aboriginal claimants.

For some liberals then, there is much to be said for realizing the good of community through the principle of freedom of association, and that it entails a not inconsiderable scope for group autonomy within a liberal state. Any exemptions from generally applicable laws are not required by justice, so this argument goes, but may be prudent to grant for political reasons. 'Governments may not single out particular religious groups for adverse treatment', argues Barry, 'but [they] are not obliged to give them especially favourable treatment'.[38]

Liberal theorists have also argued, however, that the good of community for individuals in some circumstances – notably, in the case of cultural minorities – permits wider or stronger forms of collective rights. The twist in the tale is what kinds of conditions are attached to these rights. A liberal like Barry is not opposed to differential rights *per se*, but rather to differential *basic* rights.[39] The liberals I am about to discuss think departures from the liberal baseline of basic civil and political liberties are morally permissible, although they offer different reasons for thinking so, as well as different characterizations of the distinction between basic and other kinds of rights. This will be true of postcolonial liberalism as well.

Before tackling the issue of the kind of limits liberals place on collective rights, we need to take a step back and ask how they arrive at justifying any in the first place. Cultural pluralism in contemporary liberal democracies has generated a vast array of claims for recognizing cultural difference. Jacob Levy has identified at least eight such claims; for exemptions, assistance, recognition, representation, for 'external' and 'internal' rules, self-government and 'symbolic claims'.[40] Acknowledging the complexity of claims made by different cultural groups is important. Some involve negative rights of non-interference, some positive rights of assistance, and others a combination of negative and positive measures. Some might be compatible with individual rights (wieldable by individuals as members of a group) and some only held by the group (and thus exerciseable by their agent or representative). Slogans about 'the recognition of difference' are empty until such specifics are engaged with. Note that many of these measures are ones already being used by most of the contemporary liberal democracies under discussion in this book. So to a certain extent the general question as to whether or not we should grant such rights is moot. The real question is over the underlying rationale for them, and the best way of settling the inevitable conflicts that occur between them.

Consider three basic arguments for recognizing collective rights on liberal grounds.

(1) *The historical injustice argument*: Certain collective rights are justified insofar as they are aimed at redressing or compensating for a history of past unjustice against particular historical communities at the hands of dominant majorities.

(2) *The value of cultural membership argument*: Certain collective rights are justified insofar as membership in a culture has value for individuals, and there is a link between the welfare of the group and welfare of its members. Group rights contribute to the preservation of that culture and the welfare of its members.

(3) *The cultural diversity argument*: Cultural diversity is valuable for itself and thus entails preserving, as far as is possible, existing cultures, because (i) no one culture embodies all there is for a valuable life, and thus encounters with different cultures and ways of life corrects and expand our moral imagination; (ii) it promotes critical reflection on the culture within which one currently lives and promotes change and growth within that culture, and (iii) it is a necessary precondition of effective cross-cultural dialogue.

Before saying a bit more about each of these arguments, what do we mean when we talk about groups, and in what sense are groups 'minorities'? There are (at least) two ways of thinking about the nature of groups in political philosophy. We might think that since individuals are all that matters, the only groups that matter are those formed by individuals exercising their basic liberties to associate with each other. Freedom of association entails that groups will be formed and insofar as individuals are free to form, to not form, and to leave such groups; there is no need to supplement basic individual rights with those grounded in the value of cultural membership. But it is patently obvious from looking around the world today that a purely voluntarist conception of groups is radically incomplete, either as a normative theory of political association, or as a descriptive claim about groups in political life generally. Hence, we should accept that groups made up of individuals who share an identity by way of certain characteristics such as language, culture or a shared history are also relevant.[41] This need not mean accepting that groups are static, inflexible entities. Individuals should be as free as possible to affiliate or not with their community, and group identity need not to be exclusive or all-encompassing. The point is more to do with recognizing the salience of cultural and historical communities. What follows morally from such recognition is precisely the issue at hand.

When does being in a minority matter? We are concerned with 'minority' groups in so far as being a minority affects the interests of members in morally significant ways. Supporters of the Montreal Canadiens hockey team are a minority relative to the population of Australia as a whole, but not in any way relevant to a theory of justice (unless they were persecuted in a morally relevant way as a result of that identity). Women are not a minority relative to the population at large, but are relative to (say) senior academic positions, and this might be relevant for considerations of justice. Aboriginal people are clearly a minority relative to the population at large, and also vulnerable in virtue of this status due to the threat posed by majority decisions to certain interests they have in relation to land, culture and self-government. Determining which aspects of their ways of life or cultural frameworks are eligible for protection by the state – if any – depends on beliefs about the relation between membership in a group and the fundamental interests of persons.

Let us return then to the three liberal arguments for recognizing group rights. All three are intended, in different ways, to address claims about the disadvantage suffered by particular groups and individuals in being excluded from or discriminated against within the public institutions and discourses of society. The argument from the value of cultural diversity is a classic liberal argument, articulated most famously by J. S. Mill and more recently, on rather different grounds than Mill, by

Bhikhu Parekh.[42] Some general commitment to the value of cultural diversity seems absolutely necessary for postcolonial liberalism. For a purely instrumental approach to the value of culture – i.e. that cultural diversity is valuable because it increases the range of valuable options for me, or that it contributes to truth-seeking, or that it creates a rich and pleasing world – leaves those cultures which are not really live options for us, or which are not thought to contribute to the pursuit of truth or richness, vulnerable. Moreover, why should those who do not seek greater choice or variety in their lives be persuaded as to the inherent value of cultural diversity? For Parekh, cultural diversity is valuable in itself ultimately because it fosters certain basic preconditions necessary for human well-being, whether or not it provides real options for us.[43] No single culture embodies all there is to the good life, but different cultures challenge and expand the horizons of each other and contribute to a deepening of our reflection upon the nature of human well-being. Closed and homogenuous cultures become static and rigidified, they do not challenge or develop the intellectual or moral capacities of their adherents, capacities which are required if the culture in question is to survive and adapt to contemporary circumstances. An openness towards and engagement with 'unassimilable difference' stretches and challenges our moral imagination. It forces us to step outside our own cultures – if only for a moment – and moderates our tendency to absolutize our cultural frameworks. This is a crucial precondition, Parekh argues, of respectful and effective cross-cultural dialogue.

However if cultural diversity is valuable for itself, then it is not clear why any *particular* culture should survive if its disappearing, for example, allowed other and a greater number of cultures to flourish elsewhere in the world. In other words, how does the argument from cultural diversity match up with the demands made by particular cultures for survival or resources? One can imagine a spokesperson or leader of a cultural group saying: 'I don't just want there to be lots of cultural diversity, I want *my* tribe's culture and language to survive because it has value for *us*, whatever else it might mean to you'. Of course, that is not to say the value of cultural diversity should just be ignored. Part of the liberal justification of the state is that it is best able to provide for the flourishing of a diverse range of cultures within a political community.[44] Such diversity is unavoidable, think liberals, given a liberal commitment to the protection of people's basic liberties – including their freedom (and 'higher order interest') to reflect upon and pursue their conception of the good. The argument from cultural diversity is, however, incomplete. If more cultural diversity is better than less, then either all cultural beliefs and practices are multiculturalism-enriching and deserving of toleration or respect, or only some are. The former cannot be true, and the latter forces us to identify the properties that make some cultural practices valuable and others not. And this leads to the 'historical injustice' and 'value of cultural membership' arguments.

Though the historical injustice argument and the welfare argument are often linked, they appeal to different intuitions about justice. One is grounded in intuitions about the need for restitution, and the other in matters of redistribution. These intuitions overlap, but as we shall see in Chapter 5, they are also often at odds with each other. They shape one's response to cultural claims. Categorizing Aboriginal land claims, for example, as a matter for a theory of restitution as opposed to a theory of justice is to make a substantive judgment about these claims, and not simply a logical point.

The historical injustice argument is relatively straightforward. In light of past gross injustices committed against a particular historical community – injustices which have impaired and continue to impair the ability of members of that community or culture to lead decent lives – there are moral reasons for recognizing some form of group or collective rights aimed at protecting and/or assisting that culture to survive. The important point is that it is the logic of compensation or restitution that carries the weight of the argument, rather than the value of cultural membership generally. For some, this means that Aboriginal land claims, or claims for the recognition of customary law, raise not so much issues of culture, as matters of law. Relatedly, claims based on historical injustice are read down in light of the passage of time and the difficulty of verifying counterfactuals, as entailing mainly 'symbolic' rather than 'real' compensation.[45]

The value of cultural membership argument has received perhaps the greatest amount of attention recently, and thus has many different permutations.[46] The basic thrust is that cultural membership has value for individuals insofar as access to a culture (or cultures; the difference is significant, as we shall see) is tied to the value of freedom or well-being.

The connection between cultural membership and individual freedom is central to Will Kymlicka's influential argument. Much has been written about his justification of a liberal theory of group rights, which I don't intend to survey here. Instead, I want to discuss two crucial elements of his argument; first, the link he draws between culture and freedom, and second, his conception of a societal culture.

Kymlicka argues that cultural membership provides individuals with a 'context for meaningful choice'.[47] It makes salient a range of possible goals and options, and imparts meaning to these options. It animates and illuminates the possibilities of a life and thus makes freedom meaningful in the first place. What is a 'societal culture'? It provides its members with 'meaningful ways of life across the full range of human activities, including social, educational, religious, and economic life, encompassing both public and private spheres'. It also includes common institutions and practices, embodied in 'schools, media, economy, government, etc.', as well as a shared language. Societal cultures are, by and large, national cultures, usually territorially concentrated, and thus linked to processes of 'modernization'.[48] But at the same time, Kymlicka argues, these cultural frameworks need to be seen as pluralistic and permeable. National minorities must remain fluid and non-exclusive in their conceptions of identity, avoiding the primacy of blood and descent. They must remain, in a phrase, 'civic and post-ethnic'.[49] So a societal culture is a source of both beliefs about value and a sense of identity. To lack secure access to a societal culture then, or to be coerced into giving up one's commitment to a societal culture, in some circumstances, is potentially a threat to one's freedom and well-being.

Thus, according to Kymlicka, certain national minority groups are entitled to the means to protect their societal culture when those cultural frameworks are under threat from being unjustifiably assimilated into the majority culture. This is true of national minorities as opposed to migrants, because the latter have usually chosen to integrate into the majority culture, or at least maintain their cultural commitments in less comprehensive ways.[50] Whereas national

[minorities] mobilize as nations because they cherish their own national identity and national institutions, and wish to maintain them into the indefinite future ... minority nationalism is not necessarily, or even typically, adopted as compensation for exclusion from the majority nation. Rather it is adopted because of an intrinsic commitment to the maintenance of the minority's own national identity, culture and institutions.[51]

The kinds of rights such groups are entitled to will vary. Return to the example of indigenous peoples for a moment. Aboriginal peoples in North America and Australasia are entitled, on Kymlicka's argument, to certain collective rights up to and including forms of self-government.[52] This is in virtue of the threat posed to their cultural structures and way of life by dominant majorities, and in virtue of a long history of domination and oppression (note the cross-over of arguments (1) and (2) above). These rights might include entitlements, as members of a group, to public subsidies for the preservation of their language, or exemption from certain aspects of generally applicable laws. Or they might involve more 'prescriptive' rights,[53] such as the right of a tribe or Band to prohibit non-members from settling in a particular territory, or members of the Band from selling land to non-members. The latter kinds of rights are vested in the group rather than the individual, though again, their purpose is aimed at protecting goods (e.g. land) valuable for individual members.

Problems with Kymlicka's argument emerge with regard to the tension between recognizing the 'deep bond' people have to a particular social group and set of practices (perhaps including a homeland), and moral claims about the value of autonomy or self-respect.[54] He attempts to negotiate this impasse by distinguishing between a societal culture's *structure* and its *content*. The structure of a societal culture provides the meaning and orientation in life that a liberal theory of justice should be concerned to protect, or at least compensate for if found lacking. But the structure of a culture is not the same thing as the ends or shared meanings a particular cultural group may hold at any given time, which may or may not be compatible with liberal ends.[55] The distinction is controversial, however, since if a societal culture is to be meaningful to people and something to which they feel a 'deep bond', then it must have *some* content. It is not clear in Kymlicka's argument whether people are entitled to value their cultural membership for reasons other than to do with it providing them with a context for choice.[56] This seems to limit the theory to providing rights for generally already liberal groups, and hence gives some credence to the postcolonial critic's concern with the inherent limits to liberal multiculturalism.

Kymlicka's argument is vulnerable to attack on two fronts. First, though he opposes any 'official' discrimination against women or dissidents within minority groups, he leaves himself open to tolerating more informal rules or practices that are discriminatory, especially if group rights empower men, for example, or a narrow elite, within the group.[57] Kymlicka is either too hard on national minorities (disallowing the distinctive ways in which they might organize their communities and the way they reason about their good), or too soft (tolerating internal rules that might be discriminatory of persons' basic rights).

Note that this is also a problem for those who reject special cultural rights of any kind, and insist that individual rights of freedom of expression or association are all that is needed.[58] For if freedom of association and religious belief entails that religious or Aboriginal communities should be free to get on with their lives as they wish, then we still need an argument as to why that account of freedom outweighs the unfreedom of particular members who might be discriminated against within those communities. If we reject the value of autonomy or freedom as grounding liberal group rights, and assert that a culture is valuable to individuals only insofar as they choose to acquiesce in it, then we are back to problems first encountered in the discussion of Walzer. How can we be sure that the micro-processes of consent are not distorted by relations of power and processes of socialization? The freedom to exit is an empty option in circumstances where relations of power are such that the weakest and most vulnerable members are least able to question or criticize the social roles imposed on them.

Thus criticisms of Kymlicka's argument have focused on two general areas. First, that his conception of societal culture is problematic, even incoherent.[59] And second, that he cannot derive the justification of group rights from his claims about the connection between the value of cultural membership and individual freedom.[60] These criticisms are obviously related, but the problems with his notion of a societal culture are most relevant here, so I shall focus on them. If Kymlicka is wedded to a conception of societal culture in which a culture is said to be 'more or less institutionally complete', and that it must be comprehensively 'embodied, in schools, media, economy, government, etc.' (linked as it is to 'processes of modernization'), then he actually undermines the claims for minority rights of a much larger number of vulnerable cultural minorities than he thinks – including Aboriginal peoples. For example, Aboriginal cultures emerged long before modernization and few of their political communities have the capacity to maintain their languages or build and support a societal culture in the manner Kymlicka suggests (as much as they would like to).[61] As Joseph Carens puts it: 'If the sole justification for group-differentiated cultural rights is that they can contribute to the maintenance of a societal culture, then how can a group be entitled to such rights if it does not have the capacity to sustain a societal culture?'.[62] Carens goes on to suggest that most of the world's national minorities are far from being in a position like the Quebecois – Kymlicka's norm for a societal culture. National minorities are usually not 'more or less institutionally complete', but vary according to degrees of incompleteness, and hence liberal states with national minorities and migrants do indeed face a 'strange multiplicity' of demands that cannot be reduced to either self-government or non-discriminatory assimilation.

Moreover, to return to the second set of criticisms of Kymlicka's argument (to do with the connection between culture and freedom), it follows that there is not simply one 'context for choice' provided by *a* societal culture but rather a multiplicity of them. Language might play an important role, but so too religion, and so might moving between different societal cultures. Evaluating which elements of these various contexts of choice will require recognition by the state (and other citizens) in the form of accommodation rights, differential citizenship rights or self-government, requires showing the relation between these different mechanisms and the human interests said to be served by granting them. Recognition and accommodation of identity-related differences is always a means to the realization of important human interests, not ends in themselves. This is important, because often critics of multiculturalism assume that in order to justify cultural rights you must be committed to treating cultural groups as essentially state-like, and thus more impermeable and bounded than they really are. But it does not follow that the forms of accommodation and recognition sought by Aboriginal groups, for example, entail the withdrawal 'from individual members of minority groups the protections normally offered by liberal states', in order that these groups 'should be able to discriminate with impunity against women or adherents of religions other than the majority'.[63] This is to imply that because Aboriginal communities claim certain political powers they will *ipso facto* use them to discriminate against their members, or that they will not be subject to countervailing powers from both within and outside their boundaries. But this is an absurd conclusion. Instead, as we shall see, the real issue is one of evaluating the extent to which, in certain circumstances, it is reasonable to balance the interests of the members of a cultural community with the right of the cultural community as a whole to preserve certain aspects of its way of life. Sometimes it will be, sometimes it will not. And even then, there is yet another set of questions about the best way of going about trying to secure both the interests of individual members and the group as a whole. I shall return to this important issue in Chapter 7.

So the concept of a societal culture is deeply problematic. But that does not mean giving up on the notion that the basic interests of persons are sometimes tied to their identity-related differences. Postcolonial liberalism aims for a more contextual approach, one that takes into consideration the particular circumstances of indigenous peoples, and then asks how preserving aspects of their cultural structures may (or may not) be relevant to securing certain of the fundamental interests of their members. Moreover, as we shall see (in Chapter 6), not all possible justifications of Aboriginal rights are culture-based, nor should they be. The claim for jurisdiction over territory, for example, is based on prior occupancy and sovereignty, not culture.

Another more general objection to collective rights is that the connection between individual well-being and the protection of cultural or associational groups is at best contingent, and at worst dubious. Recognizing group claims in fact usually undermines the well-being of individuals rather than enhancing it. It can do so for two reasons. First, collective rights can increase the transaction costs of communication, and may be perceived by a majority as opening the way to an inevitable proliferation of such claims, and the potential break-up of the state. And since collective rights often entail significant burdens placed on the majority population (e.g. subsidizing minority languages, or tolerating different legal standards), such rights can generate resentment against minorities, thus undermining, paradoxically, one of the main reasons for supporting group rights in the first place.

Secondly, group rights undermine individual welfare by creating conditions ripe for strategic manipulation. They provide opportunities for 'tribal political entrepreneurs', as Claus Offe calls them, to manipulate norms and rules to exclude and discriminate against not only other groups, but individuals within their group as well.[64] Overall, so this argument goes, the opportunity costs of group rights outweigh any potential benefits. Liberal individual rights, including social and economic rights, offer far greater potential for creating the conditions for genuine equal citizenship and democratic stability.

Taken together, these objections to a liberal theory of minority rights are quite powerful. But so is the intuition that questions of identity, recognition and the accommodation of identity-related differences also matter, and that people suffer genuine harm when their cultural interests are ignored or excluded from the common registers of public reasoning. One need only consider the history of nation-building in the West (or anywhere else, for that matter) and the experience of indigenous peoples in relation to it, to test this thought. There are at least two parts to this process, however, which are often neglected by critics of Aboriginal rights, and multicultural and multinational rights more generally. Claims for the accommodation or recognition of cultural practices originate first from within the various groups, as they try to make sense of their traditions and practices in light of the circumstances they face in the wider political system. They then engage in the exchange of public reasons with other citizens, either directly or through their representatives. The next part of the process involves working out what the appropriate new norm of recognition, or new institutions, should be on the basis of this exchange.[65] The parts are interdependent and interconnected; sometimes public reasoning is shaped by models of collective or group rights worked out by various claimants, but just as often those initial models or proposals are reshaped in light of public argument and debate over them. Often these exchanges in turn reshape the internal practices and discourses of the various groups. But it is still important to see these components as analytically distinct. If not, then the tendency is to assume that the claimants are being unreasonable, offering up their demands without any intention of trying to justify them to others, or of remaining open to counter-proposals and seeking some form of common ground.

I shall argue that we should see claims about Aboriginal rights in terms of an ideal of democratic citizenship, and especially as providing a distinct set of capabilities in relation to their fundamental interests in land, culture and self-government. Democracy presupposes that a people, collectively, are entitled to an equal say in decisions that affect them. To possess equal standing in relation to one's fellow citizens is to have the capacity to take part in the governance of that society, in both direct but mainly indirect ways. Still, any democratic system is based on some form of (restricted) majority rule, and so a further feature of democracy is that whatever the procedures by which decisions are arrived at, there must be mechanisms (both electoral and non-electoral) through which the 'losers' can seek to produce change in the future, or are protected from domination if they are a minority unlikely to be able to influence democratic debate in significant ways.[66] There are, in other words, certain basic interests that must be protected from majoritarian abuse if democracy itself is going to be effective.[67]

Claims by national groups can be seen then, in some circumstances, as claims about equal standing relative to a dominant majority. In multi-cultural and multinational states there will be minorities relative to a majority population who will always remain vulnerable to majority deci-sion making. Thus claims for minority rights should be understood as claims for measures that would allow such groups to participate, on fair terms, in the direction and governance of that society. In some cases, 'what is fair' may entail extensive political rights of self-government, in other cases, accommodation rights or exemptions which allow a group to protect aspects of their cultural frameworks related to the funda-mental interests of their members. In still other cases, the fundamental interests that all citizens have in possessing certain basic freedoms will trump membership interests.

In general, it is better if people are able to exercise influence over decisions and institutions that exercise influence over them. All manner of social practices, however they originally arose or were designed, can atrophy into systems of domination.[68] Benefits and harms are distrib-uted in different ways, and there will always be questions about these patterns of distribution at particular times. Thus the value of collective self-government is, as Ian Shapiro has recently emphasized, as much to do with the capacity to *oppose* a set of practices as it is to participate in them; or to say, as Foucault put it, that in so far as we are all governed, we ought 'not to be governed in this particular way, or at this price'.[69]

Focusing on the democratic dimensions of multiculturalism and multinationalism is thus crucial to the whole project of postcolonial liberalism. At the same time, this same logic should lead us – on pain of self-contradiction – to be concerned with the capacities of vulnerable individuals and sub-groups *within* the various groups pressing for accommodation themselves, to secure their equal standing in relation to the political arrangements in which they are situated. This does not jus-tify imposing on every group's way of life the institutions of liberal democracy writ small. Democratic concerns should *condition* the pursuit of communal goods, not dictate them.[70] The whole idea of liberalism going local, which is at the heart of postcolonial liberalism, is concerned to adapt to and learn from local practices and concrete forms of life, not obliterate them.

## Conclusion

I began this chapter by noting how the postcolonial critique of liberalism raised serious questions about liberalism's individualism and abstract rationalism, both of which feature in the story of its historical complicity with colonialism. I have attempted to show that, at least with regard to the charge of individualism, the matter is much more complex. Connecting the debate between liberalism and communitarianism to 'the problem of political division', I attempted to show how liberalism has the resources to accommodate the value of communal goods in any number of ways, although there are important questions about the limits within which these goods can be pursued. Determining the reasonableness of these demands, and of any limits to be imposed, requires paying close attention to the specific nature of the claims and the context in which they are made.

The charge of abstract rationalism requires an equally complex response, and is potentially more difficult to answer. For normative political theorists often do underplay the extent to which public deliberation is shot through with historical and practical features difficult to transcend or set aside. The transparency of communication presumed to be necessary for legitimating the exercise of political power is always in danger of glossing over the cultural and strategic aspects of how disagreements and claims arise and are processed in the first place. Should moral discourse, let alone public practical reason, be conceived of independently of its origin in complex practical and historical contexts? It should not, but that still leaves the question of what the relation between reason and history is. Assuming that there is no place where human deliberation is not coarsened by relations of power, where rationality is not in some way embedded or limited and we are unavoidably encumbered by our historical 'sunk costs', how can the liberal justificatory ideal possibly be realized?

# 4    Disagreement and public reason

> The threads of a thousand acts of accommodation are the fabric of a nation.[1]

## Introduction

Given the history of relations between Aboriginal peoples and the state, on what possible grounds could a liberal state ever become a genuinely postcolonial one? The terms of association would have to be ones acceptable to both Aboriginal and non-Aboriginal peoples – and therein lies the challenge. The obvious solution is dialogue: a mutually acceptable form of negotiated settlement. But how do we get from mutual incomprehension or indifference to dialogue; and then from dialogue to a mutually acceptable negotiated settlement? I might demonstrate my respect for you by engaging you in dialogue, but it does not follow that I might not still try to impose a settlement upon you if I thought it was the right thing to do, or that you were unreasonable in rejecting it. The invocation of reasonableness is deeply contested terrain in colonial contexts, and the fact that it continues to occupy an important place in contemporary theories of justice will be significant for our discussion below.

Partha Chatterjee, for example, has argued that 'the limits of liberal-rationalist theory are reached' when a particular group demands the right 'not to offer a reason for being different'.[2] The possibility for any kind of accommodation might seem to have been lost at this point. But given the strategic emphasis theorists like Michel Foucault and James Scott have brought to bear on our understanding of the relation between government (broadly construed) and cultural groups, what in fact may be occurring is the demand not to give reasons that are grounded in a particular conception of public reason.[3] This may seem to involve, at first glance, declaring yourself unreasonable. However what might be occurring is in fact a contestation of the deliberative idioms and forums within which their claims are heard and evaluated.[4] It is not necessarily a refusal to engage in public exchange of reasons.

In Chapter 1, I suggested that there simply was no *categorical* justification of our obligations to the state along the lines of consent, and this seems especially clear in relation to the situation of indigenous peoples. But what then is the link between legitimacy and the practices of public reason? The legitimacy of the postcolonial state will be one that inheres in a political argument about the role of the state in relation to its citizens that is 'without any guarantor and without any end'. In this chapter I want to consider *five* dimensions of public reason: power, procedures, practices, *modus vivendi* and affect. In so doing, one of the underlying aims will be to re-evaluate the link between consensus and legitimacy. Liberals are usually thought to presume that there is an important connection between consensus and the nature of public justification. Without consensus on constitutional essentials, or a common notion of 'reciprocity', the exercise of political power cannot be justified in conditions of deep social and political diversity. To treat people with equal respect entails seeking reasonable agreement.

But as I will argue below, the achievement of consensus is impossible and hence the ideal is fundamentally ambiguous.[5] Any form of discursive consensus is at best only partial and transitory, since any rules or norms agreed to will always be subject to re-description and change given the dialogical contexts within which they were formed. Moreover, actual consensus in collective choice, in terms of agreement not just over some public policy but also the reasons for it, is literally impossible. Even meaningful participation in collective decisions by anything other than a small minority is beyond reach.[6] So consensus can never be complete or wholly constitutive of exercises of political power. Residues of misunderstanding, non-consensuality and injustice persist through the various mediums of communicative action which have gone into the construction of consensus. The gap between agreement and its application in practice is thus central and not peripheral to such a political sensibility. It provides the means to question and contest the ground upon which apparent consensus provides a warrant for the principles or institutions appealed to in relation to the exercise of political power. Moving conflict and disagreement into the centre of our thinking about justice is a critical aspect of postcolonial liberalism. We need to take the pluralization of public reason seriously, and aim for discursively legitimated forms of agreements that do not over-idealize consensus. I shall refer to such agreements as *discursive modi vivendi:* discursive because they emerge from the constellation of discourses and registers present in the public sphere at any given time, and subject to at least some kind of 'reflexive control' by competent actors; and *modi vivendi* because they are always provisional, open to contestation and by definition 'incompletely theorized'.[7]

We turn first, however, to the five dimensions of public reason.


## Power


You might think that untrammelled public argument is, in fact, all that we have got and that we should expect in politics. If all political interaction is essentially strategic interaction, and therefore all appeals to principle are strategic appeals, then the persuasiveness of political argument is derivative of the strategic positions of the interlocutors, not the quality of moral deliberation between them. As Stanley Fish has argued, when it comes to political argument 'Who gets to say what is and is not a plausible premise?... The answers are obvious and embarrassing because they point to an act of power, of peremptory exclusion and dismissal, that cannot be acknowledged as such lest the liberal program of renouncing power and exclusion be exposed for the fiction it surely is'.[8]

One can go quite far with this emphasis on the strategic nature of public reasoning, but precisely how far? Critics of liberal public reason like Fish and Elizabeth Povinelli, whose criticism of liberal multiculturalism we encountered in Chapter 2, are prepared to go quite far. For both Povinelli and Fish, liberal norms of public reason are ultimately reducible to power and not much else. But both also appeal to moral premises in order to make their claims. For Fish, the problem is the 'peremptory exclusion and dismissal' of those who do not accept liberal premises of mutual respect. For Povinelli, it is the liberal state's hypocrisy in celebrating difference whilst all the while governing and 'scarring' indigenous alterity, thus neatly rationalizing the material and social disadvantages of indigenous people at the hands of the 'liberal common law'.[9] So in the end, for both, the hope must be that politics *can* actually generate the right moral conclusions about certain questions, if only contingently.[10] There simply are no other 'different or stronger reasons than policy reasons' in public reasoning.

But then why is exclusion or the scarring of indigenous alterity, an undesirable feature of democratic theory and practice? Simply because *I* think so? Why should you accept that as a claim about how democracy should work? Because I've convinced you that you should. How? By way of assertion? That does not seem very promising, or if it is, only by asserting something I think you might find persuasive. If it is not merely an appeal to the fact that I am bigger or richer than you, then it sounds like an appeal to certain moral premises about, say, the value of democracy, or of cultural or social alterity, or the importance of individual freedom. Why should we care if democratic institutions are justified in this manner? Because if they are not, then democracy risks becoming merely rule by force. Is rule by force really no different, for Fish, than rule through democratic institutions? If Fish, in particular, wants to reject this characterization of democracy, or even to imagine a new one, then he has a conception of the reasonable despite himself, and thus a theory of public reason that involves more than simply the exchange of threats.

## Procedure

Procedural modes of public justification are, by now, extremely familiar. In modern contractarian political theory, the contract is used as a way of expressing our beliefs or intuitions about equality and fairness, and extracting the consequences of these beliefs for the regulation of social institutions. So a theory of justice will pick out appropriate rules or norms at the constitutional level which are meant to regulate or guide procedures at lower levels to do with determining rules and policies in more specific circumstances. The point is to provide fair ground rules that set legitimate limits to the pursuit of any particular moral system's precepts, given social and political diversity. Justice is procedural and impartial. Brian Barry insists, for example, that it is a 'great mistake ... to suppose that justice as impartiality is intended to constitute a complete, self-sufficient moral system in itself'.[11] A political decision then, as long as it is arrived at via the right procedures fairly conducted, will be legitimate even if in the end, at the legislative level, it refers to a specific conception of the good. The asymmetry between impartiality at the level of general constitutional rules (or the 'basic structure of society') and the 'partiality' of specific political decisions is not a contradiction, but something we should expect. A society organized along the lines of complete first-order impartiality applied to all social and political relations would be intolerable (as well as impossible to maintain).[12]

Thus the procedural public sphere provides a framework within which a particular liberal mode of engagement or dialogue can occur, what Rawls refers to as the 'ideal of public reason'. Citizens engage in public reason when they address their collective arrangements; but more specifically, when they offer and contest reasons provided to justify the exercise of the coercive (collective) power of the state in matters of basic justice and 'constitutional essentials'.[13] But the challenge is this: how can a consensus be created around a set of basic constitutional essentials if people not only have widely different sets of nonpublic identities, but also disagree about what counts as an authoritative public reason?

Consider two general modes of public justification; consensual and distributive.[14] A consensual mode of public justification implies that public debate will be characterized by a search for consensus on the regulative principles of the main political institutions of society. Desires and beliefs are thus subject to a filtering process designed to promote such a consensus, a process which involves refining or 'laundering' preferences.[15] Public reasons (suitably defined) are thus offered in the course of public deliberation, the purpose of which is to legitimate the exercise of collectively held coercive political power.

A distributive mode of public justification, on the other hand, entails that public debate will be characterized by the search for an optimal compromise between the existing interests of individuals. Public justification thus must appeal to what individuals, given their interests, would accept; political arrangements must suit these interests and not the other way round. Public reason, in so far as it acts as a constraint on self-interest, is simply what rational prudence suggests in contexts where the cooperation (or forbearance) of others is a condition of individuals satisfying their preferences. Distributive modes of public justification thus take public reason as the lowest common denominator from which to justify basic political institutions – i.e. establishing a *modus vivendi*.

David Gauthier, for example, sees morality as the product of rational agreement, not vice versa.[16] What it makes sense for the contractor to agree to, on this account, is that the constraints of society must 'advance what one judges good' relative to a baseline of non-agreement.[17] Each must gain from cooperation in a way they could not on their own. Society is thus a 'cooperative venture for mutual advantage'.[18] It provides a means of assuring (through coercive sanctions) that others will not take advantage or free-ride on the back of your cooperative behaviour, as well as provide determinate norms of cooperation. The benefits of cooperation and the need for assurance and determinate norms provide agents with reasons to obey the norms of society; they are capable of being justified in this way to each rational agent who seeks to advance her good.

Now it is often suggested that distributive modes of justification fail to capture something essential about the nature of public justification. According to theories of justice as mutual advantage, for example, the rational constraints that emerge from the amoral premises of rational choice are justified insofar as people lack the 'power irresistible' to run roughshod over everyone else to get what they want. To paraphrase

Rawls, 'to each according to their threat advantage' is not much of an account of public justification – though it is, of course, impersonal and impartial.[19] Consensual modes of justification, on the other hand, are meant to engage the interlocutors in a process of common deliberation which aims at a morally richer and more stable form of consensus, one that is reflective of people's *prior* equal moral standing and thus a different fit between the justification of rules and the motivation to obey them. The constraints of justice are not simply the product of cooperation, but reflected in the idea of agents seeing themselves as related to each other 'in a fundamental moral relationship expressed in mutual justification'.[20]

Before considering Rawls's argument more closely, note that Gauthier has elaborated upon this argument recently in interesting ways. He writes of a 'real but limited transformation of her own exercise of rationality in deliberation when a citizen internalizes the right reason (i.e. the public reason) of an authorized public person on matters which 'significantly affect the interactions of the citizens and the public goods available to them'.[21] The institutions established to structure interaction in order to promote mutual advantage 'embody the common good' of such a society, one tied to the enhancement of the individual goods of the members.[22] Such a constitution, in so far as it reflects agreement reached through 'reasoned interchange' and 'deliberative politics',

offers each person the opportunity to advance whatever proposal he pleases, but requires him to submit it to the critical consideration of his fellows, so that its adoption depends on his being able to give it a reasoned grounding that must either speak equally to the life-plans of all the participants, or establish the parity of the proposal with similar and compatible proposals that, taken together, reflect equally their several life plans.[23]

As an ideal of justice, Gauthier admits, it is essentially negative; it is 'the virtue of the self-interested … that curbs self-interest'.[24] But things can change. Bonds of mere convenience can grow into 'ties of mutual civic [though not necessarily personal] concern'. Public or civic friendship does not supplant the agreement needed for instrumental partnerships to constrain strategically rational actions for mutual benefit, but *supplements* it, 'with the further demand that the agreement assure equal respect'.[25] By which Gauthier means that each respects the identity and aims of her fellows and willingly accords them 'equal place in their common affairs with her own'.[26] If each comes to see her share of benefits as 'fair and reasonable' then others become not merely accepted but regarded as 'friends … as persons in whom one takes [a political or civil] interest'. Hence a constitution – the framework for structuring interaction to promote mutual advantage – becomes 'an affirmation of civic friendship, and not a mere treaty or compact of alliance'.[27] It comes to reflect the commitment of individual contractors to the equal value of those with whom they cooperate in political society.[28]

Gauthier emphasizes that he is not suggesting 'deliberation' or 'reasoned interchange' is opposed to his well-known emphasis on strategic interaction, but that is intended to supplement it (in the course of an argument concerning how a constitution comes to embody 'higher law'). The opposition between reason and force is a false one; 'reason and force coexist in all human interaction'. Deliberative agreement is thus 'strategic bargaining under full information',[29] proceeding from a baseline not necessarily of equality of condition but one in which there is a desire for mutual advantage, and also which 'invites' a desire to 'manifest civic friendship through the expression of equal respect'.[30]

In his major work on distributive justice, *Morals by Agreement*, Gauthier argued that only someone with a settled disposition to act justly will be invited to join in cooperative ventures, and that this provides a rationally compelling reason – grounded in self-interest – to adopt such a disposition. This argument, and the account of justice accompanying it, has been subject to considerable criticism. A big problem for any theory of justice grounded mainly on self-interest is showing why people should be just, or obey political norms generally, when the cost of not doing so is less than compelling. But note how, in the passages discussed above, Gauthier seems to be in search of extra-contractual help in securing the basic structure of a political society organized according to justice as mutual advantage.[31] Strategic interaction is supplemented by ties of civic friendship, which means that Gauthier is sceptical of the viability of a simple or static form of *modus vivendi* as the grounds for a framework of political cooperation over time. But nor does he presume away the ubiquity of strategic behaviour in human interaction.

Now consider Rawls's ideal. For Rawls, the 'liberal principle of legitimacy' states that

> our exercise of political power is fully proper only when it is exercised in accordance with a constitution the essentials of which all citizens as free and equal may reasonably be expected to endorse in light of principles and ideals acceptable to their common human reason.[32]

'Common human reason' alone, however, does not lead to convergence on the best possible principles. It has to be focused on a specific set of questions and grounded in a specific political conception of justice and accompanying ideal and ethos of citizenship. Hence the account of public reason:

Public reason is characteristic of a democratic people: it is the reason of its citizens, of those sharing the status of equal citizenship. The subject of their reason is the good of the public: what the political conception of justice requires of society's basic structure of institutions, and of the purposes and ends they are to serve … Public reason is the reason of equal citizens who, as a collective body, exercise final political and coercive power over one another in enacting laws and in amending their constitution.[33]

The accompanying ideal of citizenship imposes a duty of civility to 'explain to one another … how the principles and policies they advocate and vote for can be supported by the political values of public reason'. This duty also implies a willingness to 'listen to others and a fair-mindedness in deciding when accommodations to other views should reasonably be made'.[34]

A reason is a public reason when offered as a possible authorization of the exercise of coercive political power which others might endorse 'as consistent with their freedom and equality'.[35] Thus public reason has 'special subjects'. It does not apply to the specifics of tax legislation, or the regulation of the environment, or the funding of the arts, but to constitutional essentials and matters of basic justice (which will have, needless to say, consequences for the *way* such policies are arrived at, and thus ultimately do affect those matters). This is not to say that we do not, in our 'personal deliberations', as Rawls puts it, or in our deliberations within families or cultural and other kinds of associations, reason on the grounds of a whole range of 'background' philosophical, moral, religious, political, and cultural beliefs. But that when arguing about and proposing (including voting on) matters to do with constitutional essentials, citizens should offer public reasons that others could reasonably be expected to accept, consistent with their freedom and equality. Nor should we appeal to what we see as the truth of a particular philosophy, religion, or other 'comprehensive doctrine', but instead confine ourselves to 'plain truths, now widely accepted, or available, to citizens generally'.[36] A belief in the superiority of one's religion, for example, is not a basis upon which reasonable arguments can be advanced as the grounds for society's basic political institutions.[37]

Convergence on the idea of public reason seems to *follow* the process of converging on the political conception of justice, or in other words, that we use the contents of the political conception of justice to work out the determinant content of public reason. But Rawls now thinks this includes a *family* of possible doctrines, rather than just the one presented in *Political Liberalism*.[38] This implies that he accepts the fundamental plurality of political deliberation.[39] Thus, to a certain extent, it will only be *through* some form of public reason that we will arrive at a suitably political conception of justice. For how can we prejudge the kinds of authoritative reasons citizens might accept, on the basis of a pre-loaded overlapping consensus on basic constitutional principles? [40]

Now consider Rawls's contrast between the political conception of justice and a *modus vivendi*, which is 'political in the wrong way'.[41] Rawls's account of a *modus vivendi* is essentially static; it equates to an equilibrium point between two warring factions, analogous to a treaty neither party currently has an interest in violating, but may if circumstances change. It is static in the sense that the underlying interests of the parties are assumed to remain the same. Thus a political deliberation grounded exclusively on political bargaining results in social unity that is 'only apparent, as its stability is contingent on circumstances remaining such as not to upset the fortunate convergence of interests'.[42] If society is to be a fair system of cooperation, a simple balance between competing political and moral forces will not do.

So why should citizens honour the limits of public reason? To a certain extent, the requirement to act in accord with public reason is grounded in the fact that people are reasonable in the first place – that they already have a higher-order motivation to offer public reasons to others in the first place. The concept of the person, in other words, seems to presuppose the particular form of practical reason required.[43] Two things could be said to follow from this. First, it appears as though Rawls is appealing to a controversial conception of the person, which undermines the strategy of political liberalism. Second, if Rawls is not appealing to such a conception of the person, or to the truth of this conception of practical reason, then either his argument risks circularity or he thinks that an account of practical reason can be separated from comprehensive views and still be persuasive for people who hold different conceptions of the good, or even truth. He seems committed to some version of the latter; but this seems weak support for the strong claim that the political values always outweigh non-political ones in matters of basic justice.[44] It is not a case of having to find a way of justifying the exercise of political power to those who reject *any* form of public reason whatsoever, but coping with the plurality of public reasons and thus the plurality of public deliberation itself.

In the end there is no reason to suppose that the fact of reasonable pluralism applies not only to conceptions of the good, but to standards of right as well.[45] But what then follows from this? Do we thereby have to give up on the ideal of public reason altogether?

### Practice

What keeps people motivated to continue to comply with the rules of a game that continually, in their eyes, consigns them to the sidelines or are designed to make them lose? In what way, with reference to what kind of goods or in what register of justice and injustice, must I express myself in order to be heard? These are especially pressing questions at a time when social and economic disadvantage overlaps considerably with questions of race, gender, ethnicity and culture. For critics of liberal neutrality, this is evidence of the failure of this liberal ideal. The state has never been nor ever could be neutral towards groups who are consistent losers in public decision-making processes. For proceduralists, the dispiriting facts of overlap between economic disadvantage and racial or cultural groups only indicates the need for greater neutrality or impartiality on the part of the state and its agencies, not less.

A common theme explored by many defenders of Aboriginal rights, when confronted with the proceduralist arguments explored above, has been to claim that an ideal of public argument that is tied so closely to convergence on a liberal theory of justice is deeply problematic. It forms too convenient a connection between what counts as an acceptable premise in political argument and the kind of outcomes that Rawlsian liberals support, which seem to countenance denying the kind of political and constitutional interests sought by indigenous peoples.[46] The problem lies in not paying close enough attention to the situated but always dynamic practices of the actual individuals and groups involved.

An interesting recent account of public reason that builds on some of these criticisms has been developed by James Tully, who draws on the philosophy of Wittgenstein (amongst others) to provide a framework within which to rethink the relation between public reasoning and cultural diversity.[47] Without delving too deeply into the Wittgensteinian framework, we can isolate three crucial claims of Tully's argument: (1) language is aspectival; (2) understanding is achieved only in dialogue with others; and (3) that what emerges is akin to constitutional conventions rather than comprehensive rules.

The aspectival account of language and the dialogical character of understanding are put together by Tully to represent an alternative approach to modern constitutionalism. The approach has affinities (which Tully makes explicit)[48] with common law practical reasoning; i.e. the way the common law is interpreted and modified in being applied to particular cases, as well as the inherent irregularity and complexity of it as a body of law. So what emerges from dialogue between such complex situated beings? For Tully, the norms that emerge are akin to common law constitutional conventions; 'norms that come into being and come to be accepted as authoritative in the course of constitutional practice, including criticism and contestation of that practice'.[49] A convention, like a rule, can be grasped in a variety of ways, and thus being guided by a convention is conditioned not only by the context in which it is applied but also by our engagement with others.

Applying this distinctive perspective to various particular cases in Canada, but especially to the claims of Aboriginal peoples, Tully identifies three such conventions; mutual recognition, continuity and consent.[50] These emerge out of a 'living practice' of negotiation and accommodation – often breached and abused but nonetheless still relevant – between Aboriginal and non-Aboriginal peoples. They are immanent in these practices, rather than derived from intuitions or beliefs about fairness or impartiality extracted from an 'original position' or 'ideal speech situation'. And yet they are still capable, Tully argues, of acting as norms of justification which can be appealed to from the many different sides of public argument.[51]

This practical public sphere is thus an intercultural space in which interlocutors participate from their diverse cultural perspectives and work toward a form of intercultural understanding that does not presuppose a comprehensive language. The image is not of participants in an imaginary constitutional convention forging consensus on general terms which are then applied to particular cases, but rather of the particular circumstances playing a much greater role in determining what kind of political norms or rules are appropriate for coordinating the exercise of political power in the first place. Political norms and conventions, in other words, are no more derivative of formal rules and mechanisms than speech is derivative of grammar.[52]

Note, however, that for Tully the conventions of mutual recognition, continuity and consent are derived, for the most part, from the interaction between Aboriginal and non-Aboriginal peoples in North America. And thus in the Wittgensteinian sense, they are meant to be grasped according to the ways in which they have been put to use in particular circumstances. But what about those contexts in which the interactions are such that conventions of the kind Tully identifies are unlikely to emerge or emerge distorted, for example, by relations of power which are radically asymmetrical?

Of course there is always resistance to power,[53] but then how do we judge if the conventions that emerge are acceptable to the parties involved? Appealing to consent may be a necessary condition but it cannot be a sufficient one, since the conditions in which people consent to a set of norms or rules are themselves not something they can consent to and yet they often exercise enormous influence over the range of opportunities and options actually available to them. Tully's claim cannot be that the conventions of recognition, continuity and consent are regulative independently of the particular relations between peoples, since they are meant to emerge from those particular interactions. They cannot simply be imposed on the parties either, since this would be to claim that the conventions are more like comprehensive rules applicable in any number of different situations. And yet the three conventions are said to be regulative in three *other* contexts as well – the case of linguistic minorities, feminist claims and cultural minorities generally.[54] In each case the three conventions derived from the Aboriginal case apply analogously. But why? Is it because the pattern of relations between linguistic communities, between men and women and between immigrants and 'natives', is best re-described as struggles over recognition, continuity and consent? Or is it that the conventions are the necessary preconditions for a fair and just adjudication of their claims? In either case, the gap between 'common' and 'comprehensive appears to be narrowing; the conventions are looking more and more like principles of the Rawlsian kind and less and less like the context-sensitive norms suggested in the discussion of Wittgenstein and common-law reasoning.[55] To summarize: If the conventions are too context-sensitive then the challenge of forging a common normative language over difference is potentially insurmountable (or at least very costly); if they are too general, then they risk mistranslating the particularity of the claims at stake, something Tully's approach as a whole is meant to avoid.

But to focus on whether the conventions are either too context-dependent or too little is perhaps to miss a crucial emphasis in Tully's argument. This is, whatever the ultimate status of the rules or conventions they should be arrived at through dialogue between citizens occupying a range of different vantage points given by their identity-related differences. The multiplicity of vantage points and worldviews in the public sphere is thus not to be filtered or bracketed out, but recognized and accommodated. Dialogue between these differences prompts awareness of the diverse ways in which rules are interpreted and applied. This prompts awareness of the aspectival nature of public debate; each claim is only ever a partial re-description of the issue at stake from a particular vantage point. In recognizing these limits to our claims and to those of others, we actually expand our conception of what it is to follow a particular set of rules or norms. Comprehensive rules, in other words, are not the only guide to playing the constitutional game. The best way to see this, Tully argues, is to pay attention to the concrete examples of interaction between different peoples, and to study the modes of reasoning appealed to therein. The 'perspicuous representation of the reasoning that mediates [these] conflicts' consists in our dialogical re-description of these very modes of reasoning.[56]

## *Modus vivendi*

But if we begin with existing arrangements and practices rather than trying to stand outside of them and evaluate them according to an independent standard, are we not accommodating power to reason? And if the political arrangements which are ultimately agreed to are based on nothing more than a mere *modus vivendi*, then is justice merely a form of compromise, an accommodation of justice to power?

All forms of human interaction – and especially social and political interaction – are characterized by relations of power, albeit always to varying degrees. Thus *all* social and political arrangements and institutions, to a degree at least, can be characterized as resting on forms of social agreement akin to a *modus vivendi*. If institutions have histories which include not only the congealed wisdom and virtue of past generations, but also their biases and partialities as expressed in various norms and conventions, then this extends also to the procedures, norms and conventions we use to *argue* about these institutions as well.[57] Combined with an acknowledgment of deep and persistent disagreement about the nature of justice, and especially about what justice requires, these presumptions move us in the direction of trying to devise a way of proceeding that accepts the centrality of disagreement and the ubiquity of power as formal and informal constraints on ideal decision-making procedures – hence to revisiting the idea of a *modus vivendi*. Doing so does not entail rejecting liberalism, any more than it does embracing communitarianism or libertarianism.

So if we disagree about what justice is, or agree what it is but disagree over what it requires, and yet need some way of proceeding in face of such disagreement, what should we do? A *modus vivendi* at the level of conceptions of right seems to be required. But we need to conceive of the nature of a *modus vivendi* very differently from that which has hitherto been the case.

Consider two versions of *modus vivendi* compliance with political norms:

*(1) A simple or static modus vivendi*: The parties are motivated to comply with political norms only where it is in their interest to do so, where 'interest' is narrowly defined in terms of individual or group self-interest.

*(2) A discursive and dynamic modus vivendi*: The parties are motivated to

comply with political norms where it is in their interest to do so, but (a) these interests include moral interests, and (b) over time, the demands and practices of social and political cooperation may come to be seen as fair and reasonable. However the content of what is 'fair and reasonable' is always incompletely theorized and tied to the constellation of 'registers' or discourses – i.e. the various concrete practices of public reason and social interaction – present at any given time in the public sphere.[58]

As it stands, (1) is an unattractive and unpersuasive way of thinking about the grounds of political community, given its narrow and static focus on interests. The main assumptions governing much of the analysis of the shortcomings of *modus vivendi* arrangements are that the interests of the parties remain static. Rationality is almost exclusively strategic and instrumental. *Modus vivendi* citizenship here is just the strategic pursuit of one's self-interest(s) via appeals to others' self-interest by conditional offers of forbearance or cooperation. If the paradigm of successful strategic interaction is the market, then political institutions are justified on the grounds of supplanting or constraining strategic interaction where this would be advantageous to everyone, compared to the non-cooperative baseline of an anarchic state of nature.

In fact, the simple or static account of a *modus vivendi* has few takers. Even David Gauthier, as we have seen, who has developed one of the most powerful and complex accounts of justice as mutual advantage, now argues that self-interest alone cannot ground a political settlement over time, and must be accompanied by a form of 'civic friendship' that evolves beyond mere forbearance into an expression of 'equal respect' for one's fellow citizens.[59]

So consider (2). The emphasis on the relational or dynamic character of agreements concerning basic political institutions and practices is critical. If liberalism is to go local, at least in the way postcolonial liberalism envisages, then it must be flexible and context-sensitive, attuned to the historical circumstances and the local knowledge(s) of the people for whom political arrangements must not only be just, but ones with which they can actually identify. But the line between 'context-sensitive' and 'co-opted by the status quo' is a fine and difficult one to tread. The account of a discursive *modus vivendi* is intended as a first step in elaborating just how such a distinction might work. Note that our task is not to provide reasons for cooperating that would motivate an amoralist (what could?). Rather, for socialized, situated, historical beings who are interacting (sometimes peaceably, sometimes not) in the context of existing imperfect institutions and practices, and who draw on a diversity of moral sources to account for and justify the value of these interactions and institutions to themselves and others.

Hence the dynamic *modus vivendi* presupposes a different account of social and political pluralism to that of the Rawlsian story. For Rawls, the world of liberal democracies is characterized by a reasonable pluralism of 'comprehensive' doctrines.

For postcolonial liberalism, on the other hand, there is both more overlap between cultural, ethical and political identities and sensibilities then usually presumed, and yet potentially less consensus available. It presupposes that political identities, in particular, are fundamentally interdependent in a number of complex ways. Relations of identity are held in place and constituted, in part, by perceptions of difference, and vice-versa.[60] So as much as political identities often seem fixed in opposition to each other, the underlying structure is actually relational, as the work of William Connolly has emphasized. Difference is essential to identity because it provides the means for it to become fixed and distinct in the first place. Hence identities are vulnerable to processes of redefinition and counter-definition, and at least always potentially unstable. This vulnerability can manifest itself in both responsive and resentful ways. It might provoke a critical responsiveness to 'otherness' previously thought intrinsically inferior or unworthy of tolerance.[61] Or it might intensify intolerance and even disgust for those against whom someone defines themselves.

To notice how political and cultural identities are constructed in this relational and oppositional way does not necessarily make it any easier to reshape or reform them. But an appreciation of this interdependence promotes a wariness about strategies that attempt to dredge out of public life the cultural densities upon which identities and attachments depend.[62] Such strategies are vulnerable to accusations of bad faith or hypocrisy as they run up against the multiple sources from which citizens draw their sense of moral and political understanding. As Connolly and Stephen White have pointed out, public disavowal of metaphysics seems to invite the eventual exposure of unacknowledged dependencies upon metaphysical claims.[63] One side seeks to protect public life from metaphysical and visceral intersubjective judgments and attachments, whilst the other sees the very possibility of meaningful community to depend upon their admittance. The only solution is to redraw a new form of *modus vivendi* between competing moral sources that doesn't pretend to have established *a priori* what counts as a genuine public reason. But as we shall see, such a *modus vivendi* must still constrain these opposing views in some ways – to provide for the conditions in which some kind of effective reflexive control can be exercised over these competing discourses.

To say that an agreement is 'incompletely theorized'[64] is not to say that it is right or just simply because it coordinates collective action. It must be subject to scrutiny and modification over time, including with reference to more general principles and ideals. But a political settlement based on incompletely theorized agreements does not necessarily evolve into a wider overlapping consensus on political values as presumed in the Rawlsian story. Incompletely theorized agreements worry Rawlsians because it means they are incompletely justified. But all political agreements, as I've been been arguing – even to do with constitutional essentials and matters of basic justice – are to some extent incompletely justified. Incompletely justified and mixed public reasons are the grounds of cooperation in conditions of socially and politically diverse liberal democracies.

But does this give up too much? Does not the lack of an overlapping consensus on a freestanding political conception create a motivational deficit on the part of citizens to cooperate and negotiate with each other, especially with the less powerful or less able?

A key question for postcolonial liberalism is thus how citizens can be motivated to continue to negotiate and make compromises in the face of frequent disagreement and lack of convergence on an independently valid theory of justice, or a 'freestanding political conception of justice'. In dropping the Rawlsian requirement to bracket our conception of the good in the public sphere, our task might seem to have been made even more difficult. How can citizens deliberate about matters of basic justice as bearers of thick conceptions of the good and particular interests, and yet do so on equal terms; i.e. recognize each other as worthy of equal concern and respect?

Brian Barry has argued that equal respect fails as means of establishing the grounds for mutually acceptable terms of cooperation because it does not by itself lead to the conclusion that disagreements over conceptions of the good should be resolved by retreating to more neutral common ground. Charles Larmore, for example, argues that the obligation of equal respect consists in our being 'obligated to treat another as he is treating us – to use his having a perspective on the world as a reason for discussing the merits of action rationally with him'.[65] Barry argues that this leaves open the possibility that as long as we argued our conception of the good was rationally superior to others, and hence a proper basis for constitutional arrangements, dismissing other views (because they will not or cannot acknowledge our rationally compelling argument) would be compatible with treating them with respect. Hence for Barry, we need an additional sceptical proviso to move us to more neutral ground. The proviso acknowledges that we can not, in fact, produce such a rationally compelling argument, and thus it would be unreasonable for us to insist on imposing our conception of the good on others.

But reasonable people will also disagree about the criteria for certainty. How does an epistemological claim get us out of moral trouble? It cannot. Barry's criticism is searching, but the addition of the sceptical proviso misses the point. It does not follow from my not being able to convince others to agree with my claim that I should be sceptical about that belief. Scepticism will not deliver us to neutral ground any more than presupposing equal respect will. The important point about the limits of my being able to convince others is, rather, that I come to see and accept those limits in some way and that I refrain from imposing them on others despite my initial convictions about them.

In what way, then, do we demonstrate our equal respect for others, if neither an appeal to consensus or a sceptical proviso about our own comprehensive beliefs does it? There are two important points here. First, we should not confuse equal respect with the equal *affirmation* of all, especially the equal affirmation of all cultures. This is impossible, both logically and psychologically. I might owe you equal consideration or respect in offering you public reasons you could endorse in light of your equality and freedom, but it does not follow that I have to positively affirm the kind of life you lead, or the culture or group you identify with. This leads to the second point with regard to conceptions of equal respect. If we presuppose too thick a sense of equal respect, argues Stephen White, then its emergence tends to take on a kind of magical quality, appearing as if out of thin air, without any sense of the affective work and 'micropolitical preparation' that goes into the realization of it.[66]

The challenge is thus not to presuppose a moral conception of respect for others, but to focus on the processes that help us *move to it* in different ways. To do this will involve seeing citizens and their practical identities as tied up significantly in the way processes of public and non-public reasoning intersect, and thus securing the conditions in which the equal and free exchange of public reasons can be carried out, all the while acknowledging the plurality of political deliberation itself. I attempt to provide such an argument in Chapters 5 and 6.

### Affect

Finally, recent poststructuralist analyses of the politics of recognition have emphasized the potentially distorting effects of the conceptual apparatus of rights or 'public reason' (whether Habermasian or Rawlsian) on our relation to difference.[67] The distortion occurs in particular when Kantian-inspired accounts of public dialogue highlight the cognitive gain of discourse with the other, at the expense of the affective change that might be induced in our ethical attitudes towards difference. The concrete particularity of others, in other words, is either subsumed in the monological thought-experiment of a Kantian universalizability test, or tamed according to a singular and universal ideal of public reason aimed at constructing mutual understanding and regard in dialogue with others.

Thus a very different account of pluralism is on offer in these critiques than that presupposed by liberals. For liberals, the 'fact' of reasonable pluralism is constituted by the freedom of individuals to form and pursue a plurality of conceptions of the good, none of which can provide the singular grounds for the justification of the exercise of political power. However for poststructuralist critics of liberalism, the problem to which liberal proceduralism is the answer is misconstrued. No such neutral ground is possible, given that individuals are already and always constituted not only by various discursive and concrete practices, norms and institutions, but through their responses to and engagement with others. In other words, the issue is not one of providing the grounds for toleration, which presupposes a plurality of self-contained identities susceptible to rational arbitration, but of cultivating an openness or receptiveness to the unknowable consequences of our encounters with difference – given the ultimate permeability and interdependence of identities. It is this pluralism – to do with the 'politics of becoming' (see below) as opposed to recognition – that matters, and indeed must be actively cultivated. To acknowledge the impossibility of our ever being able to apprehend the other without any presuppositions or preconceived notions of identity, to be able to offer 'unconditional hospitality' to them, or indeed to think that justice is always, fundamentally, both impossible and yet necessary to realize, does not mean giving up on these ideals. The aim is to foster 'better conditionality', and to remain open to the 'future to come'.[68] Acknowledging the impossibility of justice and yet also the inescapability of our appealing to it captures the appropriate ethical attitude towards the world that keeps open the possibility of new modalities of politics, identity, and justice.

These are provocative criticisms, and as we saw in Chapter 1, the 'strange proximity' of the colonial encounter – settler societies' uncomfortable experiences of radical difference – suggests that the affective dimensions of cultural and political pluralism is crucial to consider. But postcolonial liberalism parts company from these arguments in at least two ways.

First, as I argued above, postcolonial liberalism has an explicit commitment to equality, and thus interprets the demands for recognition as another way of talking about equality and freedom in light of the complex conditions of modern liberal democracies. It is not clear that poststructuralist critics of liberalism would accede to even this. The conceptual apparatus that accompanies most accounts of liberal equality may appear too conceptually intrusive and ham-fisted – not supple enough – to do justice to the kind of ethical attitudes they argue need to be cultivated in our encounters with difference.[69] Second, poststructuralist theorists often argue that the task of ethics in these contexts is to 'interrupt' contemporary politics and hold it up against a very different ethical register. Hence the focus is generally upon how the ethical shapes the political, rather than the other way around. This seems to involve invoking deep ethical claims in order to justify the value of the transformative effects (and affects) of encounters in the public sphere. But for postcolonial liberalism, the risk is always of not taking reasonable pluralism seriously enough, of departing too far from the rough ground of politics. Even if the desire to move beyond apprehending the 'concrete other' through communicative reason is only ever a critical ideal,[70] an ideal that can never be realized, and that grasping its impossibility is precisely what the appropriate ethical attitude towards the other consists in, the kind of politics it prefigures – the norms, practices, institutions and distributions – seems far too distant and elusive for the historically situated, limited and imperfect creatures that we are. It seems to call for a form of ethical responsiveness and generosity to the other that goes beyond any political experience we know of, so as to almost enter into the realm of the theological (which is for some of these writers, precisely the point).

But what postcolonial liberals and poststructuralist critics of liberalism do share is an acute awareness of the often fugitive elements of what William Connolly has referred to as the 'politics of becoming', which we discussed towards the end of Chapter 2. Connolly asks us to focus on 'how the politics of becoming proceeds when it is actually in motion'; that is, how politics proceeds not simply in the mode of demands for the expansion of the category of the universal, or through the prompting of a self-fulfilling logic already implicit in particular society, but in demanding a reconfiguration of the existing 'register' of justice/injustice. The idea of a 'register' of justice/injustice, as I argued earlier, is a helpful one. It consists, in part, of the particular conceptual scheme(s) in which we apprehend various claims to do with the nature of justice and injustice – the presumptions, for example, about the nature of persons, power, individual and collective responsibility, rights and resources that we apply to such claims. But it also consists in the affective relations we have with the claim-makers; for example, the extent to which we feel close, distant, agitated, repulsed or in solidarity with them. Think of how Aboriginal peoples' claims have been interpreted over the past one hundred years. Their claims have been rejected as uncivilized, 'repugnant to the common law'; as incompatible with liberal rights; as being fully satisfied in the extension of liberal rights; or as requiring 'special rights'. Connolly is right to suggest that our sense of what we think of as just or unjust, reasonable and unreasonable, acceptable and unacceptable, is tied to different practical and affective registers and discourses through which we interpret and process the world. Thus, the pluralization of public reason refers to the presence at any one time of a range of different constellations of registers and discourses in the public sphere.[71] But these discourses, which shape attitudes and beliefs (and if Connolly is right, gut feelings) are always open to being modified and re-configured through various forms of collective and micro-political action. Discursive legitimacy is achieved, therefore, when a collective decision is seen to be consistent with the outcome of these various constellations, which are communicated via both electoral and non-electoral avenues of influence.[72] As John Dryzek points out, changes in prevailing attitudes and beliefs towards the environment or the role of women in modern societies, for example, requires not only legislative change, but also 'alterations of the terms of political discourse in ways that come to change the understanding of state [and non-state] actors'.[73] Something similar will have to occur – and is even beginning to occur, I think – in relation to non-indigenous people's attitude toward the claims of indigenous peoples.

## Conclusion

Politics is indispensable to postcolonial liberalism. Engaging in deliberative argument and counter-redescription; bargaining and strategic machinations; rhetorical ploys; protest and civil disobedience; 'micropolitical self-fashioning' and self-questioning – all the varying degrees of interaction that characterize what we ordinarily think of as politics need to be included. Since there is no pure form of politics, no way of reducing it to an essential domain or activity, and no way of drawing any *a priori* distinction between the political and non-political (because relations of power are ubiquitous and we disagree about what justice requires in addressing these relations) we should not think of it as reducible to any one mode of interaction. There is not a choice between the market or the forum, 'bargaining' and 'politics', but rather a need to keep the different modes of engagement – these different sociabilities – in creative tension. This might seem surprising. So much of contemporary political theory seems oriented to promoting one form of interaction or mode of engagement over another, especially reasoned or deliberative argument above everything else. The ideal of deliberative democracy is valuable and important, but precisely because deliberative consensus can never be a sufficient condition for justice, other modes of interaction – perhaps idiosyncratic, perhaps appealing to or based upon radical or alternative worldviews, perhaps confronting and ill-tempered – are important too. Moreover, no amount of deliberation can ever do away with the need for hard-nosed bargaining over certain issues, and compromises that fall short of an all-things-considered (or theorized) agreement. The conditions that underpin philosophical accounts of deliberation – full information, coherent frameworks of articulation and open-ended ratiocination – are precisely what is lacking in actual politics.

One idea lying behind this chapter is that there may be certain kinds of disagreements and arguments that can actually contribute to political stability and community rather than undermine it.[74] Ignoring or dismissing arguments from particular groups who claim that the current terms of association or the dominant modes of citizenship, are overly burdensome can obviously undermine the legitimacy and stability of public institutions over time. But in societies where citizens have reasonably effective freedoms of speech and association, people learn through a combination of bargaining and arguing, to manage the conflicts that are thrown up by the inequalities and asymmetries which inevitably accompany modern market societies. Such conflicts are not only 'managed' in the sense of being pacified; they produce, in turn, demands for corrective action and reform (based on both self-interest and a concern for the common good) that can generate new social and political arrangements and potentially new self-understandings on the part of citizens as well. The 'positive residue' of conflicts that is left behind is the experience of living in a society that learns to cope with its conflicts. Social cohesion thus becomes a byproduct of certain kinds of disagreement.

I am not suggesting that the conditions for such positive societal learning are in place in relation to the situation of indigenous peoples. But it presents an alternative possibility about the emergence of social cohesion than is often on offer in public debates over the consequences of Aboriginal rights. Too often the question of social unity is either simply ignored, often by supporters of Aboriginal rights, or cast in impossible terms: sign up to *this* national story, or *these* sets of citizenship rights, or the moral basis for national unity is lost. Both are oversimplified responses.

One of the difficulties with the learning-through-disagreement-argument, however, is that it seems to involve a kind of insight that arises *post hoc* rather than *a priori*. How do we know which conflicts will produce these positive residues – effects which the participants themselves are usually not aware are being produced? And what if we are wrong? Are not some forms of moral conflict better left off the political agenda, lest they deepen social and cultural cleavages that end up leaving everyone worse off? This is one justification for liberal constitutionalism and the 'gag rules' which aim to keep religious conflict, for example, out of debates about constitutional essentials.[75] Mutual deliberation is a fine idea, so the argument goes, but doesn't necessarily move politics towards agreement and accommodation, in fact, it can move it in the opposite direction as well. In some circumstances, it might even lead citizens to *harden* their attitudes towards others when they discover, for example, just how deep the conflict between their interests and others' actually is. Removing limits on the politicization of political and cultural differences can end up making things worse, not better.[76]

These are powerful objections for any account of public reason that promotes deliberation over rules of recognition and the relevance of identity-related differences for making judgments about justice. But they are not fatal. For one thing, why assume that the underlying interests remain static when confronted with each other? Cannot politics, and the arguing and bargaining which it entails, alter those interests and move the parties to a different, more acceptable and equitable equilibrium point? Also, even if it is true that in some circumstances some things are better left off the political agenda, we still need to justify why the things we want held back from politics should be. And *that* debate seems hard to inoculate completely from politics, as public debates about the introduction of a Bill of Rights (in Australia or Canada) and major policy issues involving religion (in the USA) seem to suggest.

But having said all of this, we should not be overly sanguine about politics. And more importantly, something must be said about the conditions required for 'politics' to play the role it has been given – of producing the means to proceed in the face of deep disagreement about justice. In the next chapter I want to begin by considering the deep and often divisive issue of the nature of historical injustice. This is one strand of the constellation of registers or discourses surrounding Aboriginal rights in countries such as Australia, Canada and the United States. It is absolutely central to the claims of Aboriginal peoples, and thus to postcolonial liberalism and the ideal of public reason that animates it. John Pocock and Stuart Hampshire, amongst others, have pointed out that among the most fundamental conflicts in politics are those derived from contrasting attitudes to historical time.[77] This debate is also of central importance to modern politics in general: think of Northern Ireland, the former Communist bloc countries of Eastern Europe, as well as Bosnia, Rwanda, South Africa and East Timor (to name some recent prominent examples). Truth about the past – or at least a willing-ness to address the past – has been claimed to be a necessary condition for justice and reconciliation in the present. The problem is, people disagree profoundly over the consequences of perceived past injustices for thinking about justice in the present. The disagreement is profound because it touches on beliefs about not only justice, but about the nature of responsibility, freedom and identity.

# 5    Historical injustice

> How are we to tell whether a state is still the same state or a different
> one? ... Another question is this: when a population lives
> in the same place, what is the criterion for regarding the state as
> a unity?[1]

As I have been arguing, public reason is the reason of democratic people
seeking to justify the exercise of coercive political power *lacking* any prior
established consensus on a substantive conception of justice. A crucial
feature of the 'circumstances of politics' in the case of postcolonial
societies (and many others as well) is disagreement over the legacy of
colonial domination.[2] My aim in this chapter is twofold. First, to use an
exploration of this debate as a way of elaborating on the idea of public
reason aimed at a discursive *modus vivendi* (or more accurately, a series
of dynamic *modi vivendi*) begun to be sketched in Chapter 4. And
secondly, to begin laying the groundwork for the discussion of the postcolonial state in Chapter 6. If postcolonial liberalism appeals to the
values of equality, freedom and well being as conditioning goods – as
goods which condition but do not necessarily pre-determine the way
people live according to their own values – then there will be an important and distinctive role for the state (as well as potentially trans-national
authorities) to play. This is particularly true in the case of relations
between the liberal state and groups like indigenous peoples. But the
only way the state can play a justice-enhancing role in this instance is if
the distinctive history of those relations is addressed. And this has
proven to be a difficult task.[3]

There is also another deeper philosophical issue underlying this chapter; the persistence of the past not only in our individual lives, but in our
collective, public ones as well. How does the past persist in the present?
One obvious way, it seems, is through identity-relations, both individual
and collective. Identity claims are not simply propositions about 'current time-slice sets of values [and] institutions',[4] but also about the continuity and persistence of identity across time, and thus the legitimacy
or not of the attribution of responsibility for acts in the past as well as

the present. There is an inescapably temporal dimension to moral and normative claims based on identity relations, and therefore to many claims in politics. Our beliefs as to *what* we think we are responsible for and to *whom* we are responsible, and thus to a certain extent our beliefs about the nature of citizenship, will be affected by our answers to these metaphysical questions (as should be clear, the Rawlsian strategy of avoiding metaphysical issues by sticking to a purely political conception of public reason is an unlikely, even incoherent strategy, given this claim).

The good of citizenship, whatever else it involves, includes the capacity to participate as effectively as possible in the (re)shaping and interpretation of a community's political morality and 'ethos' as manifested in its social practices and institutions – or at the very least, to be able to *oppose* those dominant discourses. Ensuring the conditions in which citizens can at the very least effectively voice and act on their opposition to the dominant forms of public culture (either electorally or non-electorally) in the state is an obligation citizens owe to each other. What I shall go on to argue below is that historical injustice comes to bear on the content of these obligations and responsibilities through the practices of public reason. Thus citizens of ostensibly postcolonial states, such as Australia and Canada, have special responsibilities to account for past injustices. (Needless to say, these are not the only obligations they have.)

The way a community argues about the scope and limits of justice is affected by its past. The enterprise of democracy rests upon a premise of collective agency, however contestable and fluid that conception of agency is. Citizens must come to accept their own 'authorship' of the procedures (deliberative and otherwise) through which the state reaches its decisions in order to realize their equal freedom and feel 'at home' amongst its institutions and norms.[5] But how a people are able to constitute themselves in this way – how democratic institutions are able to remain stable and robust over time in the face of disagreement and political and economic change – is tied, in various ways, to how they are *already* constituted through their history and ethos. The history of relations between indigenous peoples and liberal democratic states presents a particularly charged and complex example of this interdependence.

## Public reason and history

I have been arguing for a conception of public reason that does not presuppose a prior consensus on a substantive conception of justice. We start with the imperfect, often unjust and unequal practices, norms and institutions we inherit and try to redesign them as we go. Institutions and practices are best able to be redesigned when done by those who possess the requisite 'insider's knowledge' required for intelligent and effective redesign.[6] Thus public reason has what I shall call historical and interpretive dimensions to it. What do I mean by these terms? An interpretive approach to ethics suggests a particular ordering or fit between a community's complex of institutions and practices and its scheme of values – an account of what is good about those practices and institutions. On one reading of the interpretive approach, the former is basic. As Gopal Sreenivasan puts it, 'their status as goods is recognized within the organization of that community's ethical life itself'. The validity of these goods, in turn, cannot be deduced from any 'independently valid rules or principles'.[7] If the community's concrete conception of the good life is basic, then any adequate account of the goods informing that conception has to be established with reference to the actual complex of practices and institutions that make up that way of life. Thus in interpreting our community's way of life, we are seeking to uncover and/or explain those goods that constitute our community's ethical life.

The interpretive dimension of public reason involves a particular fit between the public discourse of a community and the goods that inform that community's concrete conceptions of the good life. Public reason, in other words, is always carried out in light of the discourses, institutions, practices and understandings that make up those concrete conceptions. A prominent defender of such an approach is Michael Walzer, as we saw in Chapter 3. He argues that if the boundaries of the political and the cultural/historical community do not coincide – if there are disputes about the legitimacy of the institutions, practices and understandings of a community's concrete conceptions of the good – then distributive decisions will have to be worked out politically. And precisely how they will be worked out will depend 'upon the understandings shared among the citizens about the value of cultural diversity, autonomy and so on ...'.[8] But this is a potentially worrying response, we saw, in the context of societies where particular groups, such as indigenous peoples, have either been forcibly assimilated to and/or excluded from national citizenship. Walzer's argument implies that the viability of a minority group's claim for the protection of their cultural norms, or the revision of mainstream norms, will depend in large measure on the shared understandings of the value of cultural diversity or local autonomy – and even about how negotiations about these values should be conducted politically. However taking shared meanings about the nature of local autonomy or cultural diversity at face value, and indeed those about the nature of the political, might entail ignorance about the relations of power that hold between the state and various groups, as well as within the minority groups themselves.[9]

So as important as it is to consider this interpretive and historical dimension of public reason, it raises considerable problems. The good of the relations referred to in the concrete conception must be good not only in virtue of being shared, but also in terms of the values and practices that are actually shared. But how do we establish this? With reference solely to the concrete conception, or by giving some independent account of the good? Public reason, as I understand it, moves between these two spaces of practice and reason.

The tendency amongst most contemporary theorists of justice, in fact, is to translate the particularity of claims based on historical and cultural wrongs into more general (i.e. 'independently valid') categories of primary goods and resources. These categories establish a kind of benchmark for entry into the conversation of justice. But unless one thinks of these categories as independently valid in a very strong almost Platonic sense, the fit between them and the concrete ethical life of a community still matters. For as much as debates about political morality may be oriented around various principles to do with, for example, equality, individual liberty or fairness, they become embodied in particular institutions and practices. Hence our speaking of particular 'registers' or discourses of justice/injustice', explored in earlier chapters. This is not to say that the structure of moral experience is determined exclusively from within a specific cultural or historical context. The moral practices of cultures are far more complex and porous than that. But this raises the crucial question for this chapter: just what is the relation between the past and a commitment to those norms and principles said to be constitutive of the political morality of the state?

## Historical injustice and liberal theories of justice

Let us now turn to the specific example of historical injustices committed against indigenous peoples by settler states. These have often been at the centre of often bitter public debate about these issues in Australasia and North America. The histories are varied and complex, but they include genocide, the forcible appropriation of traditional lands, coercive assimilation, the denial and violation of basic human rights (including freedom of movement, basic citizenship rights, the denial of language rights, etc.), poverty wages, exposure to devastating diseases and the forced removal of children.[10] Although almost everyone accepts there is *some* connection between the injustices of colonial domination and the disadvantages indigenous peoples suffer from today, the exact nature of this connection is contentious. Is it causal or moral (or both)? If it is the latter, then in what *way* are the connections between past injustices and present day justice morally relevant? Many argue that concentrating on the historical nature of colonial wrongs is misplaced. 'Backward-looking' claims of injustice focus too narrowly on the allocation of blame, so the argument goes, and not enough on addressing contemporary disadvantage. If rights or primary goods are to be distributed impartially, then what has the particular history of relations between peoples got to do with it? Indigenous peoples deserve special rights, on this line of argument, because they suffer from contemporary disadvantages such that the granting of rights is a justifiable means of addressing those disadvantages (that they are 'special' is an important aspect of this mode of justification). The nature of disadvantage itself is established with reference to the goods of liberal justice. The fact that the claimants are 'indigenous', or signed an agreement in the distant past that entitled them to a specific piece of land, is less relevant than the fact of contemporary disadvantage. These questions also touch on deep disagreements about the nature of responsibility, as we shall see. Arguments about compensation or redistribution on the basis of historical wrongs runs onto the rocky shoals of contemporary debates surrounding economic policy and the welfare state – for example, debates about welfare inducing passivity or undercutting the capacity of people to take responsibility for themselves. (I shall return to these issues again in Chapters 6 and 7.)

So there is scepticism in contemporary debates (both academic and public) about the value of focusing on historical injustice as the most appropriate means of addressing the claims of indigenous peoples.[11] The basic intuition here is that the historical nature of the wrongs committed against indigenous people is either impossible to compensate for, or is not as relevant to addressing contemporary disadvantages as indigenous people and their supporters think it is. Compensation and reparations may be due for certain specific wrongs but cannot by themselves carry the burden of rectifying the kind of systematic injustice indigenous people suffer from. At most they call for symbolic gestures of public reconciliation or atonement rather than substantial distributive measures.

Consider, for example, the influential argument made by Jeremy Waldron.[12] He thinks there are two possible grounds for compensating indigenous peoples for past injustices, and both fail. The first is a counterfactual approach, where the aim is to try and bring the present state of affairs closer to those that would have obtained had no injustice actually occurred. The second approach is more straightforward. Instead of trying to reconstruct a counterfactual case for compensation, we simply ask if the entitlement that was violated all those years ago survives. If my tribe or community was entitled to land unjustly taken hundreds of

years ago, why should it not be so today? Both approaches fail, according to Waldron, because of the difficulties raised by the change of cast
and circumstances. What if returning land involves expropriating it from
innocent third parties (such as recently arrived immigrants) who had no
knowledge of, or connection with these past injustices? And what if the
descendants of those against whom the original injustice was committed are not, in fact, substantially disadvantaged? Returning land or making substantial compensation payments might harm others more than it
helps the particular people in question. The historic injustice, in other
words, may have been superseded.[13]

Waldron accepts, however, that although 'genuine' or 'full' reparations
are ruled out by his account, something is due: namely, forms of symbolic recognition and public remembrance.[14] 'Like the gift I buy for
someone I have stood up', writes Waldron, '[a symbolic payment] is a
method of putting oneself out, or going out of one's way, to apologize'.
The analogy points to the idea that addressing historic injustice falls
outside of the register of liberal distributive justice proper, however
much it might overlap with contemporary disadvantage. 'It is the
impulse to do justice now that should lead the way', argues Waldron,
'not the reparation of something whose wrongness is understood primarily in relation to conditions that no longer obtain'.[15]

Is this the best way of addressing indigenous peoples' claims for land
and self-government? I shall argue it is not. Indigenous peoples' claims
rest, in part, on the recognition of the historical injustices carried out
against them by various colonial powers. Down-playing the relevance of
historic injustice for consideration of their claims risks misidentifying
the nature of the moral wrong at stake, especially from the perspective
of indigenous peoples, and thus potentially the legitimacy and efficacy
of those institutions and distributions meant to address them.
Indigenous peoples' claims in countries such as Australia and Canada
are not only about compensation or reparations, but also about the
terms of association between them and the colonial state. The injustice
of expropriation of Aboriginal lands, for example, is not only about the
dispossession of property, or the violation of negative rights of non-
interference, but a violation or denial of just terms of association.[16]
Thus, if the institutions within which the benefits and burdens of society
are to be distributed are said to be unjust – perhaps because they do not
acknowledge alternative conceptions of property, or coordinate jurisdiction over a territory – then it is not clear how the imposition or
perception of *that* injustice has been superseded in the manner argued
for by Waldron. Insofar as it remains unaddressed, the moral rupture
that occurred in the past persists in the present. For it is clear that many
indigenous people see recognition of the past, and especially of the

injustices of the past, as important not only with regard to possible compensation, but also as informing the normative structure of relations in the present. The history of these relations remains vivid because it is a crucial part of the articulation of indigenous demands in the present; it permeates their reasoning for collective action and their culture. Addressing present claims means addressing the past. In other words, the distinction between 'forward-looking' and 'backward-looking' justice is much more difficult to maintain than is usually suggested, especially when the aim is to address political and cultural disadvantage.[17]

Waldron's argument, in other words, presupposes what is most at issue; that there is a conception of justice shared between indigenous and non-indigenous people that provides a framework for the institutions within which judgments about the relevance of the past are made with regard to the legitimacy of certain patterns of distribution and the goods distributed therein. My approach, on the other hand, presupposes no such common ground. The only common ground we have is that we share the same territory and a history of interaction upon it – however unequal and unjust it has been. And in light of this we must come to an arrangement that will not necessarily settle all these questions once and for all, but allow the different parties to coexist on terms that are as mutually acceptable as possible.

From the fact that indigenous and non-indigenous people share *a* history, if not a shared view about the normative consequences of that history, I want to argue that it is part of our obligations as citizens to take responsibility for the way the norms, practices and institutions we inherit have been marked and shaped by a particular history. The fact that we have not chosen them, or would not have chosen them – given a hypothetical choosing situation to consider – does not, I believe, absolve us of such a responsibility. But what actually follows from this claim? Again, we need to attend to both the institutional and affective dimensions of the 'strange proximity' between indigenous and non-indigenous peoples to answer this question.

Consider two senses of moral responsibility, gathered around the moral emotions of guilt and shame. On a psychological level, there is a tight connection between feelings of guilt and the demand for corrective justice. We may act or fail to act in such a way so as to elicit the anger or resentment of others and thus feel guilty. Feelings of guilt direct attention to what we have done and thus towards those we have harmed. Guilt is most readily discharged through reparation. This is the way many contemporary legal and political theorists understand claims rooted in historic injustice. Not surprisingly, the claims often appear highly implausible, since they appear to fail the evidentiary and counter-factual conditions necessary for the establishment of guilt.

But there is always a remainder to these discussions, as for example in Waldron's discussion of a secondary dimension of 'public remembrance'.[18] His suggestion is that if guilt (and thus reparations) about past injustices is out of place, there may be reasons to feel ashamed about them. But this begs the question, since shame is a moral emotion connected to moral responsibility as much as guilt is. Bernard Williams provides an interesting account of the relation between these two senses of responsibility:

> *What I have done* points in one direction towards what has happened to others, in another direction to what I am … Guilt looks primarily in the first direction … Shame looks to what I am. It can be occasioned by many things – actions … or thoughts or desires or reactions of others. Even where it is certainly concerned with an action, it may be a matter of discovery to the agent, and a difficult discovery, what the source of shame is, whether it is to be found in intention, the action or an outcome … Just because shame can be obscure in this kind of way, we can fruitfully work to make it perspicuous, and to understand how a certain action or thought stands to ourselves, to what we are and what realistically we want ourselves to be.[19]

Williams suggests that shame, in particular, is a moral emotion that refers to certain shared ethical attitudes or ideals and forms of life. And that it triggers, in a way that guilt does not, a certain form of self-reflection connected to these forms of ethical life (and not merely fear of punishment or ostracism).[20] Thus on the personal level, at least, shame seems to indicate a broader and less voluntaristic sense of moral responsibility than that associated with guilt, and more closely tied to a sense of one's own identity – 'of who we are and what realistically we want ourselves to be'. Struggling with an imperfect past not entirely of our own making, but in light of the ideals we hold ourselves by is, according to Williams, a form of ethical reflection that can be occasioned by feelings of shame or regret. It is a form of moral responsibility to do with who I am as much as it is with what I have done. And what I am is partly constituted by the historically and culturally shaped 'frameworks of articulation' that I find myself amongst and draw upon in order to articulate what I think of as good or valuable.[21] I am what I do, whether or not I have intended or chosen to do all that I have done. Williams puts it thus: 'One's history as an agent is a web in which anything that is product of the will is surrounded and held up and partly formed by things that are not'.[22]

Is there a public version of this kind of moral responsibility, a sense of public or civic responsibility for the past occasioned by feelings of regret or shame? There is, and it is tied to one's membership in a political community. A political community embodies various conceptions of membership, and thus a sense of political identity and continuity through time. And these conceptions are connected to the practices, institutions and understandings that make up the concrete ethical life of that community, and especially the history of that community. A sense of civic responsibility for the past is, arguably, connected to the way political membership is conceived.

Note that political membership can be understood along two dimensions. Citizenship can denote the rights and obligations that individuals and groups have, but also a certain affective dimension as well, to do with a sense of 'belonging to', or what I referred to above as a sense of being 'at home' amongst a society's practices and institutions. Liberals often argue that individual and group rights provide the best source of allegiance to a political community, or at least, the only source of allegiance worth defending. Critics complain that if political membership is defined exclusively in terms of rights, it can distort valuable modes of collective action and self-understanding that depart from the grounds of rights. Another worry is that liberal understandings of rights tend to distort or unfairly assimilate non-European ways of life and modes of belonging, including those of indigenous peoples.

This familiar debate between liberals and communitarians is too crude, however, since the more important question is to consider the ways in which norms of belonging and rights conjoin or come apart in particular circumstances. Arguably, rights are only effective in a political culture in which people accept and support the basic institutions intended to realize and then protect them. Rights are often needed most, of course, in contexts where existing norms and institutions, including modes of political belonging, discriminate against people unjustly. The challenge in these contexts is to generate the necessary allegiance to basic norms and institutions that treat everyone equally where the historical and cultural norms have been to do otherwise. But equally, given this interdependence between rights and norms, rights and discriminatory norms of exclusion (or forcible inclusion) can become fused and embodied in the basic institutions and practices meant to uphold the values associated with rights. The treatment of indigenous peoples in various liberal democracies presents a clear example of these kinds of phenomena.

The historical injustices committed against indigenous peoples matter for contemporary practices of public reason. The political morality that informs and shapes those practices is one that was defined, in part, by both the exclusion of indigenous peoples from common citizenship rights, as well as their forcible inclusion into the state based on the denial of the legitimacy of their own cultural and normative orders (including their capacities to adapt those orders to changing circumstances). A sense of belonging is a necessary aspect of a people being capable of willing collectively in its own interests, but it has often been promoted through discriminatory and exclusionary practices, especially with regard to race.[23] So taking responsibility for past injustices against indigenous peoples is not simply to wish that things had gone differently, but to accept the ways in which a particular history of exclusion and inclusion is linked not only to the basic institutions of society, but to its present moral character.

There are two ways of thinking about how collective responsibility for the past might be characterized. On a contractual model, individual members of a political community, having benefited from it in various ways, have *prima facie* duties to help sustain it. Thus a political community is thought of as a collective endeavour, spanning generations, which provides important benefits for its members. Its social, material and cultural infrastructure help make decent lives possible.[24] On this model, a community might be said to embody certain values or principles, but only to the extent that they are the values and principles held by the particular individuals who make it up. Thus responsibility for 'its' actions would be understood to extend only in so far as they could be linked to the actions of its citizens and officials one by one. Responsibility for past injustices, on this view, would be grounded on the basis of the specific actions of individuals, or on people having benefited from wrongful actions, or in relation to explicit agreements or treaties struck between particular indigenous peoples and the state.

The problem with this view is that although it is undoubtedly a way of conceiving of collective responsibility, it is far too narrow. We routinely talk of people being held responsible for their unintended actions, or for the actions of a group of which they are a member. Moral responsibility can not be reduced to a matter of discerning the intentions of an autonomous agent: intentions have to be balanced against other elements as well.[25] And this is even more so in the case of collective agents.

Consider a second way of characterizing collective responsibility. Here the emphasis is less on duties of fair play and more on the relation between membership, identity and well-being. Collective responsibility would inhere in the personification of the community as a collective agent, as possessing a 'unit of agency'.[26] As I have stressed, a political community is constituted not only by the actions of those in the present, but also by those in the past, through the attempt to maintain an identity over time. Even minimalist accounts of political community need some account of it as a unit of agency in order to differentiate it from other kinds of social groupings. Thus 'we', as a political community, are responsible for the past just in so far as it affects the moral character of our society, that it has an 'important effect on the claims to value and purpose in our society', and that is has shaped our society in ways both good and bad.[27] Historical injustice, in other words, is not merely regretful, but demands a response.

But how can history be constitutive of a political community in such a way so as to have consequences for the obligations citizens owe to each other? Yael Tamir refers to identity-based obligations of the kind mentioned here as 'associative obligations'; obligations towards others with whom we share special relations, including our fellow co-nationals.[28] The basic idea is that we come to value certain states of affairs *qua* our membership in a community. These values express, in part, not simply what we want but who we are.[29] But it is not the fact that the values are actually shared that constitutes political community, since no such consensus exists in any community. Rather, certain 'embodied arguments'[30] about values and practices are shared, including particular registers of justice/injustice. It is important to emphasise that it is *arguments* that are shared, since it makes clear that any obligations we have in virtue of our membership of a political community will be tied not only to our affective relations with others, but also to practices of argument and contestation that reflect upon and criticise these relations. The interdependency between identity and difference discussed in Chapter 3 is relevant here. The content of a community's political morality is not static. Critical reflection and change is prompted, more often than not, by the struggle of individuals and groups grappling with the mismatch between the sense of moral harm or injustice they feel, and the established registers of justice/injustice within which they must articulate their claims.[31]

On the second relational model then, collective responsibility inheres in our being a member of a political community and having certain special obligations towards it in virtue of that membership. I want to argue that responsibility for past injustices is a species of these kinds of obligations. It is not merely that I may be a beneficiary of wrongful actions carried out in the distant past, but that I have an obligation to try and address the past given its effects in the present in relation to matters of basic justice in *this* community, my community.

The reasons we have for valuing particular relations with others provides a source of reasons for thinking that we have certain special responsibilities in relation to them.[32] But this presumes that an account of these relations can be given that does not rely entirely on subjective attitudes towards them, since to do so would leave our public practices of responsibility open to abuse. Thomas Hurka, for example, has argued that citizens have special obligations to their political institutions and societal cultures in so far as these institutions and cultures are *in fact* good. What attaches citizens to them are the historical facts: 'this is the culture they grew up in, that their co-nationals share with them a history of being shaped by, participating in and sustaining this culture'.[33] There is no such thing as special obligations to institutions or cultures that are evil.

Whatever one makes of this last claim, Hurka's discussion raises an interesting question. If we have special obligations to our compatriots in virtue of the interactions and institutions that produce good, as he argues, are we not also responsible for the wrongs that have been produced, sometimes by the very same institutions seen to be good-producing? I believe we are. But what if some people reject their identity as citizens precisely because of the morally bad things associated with the history of nation-building? Do they thereby write themselves out of the responsibilities that, I am arguing, go along with such membership? Unless they migrate and renounce their citizenship, a radical step for most people, they do not (and even then there are limits to what people can renounce when renouncing their citizenship).[34] The tension between the associative obligations of membership in a particular cultural or political community and more general duties derivative of one's commitment to principles of fairness or impartiality is an inescapable feature of citizenship.[35] 'Special' obligations are really only special insofar as we think of them against a baseline of apparently transparent moral and political obligations, underpinned by essentially voluntarist conceptions of responsible agency. These conceptions of obligation and responsibility are connected to liberal ideals of freedom, and especially to concerns about the public distribution of responsibility.

But it is precisely this picture of the relation between ideals of responsible moral agency and freedom that is problematic. For it seems to rule out, or at least obscure, consideration of the complex interdependence between a sense of belonging and our ethical attitudes about what we owe to each other and why, including our attitudes about moral responsibility.

So if citizens have general obligations towards each other grounded on fairness or equal consideration, they also have associative obligations grounded in the history of the political relations they value.[36] Normally we think of citizenship – along both dimensions of rights and belonging – as providing the recognition and capacity not only to participate (directly or indirectly) in the shaping of laws and policies that shape us, but to pursue as effectively as possible our own conceptions of what is good or valuable. What distribution or arrangement of rights and modes of belonging then, i.e. of the goods of 'critical freedom' and the means of 'being at home' in the world,[37] are required to meet the aspirations of contemporary indigenous peoples?

It is here that an idea of public reason capable of recognizing the fact of historical injustice is required. The aim must be to generate norms of cooperation that are acceptable to all the parties. This calls for a form of impartiality in the public sphere, but one conjoined with an acute historical awareness of how public values have been invoked in the past to discriminate against indigenous peoples, as much as to emancipate them. Thus the impartial consideration of the claims of indigenous peoples is connected necessarily to consideration of the particular social, cultural and historical contexts of their relations with the colonial state. Working out, in other words, what a commitment to equality means will entail taking into consideration the facts of historic injustice. The content of what is 'reasonable' should be thought of as a function of the working out of public reason itself, rather than as derived independently of it.

Thus pursuing questions about 'constitutional essentials' in the public sphere without an acknowledgment of the historical injustices that gave rise to them risks undermining the possibilities for their just resolution along both dimensions of rights and belonging. What risks being undermined is the legitimacy and acceptability (both modal and actual) of the norms, practices and institutions meant to address social and economic disadvantage, and the social trust that is crucial for mutual coexistence in deeply diverse political communities. In other words, what risks being undermined are the conditions under which certain members of the political community could even begin to feel 'at home' amongst its practices and institutions. The reasonableness of indigenous rights – i.e. the extent to which they could become the object of collective willing – can not be established independently of the history of relations between indigenous peoples, civil society and the state.

### Contesting the presence of the past

How does the past persist in the present and thus engender a special responsibility on our part to account for it? Historical legacies are publicly 'remembered' when they are taken to present particular problems that present-day political actors have to address. So the past does not literally *determine* present-day policies, but interpretations of the past are used to support or deny various possibilities in the present.

In Australia, for example, colonial settlement was premised on the very denial of the legitimacy of indigenous conceptions of land-holding and, ultimately, self-government (we shall return to these issues in detail in Chapter 7). These premises became embodied in the common law of Australia. To argue that they are unjust and should be rejected – as the

High Court began to, at least in relation to 'native title' in 1992 – is to do more than simply slip 'native title' into an existing structure of Australian property law.[38] Rather, it is to initiate a process of reinterpreting the grounds of mutual interaction between indigenous and non-indigenous Australians that have hitherto been in place. It is to force reconsideration of the relation between a country's past and its commitments embodied in law and the practices and procedures of its embodied arguments about justice. It is to revisit the ethical bases of these relations.

The point is not to *will* shame about injustice where none existed before, a project doomed to failure. Rather, it is to suggest that a purely voluntaristic or intentional account of moral and political responsibility should be open to contestation, either as an ideal intended to govern the distribution of responsibility in politics, or more generally, as a way of understanding how our attitudes and beliefs about responsibility actually work. The less voluntaristic and slightly obscure (i.e. heteronomous) character of the ethical attitudes associated with a sense of shame and our affective relations to others, can at least begin to point to different and perhaps more fruitful ways of conceiving of responsibility politically. At the very least it points to how ideas of who 'we' are, both individually and collectively, and who we want to be, are connected to our ethical attitudes about what we owe to each other. Moreover, it points to how political identity, both individual and collective, is inherently contestable; constituted as much by relations of power, culture and history as it is by ideals of autonomy and authenticity.

In politics, of course, a public view on matters of justice has to be arrived at and decisions made in the midst of persistent disagreement. So a paralysing sense of shame (or indeed guilt, for that matter) with regard to the past is worse than useless; it can undermine the collective capacities of members of a political community to address the injustices that continue amongst them. And a sense of shame is cheap when all that it entails is a signature on a petition or attendance at a rally, as opposed to more fundamental changes in the ownership or control over valuable assets (such as land or natural resources), or in the redistribution of wealth. The political and economic questions posed by Aboriginal claims are complex and deeply contested, as we shall see.

Thus any appeal to ethical attitudes connected to a sense of shame in helping to articulate a plausible conception of collective responsibility must indeed be forward-looking, as much as it is necessarily backward-looking, if such questions are to be addressed politically in any meaningful way. But there is no such thing as purely forward-looking justice in this case. Hence my focus on the practices of public reason. The challenge of mutual coexistence between indigenous and non-indigenous communities (as well as within them) involves differences over accounts of *right*, and there is no option but to try and work these out politically, and that means through some form of public deliberation. And we need an idea of public reason, I have been arguing, that does not presume, *a priori*, that the parties already share a substantive conception of justice, but rather one premised on the very absence of such a conception.

Mutual coexistence requires impartiality, but one that respects the different sources of normativity and belonging in a polity. A sense of impartiality helps underwrite a framework of mutual negotiation and cooperation between and within these different ethical and normative orders, but it too has to emerge and be crafted out of the available practical, normative, institutional and affective materials. But it remains a form of political impartiality, and therefore must be seen to be rooted in politics itself, and not allowed to drift too far from these moorings. The kind of impartiality that is achieved in this context is political in the sense of not being necessarily about the epistemic gains of public debate, since the demand for discovering genuinely justificatory reasons for all is not the central aim of postcolonial liberalism.[39] Rather, securing the capacities for individuals and groups to express their opposition to existing norms and institutions promotes the conditions in which disagreements over justice can be seen to be handled fairly, and in ways that do not entrench the domination of majorities over minorities (or minorities over majorities). In other words, it is not only the results of democratic deliberation that matter, but the way in which those results are arrived at – the norms, procedures and practices that gave rise to them. This does not entail being overly sanguine or romantic about the possibilities of politics, as critics of impartiality often are.[40] But if impartiality is an indispensable aspect of justice, then wherever the 'circumstances of politics' are most explicitly and honestly acknowledged, then justice has the greatest chance of being done.

## Conclusion

Arguing that citizens of states like Australia or Canada have special responsibilities to address the past, and drawing in part on the affective dimensions of membership in a community to do so, does not provide a straightforward determination of any of the difficult political and economic questions raised above. But that is not the point of the argument here. Rather, it is to argue for the conditions in which any possible answer – contingent, contestable and subject to change as it will necessarily be – will have a greater chance of being acceptable to all the affected parties. Compliance with the norms of the political game cannot depend solely on coercion, nor can it be explained mainly in terms of consent (unless the idea of consent is considerably weakened, arguably to the point of theoretical irrelevance). Instead, legitimate compliance will depend on the parties accepting the outcome of a political process in which they feel their case has been heard; that they have had a genuine opportunity to shape and influence the outcome; and that if they have lost – if they have not gained everything they sought to gain – then the loss is not catastrophic or permanent. In other words, the parties feel that the processes out of which social and political 'answers' have emerged are always contingent and potentially subject to revision.

A crucial point for postcolonial liberalism, however, is that norms of fairness cannot be thought to be derivable independently of the particular context of the political process itself. If a norm is 'an informal rule that circumscribes appropriate behaviour in a particular context',[41] then norms of fairness – such as a willingness to tolerate difference, political obligation and acceptance of defeat on particular issues without feeling compelled to quit the game will shift over time. They depend for their emergence on not only the dispositions of the individual agents who are interacting, but also on institutions and practices that shape those dispositions and attitudes. Thus there is a feedback mechanism between demands for fairness and the institutions designed to enforce these standards. William Connolly's account of the 'politics of becoming' is one possible version of such a mechanism. According to Connolly, remember, new and experimental social movements seek to shift underlying norms of interaction in order to not only expand existing social and political space, but also to challenge the basic mode of sociability (or in Connolly's language, 'ethos of engagement') characteristic of those interactions. Judgments about fairness, in other words, depend not only on having appropriate and known social decision procedures against which various actions can be measured, but also on (highly contextual and historical) modes of sociability.[42] Demands for fairness can result in new institutions being established to enforce such standards (e.g. a Commission for Human Rights or a Child Support Agency), and existing institutions can in turn become the focus of demands for reform as people revise or update their beliefs about what constitutes fair treatment.

So how can fair procedures and positive modes of sociability be developed and maintained between indigenous and non-indigenous citizens given the past and more recent history of relations between them? The first step, as I have been arguing over the past two chapters, is to acknowledge the deep disagreement which exists about not only conceptions of the good but conceptions of the right, and hence the crucial role that politics – involving the expression and management of disagreement – must play in postcolonial societies. The second step is to construct an account of public reason and deliberation that does not presuppose convergence on a substantive conception of justice, but rather acknowledges the ubiquity of relations of power, and aims at more localized but inherently dynamic forms of political settlements that 'resonate' with the prevailing constellation of discourses.[43] The third step is to say more about why the politics of disagreement at the heart of postcolonial liberalism do not entail giving up on justice and simply deferring to existing relations of power. Part of the answer will be in trying to specify more precisely the conditions in which the kinds of agreements prized by postcolonial liberalism can be achieved and considered legitimate. And there is no way of doing so without appealing to more than simply procedural norms. The tension between procedures and substance in arguments about justice is unavoidable. The strategy of postcolonial liberalism then is to accept that no account of what makes one set of norms, procedures and institutions for dealing with disagreements over justice more acceptable than another can be made without appealing to potentially controversial moral premises. A premium is thus placed on providing an argument about the conditions in which disagreements about not only substantive conceptions of justice but also disagreements about the vehicles of dispute resolution themselves can best be handled. Providing an account of these conditions is the main aim of the next chapter.

# 6    The postcolonial state

> What is at stake then is this: How can the growth of capabilities be
> disconnected from the intensification of power relations?[1]

James Tully has argued that there are two crucial 'hinge propositions'
that structure debates over Aboriginal rights in contemporary liberal
democracies, and that limit our thinking about them.[2] First, that the
jurisdiction exercised over indigenous peoples by the state is not only
effective but legitimate. And second, that there is no alternative. Either
the state exercises *exclusive* jurisdiction or the indigenous nation does —
there is no in-between, no shared or co-ordinate form of sovereignty
possible. To find a successful way of dealing with the issues we have been
discussing, however, our thinking must change.

Consider the first proposition. To evaluate whether or not the burdens
and costs involved in securing Aboriginal peoples' interests are reasonable, there is a prior question of the legitimacy of the institutions within
which those distributions are located. If the sovereignty the state claims
to exercise over indigenous peoples and their territories is illegitimate,
the question about to what indigenous peoples are or are not entitled
within that state presupposes precisely what is at issue.[3] Their claims for
self-government and for the lands taken from them, or for compensation
for dispossession, are legitimate in so far as they were and continue to
be self-determining peoples forcibly and unjustly incorporated into
European settler states. This is a powerful challenge. In fact, I think it is
decisive in many ways. But as I have been arguing, it is important to see
the complex strands of this claim. It does not rest exclusively on a claim
of prior occupancy of lands, or the fact of exercising prior sovereignty, or the persistence of indigenous cultures. What I shall call *the
normative thesis* underlying Aboriginal rights draws on each of these
arguments, but goes beyond them as well. The normative thesis claims
that Aboriginal rights are justified with reference not only to the self-
understandings, laws, practices and particular historical circumstances

112

of indigenous peoples, but also to more general principles of equality, freedom and well-being. Relying exclusively on historical arguments renders them vulnerable to counter-claims that take advantage of their inherent incompleteness.[4] As I argued in Chapters 4 and 5, the point is not that the normative argument trumps the historical argument (or vice versa), but grasping how these temporal and normative strands are intertwined.

The ideal postcolonial liberalism embraces in order to flesh out the normative thesis is *complex mutual coexistence*, since although indigenous peoples conceive of themselves as peoples or nations, they tend to seek rights of self-government that fall short of statehood. But what does this mean in terms of the normative shape of a liberal postcolonial order? If we disagree about justice and yet assume that relations of power are ubiquitous, how can we craft collective decisions that not only acknowledge reasonable disagreement about these matters, but also address the serious challenges faced by indigenous peoples today? These are the central questions I want to address in this chapter. The gist of my argument has been that we should focus on the conditions of the struggles of citizens for both recognition and particular forms of distribution (the two are necessarily linked),[5] rather than on identifying a theory that aims to settle these kinds of claims in advance. The matter is complicated, however, because in focusing on the struggles themselves rather than on their endpoints, we must still say something about what is required to ensure they can be played freely, and say something about what we mean by 'freely'. In spelling out what these conditions are, we touch on substantive questions of justice, among other things. Simply agreeing to disagree is not an option because the kind of disagreement in question is one that concerns the terms on which people interact. So to be clear, and as I have argued in earlier chapters, the postcolonial state is one committed to treating its citizens with equal respect; with minimizing domination and promoting freedom; and to providing the conditions in which people can construct and pursue meaningful lives.[6]

Defending such a vision runs up quickly against a number of powerful philosophical objections, which I will consider in detail below. But there is more than just philosophical issues at stake here. The kinds of objections that philosophers have been making against cultural rights in recent years have been echoed in public debates about Aboriginal rights in Australia, Canada and elsewhere. In fact, there is clearly a backlash occurring against Aboriginal peoples' claims, in part due to the vicissitudes of changing political climates, but also due to a sense of deep misgiving and apprehension about the language of 'special measures', self-determination and cultural autonomy. When Bill Jonas, the Australian Aboriginal Social Justice Commissioner, argued in a newspaper interview recently that equal treatment did not always entail identical treatment, the letters flowed in. One writer commented: 'So the Aboriginal Social Justice Commissioner ... wants Aboriginal people treated differently from other Australians. Well in terms of money spent on Aboriginal welfare, land rights etc., they clearly already are ...'. Another wrote: 'Your distinction between treating people equally and treating them the same is a point which escapes me, and I suggest also escapes most other citizens in this country. Different treatment for any particular racial group strikes me as a sure-fire formula to intensify/ foment ongoing social discord'.[7]

It is tempting and not surprising that defenders of Aboriginal rights, at this point, often respond to these objections by pointing to the fact that Australia is a signatory to an international convention or treaty that upholds the legitimacy of using tools like special measures to combat racial inequality. Or that this more complex idea is already at work in many other aspects of public life that most people accept and even cherish. Pointing out that people cannot reject a principle or norm for others that they accept for themselves, on pain of self-contradiction, is an effective but ultimately limited argumentative strategy. Logical consistency is a virtue (and one philosophers are keen to praise), but it has limited political purchase, to say the least. It has to be applied to claims with propositional content. So the substantive normative arguments have to be made and re-made in light of changing social and political circumstances. For it is not just the middle classes that need convincing, but also the families struggling on average weekly earnings, or the unemployed suburban fringe-dwellers coping with poor housing, lousy public infrastructure and 'work for the dole'. It is no easy task. And it gets more difficult when economic circumstances deteriorate and political parties search for divisive, 'push-button', racially sensitive issues to distinguish themselves from their opponents. Media commentators, columnists, and talkback-radio pundits, among others, join in to press upon and pull at people's insecurities and fears about cultural and social difference and change.

In this chapter I want to outline the normative character of what I shall call a postcolonial political order. It is an attempt to try to put the defence of Aboriginal rights into a wider context than is often attempted, beyond the legal doctrines and arguments that tend to dominate academic discussions of these questions. And I will try to answer some of the questions that have been raised in the previous chapters about exactly how a commitment to liberal equality can be translated into support for Aboriginal rights. In the first half of the chapter I outline two different ways of conceiving of equal respect, and then link this discussion to a powerful *egalitarian* objection against recognizing any special claims for Aboriginal people beyond basic liberal rights. I consider this objection, reject it, and then go on in the second half of the chapter to develop the normative argument more positively. In Chapter 7, I shall try to show how these arguments might actually guide our thinking about some difficult practical issues that arise when different normative orders collide within the same state. This is an important task, since many of people's fears and insecurities about Aboriginal rights have to do with uncertainty over what it actually entails on the ground.

But first: what do I mean by the state?

## The state

Minimally, the state is whatever actually and effectively monopolizes the legitimate use of violence.[8] The modern state, however, has a range of functions that vary over time and space. It is considered legitimate, as we have seen, in both a functional sense and when it is seen to possess the appropriate moral standing. Thus a state offers protection when it secures you against the grave disadvantages of an unregulated free-for-all. The rule of law provides security, but this can only be secured in turn by an effective sovereign. A Lockean variation on this story would be that the state and its institutions are justified when all those subject to them consent to their establishment as a means of securing not only their basic interests in security, but also their moral interests in being a member of a mutually advantageous cooperative scheme. Kant takes this one step further. The justification of the state must rest on moral grounds because the innate freedom of every person entails an obligation on each to recognize the freedom of every one else. Thus each person should choose to live in a condition that can institutionalize the peaceful exercise of freedom by everyone – i.e. the juridical condition established by the idea of the social contract. The state literally makes freedom possible through the provision of the rule of law, without which there would be the lawless and violent (hence non-freedom conducive) conditions of the state of nature. In these instances the state is both protective and enabling.

These prudential and moral justifications of the state are only part of the story, however, since it is clear the state did not emerge, nor does it operate, according to the instructions laid out by normative political theorists. Moreover, an exclusively normative approach to the state risks missing the way power circulates in contemporary circumstances, a crucial issue for our discussion of indigenous peoples' claims. What I am referring to is what Michel Foucault called the 'governmentalisation of the state' – namely, locating the state and its agencies in a much wider process of the proliferation of forms of government in a variety of contexts, which we touched on in earlier chapters. Foucault's approach to the state, and to power in general, is also useful for putting the claims about the nature of the state into context given the forces of globalization. David Held defines these as 'a set of processes which shift the spatial form of human organization and activity to transcontinental or interregional patterns of activity, interaction and exercises of power'.[9] In general, globalization puts each of the basic elements of the modern state under pressure. The state is increasingly enmeshed in global economic and political processes which displace and qualify its sovereignty. It is also challenged by deepening multiculturalism, in part due to the increasing global movement of peoples, as well as the aspirations of stateless nations and other groups for forms of self-determination. The ability of democratic states to maintain singular, coherent and inclusive national cultures is made more complex and difficult these days. Moreover *both* governmental and democratic practices have been dispersed via globalization. Keeping with Foucault's broad ranging sense of 'government', it is clear that there are governmental practices that cut across and constrain the sovereignty of nation states, but equally, there are attempts at resisting or modifying (and in some cases democratizing) those very practices of government as well, and which also cut across national boundaries.[10] These developments can be overstated – the state is hardly withering away – but they are significant nonetheless.

This particular situation creates challenges and opportunities for Aboriginal peoples. The challenges, to say the least, are considerable. They involve contesting the legitimacy of the state and the various normative conceptions of equality, justice and freedom said to underpin that legitimacy. But they also involve struggles against the broader forms of governmental power mentioned above, including those symbolic and affective dimensions of social existence that inform norms of interaction, reciprocity and sociability. These include the historical reference points informing and shaping public discourse, as well as the psychic and social boundaries of ways of life and cultural practices said to be tolerable in a 'civilized' society. Finally, the globalization of neo-liberal economic policies has placed tremendous pressure on the capacity of states to use discretionary spending in socially directed ways, to properly manage the development of natural resources, and to effectively regulate the operations of large multinational corporations.

Keeping both the practical and normative dimensions of the postcolonial state in view simultaneously is crucial to the contextual spirit of postcolonial liberalism. As I emphasized in the Introduction, the

Aboriginal peoples of North America and Australasia have been treated as less than equal citizens, however equal citizenship is defined. But they have also often experienced injustice at the hands of apparently well-intentioned policies and programs justified *in the name of* equal treatment and non-discrimination.[11] Ideals of equal citizenship, for example, have been used to justify forms of coercive assimilation.[12] This is a function of the way political and legal institutions charged with implementing and enforcing social and political norms are simultaneously cultural institutions, and thus how general norms of non-discrimination and equal rights can be interpreted in a variety of particular, and often conflicting, ways. The fact that principles and norms are mediated through various concrete social contexts does not mean that the principles or norms are therefore a sham, or that different cultural orders are necessarily incommensurable. Relativism does not follow the fact of social and cultural mediation. But what does follow, as Joseph Carens has argued, is that we need to see if there are alternative forms of mediation that are less distorting and alienating for those subject to them.[13] One important reason for doing so is that we want people – at least ideally – to be able to freely endorse the norms to which they are subject and not merely put up with them, or worse, see them as a mere alien imposition.

Having set out some of the basic elements of our understanding of the state, and some of the practical constraints it faces today, let us now turn to sketching the normative dimensions of the postcolonial state.

### Equality

Egalitarianism involves a cluster of ethical commitments. It involves not only a commitment to the equal distribution of stuff – of resources or welfare – but also to *civic* equality, to the idea that every single person is worthy of equal respect and equal standing.

To treat someone with equal respect is to treat them, first of all, as someone of equal worth. No person is less worthy than another on the basis of their cultural or religious beliefs, ethnicity, sex or race. As Charles Larmore has argued, to treat someone with equal respect is to be 'obligated to treat another as he is treating us – to use his having a perspective on the world as a reason for discussing the merits of action rationally with him'.[14] What does this actually mean? There are (at least) two ways of grasping the meaning of 'equal respect'.[15] We can show respect towards someone when we defer to their beliefs or worldview, or when no one party is allowed to dictate or set the terms of their interactions unilaterally. It follows then that a state may be said to treat its citizens equally when it simply defers to their judgments about their best interests and the life they want to lead. Or, when it ensures that no one group or person is able to unilaterally set the terms in which others must live and go about their lives. As Arthur Ripstein has argued, in this latter conception of equal respect the emphasis is on *equal* respect; to simply defer to the beliefs of individuals is to risk allowing that party to veto whatever standards he does not like, standards that might be necessary to ensure that others are treated equally. This means we need to hold people to a common standard, 'one that protects them equally from each other', or more positively, that requires persons to interact on terms that 'are acceptable to persons who respect each other'.[16] Here, equal respect is linked to practices of mutual justification, which we argued in the Introduction is central to much of contemporary egalitarian liberalism.

What happens if I reject the premises of the justification made for coercing or regulating my behaviour? If we are committed to the principle of equal respect based on 'reciprocity' rather than 'deference' then we think that coercion is justified, in some cases, even if the party at whom it is directed rejects the basic reasons for doing so. For some critics, this means liberalism is trapped; it claims to be inclusive and offer reasons for the exercise of political power that almost everyone (save for the fundamentalist or extremist) can accept, but it cannot, so in the end it is simply one sectarian doctrine on all fours with others, and liberals should admit it.[17]

We should expect disagreement and contentiousness about this idea of equal respect as reciprocity. But liberalism is not therefore trapped in appealing to either; all the critic has shown is that you cannot appeal to premises and conclusions that do any work and not be – in some instances for some people – controversial. Liberalism is not neutral about how the world should be organized and the norms that should govern social and political interactions. The crucial question is: what set of norms and values are most likely to be able to reach across and live amongst the diversity characteristic of our political societies? Democratic negotiation seems to be the only possible way of preserving both the practice and ideal of equal respect, along with recognition of disagreement over and contestation of the ideal itself. As both Habermas and Rawls have recently emphasized, there is a double character to the relation between democracy and the rule of law; the public autonomy associated with participation in law-making is co-dependent on the private autonomy secured by the rule of law.[18]

Hence, as I have been arguing, we should focus first on the conditions in which citizens struggle and argue over particular modes of recognition and distribution, as opposed to trying immediately to articulate a complete theory of justice that might be capable of adjudicating between all the conflicting claims. But in order to ensure that any provisional settlement that emerges out of this process is not simply arbitrary, or the product of relations of domination, we need to appeal to some substantive claims, and especially to do with equality. Thus, the kind of equal respect the postcolonial state should promote is one grounded in a norm of *reciprocity*: equal respect entails that the terms of engagement between citizens should not be dictated unilaterally by any one party. The next step, however, is to say some more about the stuff of equality being appealed to: *what* should we be aiming at when we talk of making people more equal, and *whom* are we discussing when comparing the situation of people with regard to these targets.

Critics of liberal political theory often focus, as we have seen, on the apparent abstractness and formality of liberal notions of freedom and equality. In much of the postcolonial theory literature, for example, liberal notions of equality are often criticized for either not extending equality to people who somehow do not fit the norm against which judgments of equality are made, or for not adequately theorizing how recognizing social and cultural difference (both philosophically and institutionally) can be a means of treating people equally. In other words, liberal equality is often taken to mean identical treatment or 'difference-blind' treatment. It is undoubtedly true that many liberals do take this line. Indeed there is something of a backlash occurring against various liberal attempts to reconcile multiculturalism with liberal equality, and a strong reassertion of a difference-blind or impartial norm of non-discrimination.[19]

I shall argue that both the postcolonial criticisms and the liberal backlash are overstated. In the first case, recent work on liberal equality shows that many of the concerns of postcolonial critics are actually shared by some liberal egalitarians. This is true, for example, of those liberals concerned with ensuring that people have the right kind of resources as well as *capacities* in order to pursue whatever conception of the good they have. Hence these theorists are concerned with what people are actually able to *do* and *be* as much as they are with what they have, and with the effect that circumstances beyond their control – such as structural features of society to do with the economy, family, legal and educational institutions – have on their basic capacities.[20] In other words, they accept that human capacities are socially and historically constituted and shaped, and are concerned to account for these facts in their arguments about distributive justice. The consequences of this important (and quite radical) claim are often not fully developed in these discussions, but this invites further exploration rather than whole-sale rejection. If being committed to postcolonialism means rejecting equality as either impossible or as a mere Western construct, then so much the worse for postcolonialism. We need to rethink how a commit-ment to equality can be squared with the claims of Aboriginal peoples, not abandon it.

On the other hand, it seems clear that the particular circumstances of Aboriginal peoples pushes liberal notions of equality in places liberals often fear to tread. More specifically, indigenous claims are distinct from those of other ethnic, cultural or racial groups in that their equal treatment is not entirely captured through special affirmative action programs, or additional mechanisms for 'voice' in legislative institutions. These are sophisticated variations on difference-blind equality argu-ments, meant to address the persistence of inequality and social subor-dination despite the entrenchment of formal equality.[21] But the kind of structural and constitutional protection of difference sought by indige-nous groups is not tied exclusively to the amelioration of social and eco-nomic disadvantage, as important as that is. It presses directly against the ideal of difference-blind equality itself, since it calls for an accom-modation of more permanent forms of differentiated citizenship.

But first, what does liberal equality actually entail – i.e. equality of *what*?[22] An influential conception of equality in recent liberal political theory, and especially with regard to multiculturalism, has been the idea of equality of *resources*. A resourcist approach to equality and justice says that what should be distributed equally are those resources and capa-bilities required for anyone (in the specified set) to pursue whatever conception of the good they want to (consistent with the rights of oth-ers to do likewise). Equality of welfare, on the other hand, aims at the distribution of equal welfare or desire-satisfaction.[23] 'Welfare' can be interpreted either in terms of what the agent herself thinks of as valu-able, or in terms of what is deemed to be objectively valuable or worth-while for people to value.

The intuition underlying resourcist arguments for equality is that each individual should enjoy not only an extensive set of rights and liberties but also a certain distribution of resources. The preeminent versions of this argument are provided by John Rawls and Ronald Dworkin. A key aspect of these discussions for us is that both Rawls and Dworkin accept that the distribution of talents and capacities we begin with – as much as the wealth and income we begin with – is morally arbitrary.[24] That is, we can hardly claim to *deserve* our place in the natural and social distribution of talents and wealth. This presents a key theme for our discussion of postcolonial liberalism. The claim seems to commit Rawls and Dworkin to a thesis about the *socialization* of our capacities – of our ambitions, tastes, preferences, powers and opportunities. And yet ultimately, both pull back from embracing the full consequences of such a claim.

For Rawls, individuals are treated equally and justly when they are guaranteed an equal distribution of a bundle of primary goods. These 'social primary goods' include not only income and wealth,[25] but also the basic liberties, freedom of movement, choice of occupation and the 'social bases of self-respect'.[26] Despite reasonable pluralism about the good, Rawls argues, citizens should be able to agree on a set of resources that should be distributed equally to everyone in order to enable them to pursue whatever conception of the good they want to pursue, consistent with the rights of others to do likewise.[27]

Dworkin agrees that resources are relevant to distributive justice and include not only external resources, such as material goods, but basic capacities as well.[28] A distribution is equal when the value of each bundle measured in terms of the opportunity cost it imposes on others is the same. Dworkin's discussion is complex, but the basic idea is that we should start off with not only equal purchasing power (the thought experiment involves resources being put up for auction and then bid to an equilibrium), but also with equal 'assets and endowments'. These assets and endowments include not only the capital or goods one begins with, but also the 'internal' capacities and talents one has. Dworkin's claim is that although we can not completely equalize these circumstances, we can try to compensate people for their unequal starting points, the process of which he demonstrates through a complex hypothetical insurance process that underwrites a progressive taxation system. In other words, those who end up disadvantaged due to circumstances beyond their control should be compensated by those who have been advantaged by circumstances beyond their control. Physically or mentally disabled people should be subsidized in order to equalize their life chances in relation to those who suffer no such disability, and so on. Note that the focus is on equalising resources; the responsibility for maximizing welfare is left up to individuals. Whether or not the resources in question actually *do* increase individual levels of welfare is not Dworkin's primary concern.

Dworkin's particular scheme has been extensively discussed.[29] One serious problem with it is how we measure in the real world just what people's relative advantages and disadvantages are. If we accept that some capacities are socially and historically constituted, and yet we also expect people to take responsibility for their choices in light of their capacities, then what force does the distinction between choice and circumstance actually have? How can equalizing resources give people genuine equality of opportunity? How can we draw the line between what is within our control and what is not? And if we cannot, what happens to Dworkin's distinction between choice and circumstance? How can we be held responsible for our choices, but not for our circumstances, if the choices we think we have are, in fact, a product of social, cultural, economic, and political circumstances beyond our exclusive control?

Rawls tries to modify the potentially unsettling consequences of these worries by arguing that tastes and ambitions are actually something people *do* have control over, hence can be held responsible for. But this is a deeply unsatisfactory move. How can we distinguish between preferences and capacities so easily, given that the ambitions and talents we have must surely be linked to the capacities and powers we begin with and are able to develop (or not)? Dworkin makes a similar move when he tries to distinguish between 'tastes and ambitions' and our 'physical and mental powers', even after accepting that the distribution of 'physical and mental powers' is arbitrary and hence legitimate objects for a theory of distributive justice.[30] But the doubts we had about the plausibility of Rawls's move apply equally to Dworkin's as well. How can we determine which beliefs and preferences we have, and thus which choices we make, are genuinely ours and can be held responsible for, and which are not? And if the distinction collapses, then how can we talk about people being genuinely autonomous or self-governing?[31]

One response to these difficulties is to shift the focus away from resources *per se* to what Amartya Sen calls 'capabilities' and 'functionings'. The intuitive idea here is that Dworkin and Rawls miss how a person may have adequate resources, such as a set of basic freedoms or income, but still lack the *capability* to make use of them in the way she wants, or according to an established benchmark of human flourishing or well-being.[32] Capabilities are conceived by Sen as 'real freedoms' to do or be. The actual 'doings and beings' which people choose to achieve are what he refers to as human *functionings*. To achieve any set of human functionings one needs the capabilities required to do so. The advantage of this approach, argues Sen, is that in evaluating people's circumstances, it makes sense to focus on the good they derive from a resource rather than on simply the amount of the resource they have, or the subjective satisfaction they get from consuming it. Thus it is a critique of both standard resourcist and welfarist approaches to equality (although it remains generally within the resourcist camp). The capabilities approach is sceptical of focusing mainly upon peoples' extant preferences, because it thinks these can be 'adaptive', hence potentially distorted by relations of power. Moreover, it emphasizes that capabilities must be guaranteed *for each and every person*, and thus is opposed to utilitarian strategies of aggregating across persons in order to measure overall welfare satisfaction.

However there is a tension in justice as capabilities between the insistence that capabilities be the focus of a theory of justice, and that there is a unique set of human functionings central to any decent human life. The argument seems perfectionist in inclination; we treat people equally when we ensure an equal distribution of capabilities, or real freedoms, that enable people to lead good lives. A theory of the good helps us pick out which capacities are valuable and need to be equalised. The obvious question is, just how thick is this theory of the good? Is it compatible with the reasonable pluralism of contemporary liberal democracies? Sen might have provided an answer to a problem inherent to resourcist conceptions of equality – how do we actually measure people's relative advantages and disadvantages – but at what price?

This question has been addressed recently by Martha Nussbaum. The crucial move she adds to the capabilities approach is to embrace Rawls's strategy in *Political Liberalism* with regard to valuable human functionings.[33] For Nussbaum, there is no single best set of human functionings. Instead, the aim of justice as capabilities is to provide a threshold of basic capabilities for each and every person that are necessary for any kind of decent human life. There is still a conception of the good being appealed to, but it is 'thick and vague' rather than thin and specific. Moreover, it is political rather than metaphysical; that is, the basic social minimum is tied to specifically political goals rather than any comprehensive doctrine of the good; Millians, Aristotelians, Rawlsians, Deleuzians and Kantians should all be able to pursue their own valued functionings once they and others are guaranteed their basic capabilities.

The threshold itself, Nussbaum argues, should be set as per the procedures and norms of local democratic institutions, which are best suited for taking into account the particular historical and cultural features of that polity. How can we tell if a local interpretation of a basic capability is legitimate or not? On the one hand, universal norms underlying the list of basic capabilities can become embodied in international instruments such as treaties and international law, which provides a benchmark against which to judge local departures from the threshold. On the other hand, these universal norms can not simply be imposed (except *in extremis*). Nor can they determine what is acceptable or unacceptable in every instance; local specifications and interpretations will have to take over in many instances. Thus, for Nussbaum, as distinct from Sen, we should aim to equalise *capabilities* rather than *functionings*.[34] The point is not to impose particular functioning on people, but rather to empower them with the capacities they need to live a decent life, given reasonable pluralism about what constitutes a good life in the first place.

## Aboriginal rights and equality of resources

As we can see, liberal arguments for equality are thus much more sensitive to context, circumstances and structural inequalities than some postcolonial critics lead us to think. The formalism and abstractness of the notion of equality is as much a concern for many liberals as it is for their critics. And the importance of taking into consideration the socially constructed nature of both internal and external capacities is also at the heart of recent liberal discussions of equality. In fact, when we turn to the most influential liberal discussions of Aboriginal rights, some variation of the resourcist argument is usually being appealed to.

The classic resourcist defence of Aboriginal rights is provided by Will Kymlicka, whom I discussed in Chapter 2. Kymlicka adapts Dworkin's argument for the task of justifying collective rights for Aboriginal peoples, including to land and self-government. Recall that his claim is that collective rights enable indigenous people to secure access to their societal culture, which in turn secures important goods for individuals. Cultures provide a 'context for choice', and provide people not only with options to choose from, but beliefs about value that make those options meaningful and valuable in the first place. Hence to lack secure access to a culture is to be disadvantaged in a way relevant to considerations of distributive justice. In other words, where the lack of access to a societal culture is not a product of one's *choices* but rather of one's *circumstances*, and thus something that should be equalized.

How do particular cultures get into such trouble? Sometimes they are simply oppressed and dominated by the state. In other instances, a lack of significant influence over policy decisions and resources that affect their well-being means that members' capacity to sustain their culture, and hence the meaningful options it provides, is undermined. Basic democratic procedures and equal citizenship rights do not provide enough protection, so the argument goes, since members of the majority culture can out-manoeuvre or out-vote minorities regularly on matters that affect the use of resources central to minority cultural practices.[35]

There are a number of problems with this influential argument, as we explored in Chapter 2. For one thing, the link between freedom and access to a secure societal culture is problematic. If I am a member of a culture that is in the process of being assimilated to another, say larger, culture then it is not clear I am going without beliefs about value, but rather that they are *changing*.[36] How is that a threat to my freedom? Where the process of assimilation is so coercive and oppressive that the result is the outright elimination of the culture, then it clearly can be freedom-constraining in the worst possible sense. Destroy the culture, destroy the people, at least in some circumstances.[37] But applied to the justification of Aboriginal rights, this argument makes it too dependent on the fact of suffering; to have suffered great harm in the past is surely one important consideration in evaluating a claim for collective rights, but it is not the only one. Moreover on its own, this argument leads only to remedial rights, not more permanent or structural ones, and this seems to miss crucial aspects of the normative thesis underlying Aboriginal rights.

Another version of the resourcist argument is to tie the lack of a secure cultural structure to the literal *incapacity* of members of the group to cope with the wider society within which they live. According to this argument, minority language groups, for example, may be granted language rights if, because of their particular circumstances, it was unlikely that members of that culture would be able to master the language of the majority, and thus unable to pursue a range of important human activities without some provision being made for the survival of their cultural structure.[38] Applied to indigenous peoples, the argument would be that the nature of indigenous difference is such that without the preservation of their culture, they are left at a severe disadvantage in terms of coping with Western institutions and practices.[39]

The main problem with exclusively culturalist defences of Aboriginal rights, I shall argue, is that they are incomplete. The justification of Aboriginal rights, in other words, is tied too narrowly to the preservation of culture, as opposed to a bundle of claims to do with not only culture, but with interests related to land and self-government. Another danger of cleaving too closely to a culturalist defence of Aboriginal rights is that it leaves it open to various manifestations of the 'expensive tastes' objection, which we shall now consider.[40]

### Are Aboriginal rights akin to expensive tastes?

If we are committed to some version of equality of *welfare*, then we are committed to subsidizing people for the tastes and preferences they have, even if those tastes or lifestyles are very expensive to maintain. How can someone committed to egalitarianism be committed to using scarce resources to subsidize people's expensive tastes? Why should a beer lover be forced to subsidize the tastes of a wine snob? Equality of resources arguments are meant to block this objection by focusing on the equal distribution of *basic* resources, such as rights, income, and opportunities, as opposed to the equal satisfaction of preferences, whatever those happen to be. In stretching the language of resources to include culture, the worry is that something like the expensive tastes objection re-emerges.

In order to avoid this objection, Kymlicka has to show that minority collective rights can be defended as a response to unequal circumstances, as opposed to shared choices.[41] But deep problems bedevil such a move. Consider: If societal cultures are valuable because they provide meaningful beliefs about value, as well as options corresponding to those beliefs, then if a culture is in decline because its members are taking up another set of cultural practices (with corresponding options), then – as we have seen – no one is going without beliefs in value. If it is in decline because the options it provides are costly or expensive to maintain, then the expensive tastes objection may apply. Why should others subsidize the maintenance of those options if everyone has relatively equal access to meaningful beliefs about value?

We can respond to the expensive tastes objection in at least three ways. First, we can simply reject the distinction that Rawls, Dworkin and Kymlicka make between choices and circumstances. In other words, embrace the socialization of capacities thesis much more fully than most egalitarian liberals do. But does this mean abandoning liberalism? I shall return to this point below.

Second, we can reject the analogy between expensive tastes or preferences and one's cultural beliefs, and argue that it is not as clearcut as it seems. One need not claim that cultural beliefs are literally akin to physical handicaps to think that, at least in some circumstances, they are burdensome for people in such a way so as to raise a legitimate question of fairness and justice. Fairness considerations enter into the picture because it is clear that indigenous people often face being pulled in different directions by alternative sources of authoritative legal, social and political norms. In so far as this dilemma is a genuine one, some aspects of the particular content of citizenship may place an undue burden on indigenous people, that is, significantly constrain them from living their lives according to their own customs and practices.[42] *Prima facie*, this should be a concern for any liberal 'fully committed' to the freedom of association,[43] or like Rawls in *Political Liberalism*, to ensuring that citizens can adopt the political conception of justice from *within* their own 'comprehensive view'. Of course, determining what will count as sufficiently burdensome, and what kind of remedy is required, if any, will inevitably depend on what else is at stake.[44] (I will tackle this issue in more detail in the next chapter.) Much will depend on the costs – material, social and psychological and so forth – that members of a minority group face if they cannot live according to their cultural or religious beliefs, or that the rest of society would have to bear if they do.

It is not impossible, of course, that indigenous people could, over time, choose to assimilate to Western institutions and practices, if they wanted to. And one could imagine a scenario in which various forms of transition assistance could be provided by the state to ease such a process. (In fact, this supposedly 'benign assimilation' scenario has been recently re-floated in Australia by various critics of Aboriginal rights.[45]) But as I understand it, most indigenous people continue to want to protect their lands and ways of life as much as possible. They do not accept that the choice is between assimilation or separatism. Moreover, we know the terrible consequences of the long history of attempts by the state at eradicating their ways of life, such that to classify their desire to preserve them as a form of 'expensive taste' is arguably deeply misconstrued.

We need not oversimplify what we mean by assimilation. No culture or people is immune from contact or influence from outside itself, because all cultures and peoples are internally differentiated and thus always open to reshaping and reorientation from the both the inside and outside. In a world in which social, cultural, political and economic processes are increasingly transnational, the ability to immunize oneself from any kind of social, cultural or political influence from the outside is very difficult, if not impossible. But that does not mean we can presume that assimilation, *in every instance*, is inevitable, or benign, or desirable. People value their cultural practices enough to want to preserve them, even when the obstacles to integration with other cultures are relatively small.[46]

This leads to my final point concerning the expensive taste objection. If we accept, as I have been arguing, that Aboriginal rights do not rest *solely* on culturalist arguments, then the expensive tastes analogy fades. For the right to self-government is not only about the freedom to engage in various cultural practices threatened by assimilation, but also the freedom to exercise various forms of governmental authority. This raises jurisdictional claims about the constitutional and institutional structure of the state as a whole, and challenges the distribution of legislative authority between different orders of government and the administration of justice. These kinds of jurisdictional and institutional claims are not fully captured by the language of liberal culturalism. Understood properly, they pre-empt charges of 'expensive tastes' because they challenge the very premises upon which the analogy is based. Namely, that the claims of indigenous groups are commensurable with or identical to the claims of other minority groups within the political community. Thus it is important to see that we cannot engage in these kinds of judgments about cultural beliefs and expensive tastes independent of the particular circumstances of the groups making the claims. Not all peoples claiming self-government rights are claiming the same thing for the same reasons. Quebecois nationalism cannot be reduced to Aboriginal nationalism, for example, however much they both appeal to normative claims about the value of self-determination and self-rule. Hence there will be different forms of accommodation and institutional arrangements required to meet these different claims.

## The capabilities approach and Aboriginal rights

At this point, someone with generally liberal egalitarian intuitions might be willing to grant that Aboriginal rights are not necessarily akin to expensive tastes, but that what is not clear is whether or not they are compatible with the kind of outcomes egalitarian liberals generally seek.

As we saw above, the dominant approach to equality in the Rawlsian tradition is resourcist: people should start with a roughly equal bundle of primary goods or resources and then be free to use them as they see fit. A general criticism of this approach is that it focuses too much on *access* to basic social goods, and not enough on the attainment of actual outcomes. One tack is to suggest that the resourcist approach, on the whole, underestimates the effect of the structural features of social, political and economic life. These structural features shape distributive patterns in the first place, and thus cannot be addressed by theories of distributive justice that take these patterns for granted. This point has significant importance for indigenous peoples since, as we have argued, the basic institutions within which the distribution of primary goods take place can be such so as to severely disadvantage them. What counts as a primary good, the legitimacy of the basic distributive institutions, and what constitutes an acceptable move in the public conversation of justice, all have important consequences for consideration of their claims. Power, both direct and indirect, always shapes distributive justice, however much it is supposed to work the other way round.

These problems can be exacerbated by focusing upon only a narrow range of primary goods for the purposes of interpersonal comparison. How do these resources relate to the relative well-being of people in terms of what they are actually able to do and be?[47] The worry is, as Martha Nussbaum has put it, that the resourcist approach does not go 'deep enough to diagnose obstacles that can be present even when

resources seem to be adequately spread around'. In order 'to do justice
to A's struggles', argues Nussbaum, 'we must see them in their social
context, aware of the obstacles that the context offers to the struggle for
liberty, opportunity, and material well-being.'[48] These struggles include
physiological or biological factors (the different kind of needs associated
with being pregnant, for example), but also the effects of pervasive social
norms on the ability of people to achieve various kinds of freedoms.
What we require is both generality and particularity; detailed knowledge
of the context and circumstances in which the agent acts and yet at the
same time, a less subjective and more comprehensive account of her
basic needs and capabilities. A focus on capabilities as opposed to
primary goods is said to provide this. A person's 'capability set' indicates
the alternative combinations of possible functionings, or modes of living,
actually available to them.[49] Thus it is concerned with what people are
actually able to achieve with their freedoms, whilst at the same time,
accepting reasonable pluralism about the good.[50]

The capabilities approach has its own problems, of course. The first
is to do with its perfectionist and paternalistic tendencies.[51] Despite
embracing political liberalism, there is still a general question as to
whether or not it actually takes reasonable pluralism seriously enough,
although the pluralist challenge presents problems for any standard of
interpersonal comparison. The second set of problems is to do with the
abstractness of any general list of basic capacities; Nussbaum provides
very little guidance as to the priority rules or ordering principles that
should apply to the various components, save to say that they should be
guaranteed for each and every individual. Both are serious concerns for
the postcolonial liberal. And as we shall see, the ordering problem is a
particularly serious one. But set them aside for the moment. The attraction of the capabilities approach is the aforementioned combination of
particularity and generality. It provides a framework for developing critical cross-cultural judgments about the central capabilities of persons,
and yet also seems to leave room for particular interpretations of those
capabilities attuned to local circumstances. It seems to provide a framework, in other words, for elaborating what it might mean for liberal
equality to 'go local'. Consider five features of this approach which lend
themselves to the normative heart of postcolonial liberalism – the ideal
of complex mutual coexistence:

1. *The idea of a basic but contestable threshold.* A threshold is less than a
   complete theory of justice, but it identifies those basic human capabilities central to living a life that is recognizably human, in the
   broadest possible sense. Focusing on a threshold of central capabilities provides some critical grip for cross-cultural interpersonal
   comparisons with regard to equality, without necessarily claiming to

embed them within a fully worked out theory of justice.[52] Any such list is controversial. The crucial question is the extent to which such a list is compatible with the normative thesis underlying the justification of Aboriginal rights. And the answer to this question can only be discovered through actual deliberations between indigenous and non-indigenous people.

2. *Multiple realizability and normative flexibility.* Although the central capabilities denote the relevant space for interpersonal comparison between all citizens, the approach allows for the 'multiple realizability' of those capabilities according to local beliefs and circumstances.[53] This follows from the central importance given to freedom, and especially capabilities for action, in the capabilities approach. Human beings are conceived of as agents, not just passive bearers of preferences. The conception of practical reason underlying this approach is thus focused directly on principles of action first, and only then in relation to a variety of functionings the agent may have reason to value.[54] Thus, except in the most egregious circumstances, implementation of the basic capabilities is left, for the most part, to local institutions.[55] The approach acknowledges that the threshold level of each capability will always need more precise determination as it is worked out for political purposes between different local, national and international actors over what constitutes the appropriate standard or threshold, and who is best able to deliver them. Thus the process of political justification always remains incomplete. This places a premium on democratic discussions occurring within and between nations (and thus on the presence of certain basic liberties and opportunities available to those subject to those governments; see 3 below). Nussbaum cashes out this interpretive and justificatory flexiblity in the Rawlsian language of reflective equilibrium and overlapping consensus.[56] But we can also appeal to the argument made in Chapter 4, which replaced the aim of achieving an overlapping consensus with that of a discursive *modus vivendi*.

3. *A norm-suffused and contextual account of rights.* The language of capabilities arguably gets more directly than rights-talk does at the conditions required for the *effective exercise* of the kinds of capacities and interests rights are often thought to promote, whether political or economic.[57] Since people disagree about both the right and the good, any argument about the merits of one particular set of rights over another ultimately rests on controversial moral beliefs. Rights are thus derivative from these beliefs, not foundational. They also require some mechanism for their effective realization and enforce-

ment, without which they are vacuous. The capabilities approach is no less vulnerable to the fact of reasonable pluralism than rights – discourse is, and needs a story about how its basic capabilities can be actualized no less than rights-discourse does. But it arguably comes at these issues more directly.[58] For one thing, the approach openly ties its list of human capabilities to a conception of the good, albeit one that admits of potentially enough variability and local specification so as to be amenable to many different cultures and contexts. Furthermore, in focusing on human capabilities, it is focused on the potential for specific kinds of (valued) human action, and also upon the social bases of these forms of human action. Thus it is able to distinguish between someone having a nominal right to political participation, for example, without really having the capability for it. Different kinds of positive governmental or social action may be required to ensure that I am able to act on my basic capability to participate meaningfully in the political system of which I am citizen.

4. *Socialization of capabilities.* As we saw above, Rawls and other egalitarian liberals try to neutralize the consequences of the socialization of capacities thesis by drawing a distinction between choice and circumstance. But it is very hard to reel in the effects of the powerful Rawlsian claim that differences in natural abilities and contingencies of upbringing are morally arbitrary factors that should not determine the rewards (or punishments) people receive. If the distinction between what a person can be genuinely held responsible for and what she cannot is unstable – and I have suggested it is – then this is a potentially intractable problem for deciding when and how various forms of egalitarian interventions are justified. Another option, however, is to embrace the socialization thesis. Again, the capabilities approach is helpful in this regard. In distinguishing between 'basic', 'internal' and 'combined' capabilities, Nussbaum shows how difficult it is to maintain a strict line between choice and circumstance. Consider how the three kinds of capability are related. *Basic* capabilities refer to what is essentially the 'innate equipment' of individuals – for example their sense of hearing, or capacity for seeing – but at a very rudimentary level. *Internal* capabilities are those developed states of the person that are 'sufficient conditions for the exercise of the requisite functions'. *Combined* capabilities, finally, are internal capabilities combined with suitable external conditions for the exercise of the functioning.[59] What is important is how these different kinds of capabilities interact. Many internal capabilities require favourable external conditions, and

their exercise can be thwarted not only by changing material and social circumstances, but often distorted and reshaped by them as well. Most of the capabilities on Nussbaum's list of 'Central Human Functional Capabilities' are combined capabilities, and thus most of those we associate with basic human rights are too. Does embracing the socialization thesis undermine liberal intuitions about the importance of self-government and self-ownership? Well, in some ways it does. But both self-government and self-ownership are radically indeterminate notions open to a variety of often conflicting interpretations. Neither can be taken as, alone, *the* central value of liberalism. The virtue of embracing the socialization thesis is that it provides the conceptual tools to pick out, or at least remain alert to, potentially arbitrary arrangements hiding under apparently natural conditions. Instead of being focused mainly on questions about the legitimacy of various kinds of entitlements to what is produced, for example, our attention shifts to 'pursuing justice in the power relations surrounding production'.[60] This can be generalized for the evaluation of a range of other institutional arrangements as well. 'Constructive social power' is unavoidable and ubiquitous in modern societies.[61] It is, in part, a consequence of people being able to act freely in the first place. We cannot help acting on others as we are acted on by them, whether in asserting or dissenting from our practical identities, or participating in various social practices into which we are born and/or continue to uphold. We can never step wholly outside of these relations, but we can try to evaluate the consequences of the various particular distributions of social power we encounter, and try to address the asymmetries that inevitably arise and affect citizens' freedom and equality.

5    *A practice-dependent conception of freedom.* The focus on what people are actually able to do and be leads to a distinctive account of freedom. On the capabilities approach, securing negative freedom – the removal of external hindrances to doing what one pleases – is an important but only partial aspect of human freedom. To have the capability to do $x$ is to be free from external hindrances to do $x$, but also to have the material and institutional resources to do $x$ effectively – to have the 'effective power to achieve chosen results'.[62] Thus freedom is tied closely to principles of *action*, and especially to the material, institutional and social conditions required to act freely, both individually and collectively, since these two modes of freedom are interdependent.[63] To act freely is therefore not only to have the material and institutional means to convert opportunities into achievements, but also the capability to contest and question

those norms of recognition and distribution that govern access to those various means.

Putting these five features of the capabilities approach together provides a way of conceptualizing the shape of the kind of political order postcolonial liberalism aims to promote. A postcolonial liberal order should aim to secure those capabilities required to participate effectively in collective practices of public reason that affect one's fundamental interests. What counts as a fundamental interest includes not only those very basic physiological and psychological needs that human beings everywhere share, but is also shaped by the particular forms of constructive social power – or constellation of discourses – circulating in the public sphere. The way capabilities are picked out and described is therefore crucial. Thus any proposed list or threshold of central capabilities has to be adequately deliberated and subject to contestation. That is, it has to emerge from a process in which the reasons that become authoritative in shaping governmental or social action in a particular domain can be shared by those subject to them. The focus then is not only on trying to identify those central capabilities that are required for being a 'normally cooperating member of society',[64] but also the conditions under which agreements about these descriptions are said to be legitimacy-conferring. Note that there is a dynamic relationship between these two demands. People need the capabilities and opportunities required to engage in these practices of freedom, but these practices in turn reshape and reconfigure what counts as a central capability or valued functioning in the first place.

So Aboriginal people, like all people, need those basic capabilities required for bodily and psychological well-being, such as freedom from premature mortality, from persistent violence, from preventable morbidity, and from inadequate nourishment.[65] They need those capabilities associated with engaging in practical reasoning, both public and non-public; not only the ability to imagine, think and reason in ways informed by an adequate education, but also to form and pursue conceptions of the good and be able to reflect critically upon them. They require some form of mutual recognition from others, and thus having access to the 'social bases of self-respect' and non-humiliation.[66] They need to be able to pursue their interests responsibly, that is, with regard to the interests of others, and to be able to comprehend the kinds of constraints that imposes upon their actions. If people are to have the capabilities required to choose between any number of possible functionings in modern, market-based liberal democratic societies, then they will also need some set of 'saleable skills and capacities', given prevailing economic circumstances, that will allow them to participate in the real economy of their society in some way.[67] To blame people for being a net

drain on society's resources without giving them the capabilities or genuine opportunities to contribute to that society, or provide for themselves, is deeply confused. (We shall return to this issue with specific
reference to debates over Aboriginal people and 'welfare dependency' in
the next chapter.)[68]

But note immediately that much more complex elaboration is
required. For example, what do I mean by *adequate* levels of nourishment
or education? What *kind* of mutual recognition is required to secure the
social bases of self-respect? *Which set* of 'saleable skills' exactly, prevents
people from being excluded from the economy and enables them to take
responsibility for themselves? And which capabilities should take priority in what kind of circumstances? This kind of elaboration can only
occur at the level where those most affected by these descriptions have
the opportunity to contribute to their formulation. But in order to make
such a contribution, certain basic capabilities must already be secured.
In other words, there is no escaping the fact that capability sets must be
discursively constructed and legitimated, but one must also secure the
conditions in which such processes of discursive construction and legitimation are accessible to all those affected by the authoritative reasons
that emerge from them.

Second, the capabilities here are all, by and large, 'combined capabilities' in Nussbaum's sense of the term. Their realization requires a
combination of internal and external factors. Achieving reasonable
health, educational, and employment levels requires more than simply
negative rights of non-interference. Evaluating whether or not someone
has the requisite capabilities – or real freedoms – for functioning will
require more than the presence of a range of permissible options from
which to choose. It will also require an analysis of the kinds of constraints and incentives that exist, and which lead some people to take up
some options but not others, including ones that, in principle, they
could freely take.[69] This means looking at the relationship between
extant social, legal and political norms and practices and people's ability to convert resources into valuable functionings. Are there pervasive
norms of social discouragement, for example, that affect young women's
ability to achieve some level of economic independence? Are there material, social or cultural factors that interfere with the delivery of better
healthcare, for example, which result in grossly unequal outcomes for
different groups in society? A society cannot will or guarantee good
health or self-respect, but it can provide the social bases of these goods
by promoting the capabilities required for people to be both physically
and psychologically healthy.

How does all of this relate to Aboriginal rights? As we saw earlier,
these rights originate from the prior presence of Aboriginal peoples and

their distinctive laws and practices, as well as through the complex inter-societal negotiations between them and European settler nations. What I want to argue is that we see these rights, normatively speaking, as securing a particular kind of capability set in relation to Aboriginal peoples' interests in land, culture and self-government. These capabilities enable indigenous people to pursue their conceptions of the good and ways of life equally, since they promote a distribution of formal and constructive social power that takes into account the distinctive histori-cal and social facts of their situation, both in the past and today. Securing Aboriginal peoples' interests to land recognizes their pre-exist-ing territorial rights and protects their property interests, just as the law protects those of non-Aboriginal people. Securing their cultural inter-ests enables Aboriginal people access to equal resources to maintain, adapt and reproduce their cultural identities, given the challenges they face in doing so. Securing their sovereign interests acknowledges Aboriginal nations as equal partners at the time of European contact,[70] and contributes to their capacity to improve the substantive material and social inequalities their communities face today. Moreover, indige-nous peoples have good prudential reasons for being sceptical of giving up their sovereign interests, however limited, given the costs of incorpo-ration and inclusion that have been imposed upon them over the years by liberal states.[71] Thus a postcolonial liberal order tries to ensure that the spillover effects of interactions between indigenous and liberal nor-mative orders are, as much as is possible, mutually acceptable.[72] In so doing, it helps secure the equality of 'effective social freedom' for indige-nous peoples, and thus the equal capability for 'adequate public func-tioning'; that is, effective use of the political opportunities and liberties required to make their concerns known and initiate public debate about them.[73]

So what are the advantages of using the capabilities approach for justifying Aboriginal rights?[74] They stem from the five features outlined above. The approach ties generally liberal notions of equality and free-dom to a much richer set of social, material and cultural considerations concerning what is actually required for people to achieve effective social freedom, whilst accepting the pluralist challenge to ideals of human flourishing.[75] Note also that it leaves open the precise calibration required between individual and collective rights. Some kinds of capa-bilities will best be promoted by securing the capacities of groups to act in various ways; in other instances, only by empowering individuals. In the case of indigenous peoples, it will always be a matter of strug-gling to get the mix right, for it is clear that an exclusively individual-rights or group-rights approach will be inadequate, given the complex circumstances they face. Thus the capabilities approach, applied to the circumstance of indigenous peoples, offers a break from 'difference-blind' liberal equality – since it takes the social, cultural and political differences people face in achieving real freedom very seriously – without breaking with equality completely.[76] What it does is encourage a more pragmatic approach to getting the calibration between individual and collective rights correct, albeit always a value-infused kind of pragmatism.

Aboriginal rights, by and large, have usually been conceived of as involving collective rights – to property, to the means for preserving cultural practices, and to self-government as self-determining peoples. But since Aboriginal people are also citizens of the wider state (assuming, for the moment, that their sovereign interests do not preclude them from being so), they also enjoy certain basic individual rights too. Translating Aboriginal rights into effective public policy involves, as Tim Rowse has argued, a persistent interplay between the 'individuating and communalising' modalities of liberal government and law'.[77] A policy of self-determination does not merely acknowledge the communal character of indigenous interests and practices, for example, but actively solicits the formation of specific kinds of groups – regional associations, land councils, corporations – with whom the state can deal. As Rowse points out, '[t]he phrase "self-determination" poses the question: what self or selves?'[78] The statutory and institutional requirements attached to the formation of these bodies, although intended to allow for the continued expression of indigenous interests via their customs and practices, are also intended to translate those collective interests into forms recognisable to established practices of government. The spillover effect of these translations can involve the reshaping of both public and private space by liberal norms.[79]

Here we encounter a deep challenge faced by Aboriginal peoples in contemporary liberal democracies raised in earlier chapters and above. Aboriginal rights are particularly vulnerable to co-option, or as John Borrows puts it, to 'domestication' under the guise of legitimate recognition. This is frequently commented on by Aboriginal activists and theorists.[80] It falls somewhere between exclusion and assimilation. As Borrows argues: 'Aboriginal peoples can now legitimately question the injustice of colonial encounters and thereby lay claim to pre-existing rights in the nation states in which they live … Nevertheless, it is becoming increasingly clear that these same states can extensively modify, infringe, or extinguish indigenous rights'.[81] Aboriginal claims are taken up within the framework of public reason, but the nature of the uptake becomes problematic. Crucial premises are not so much lost in translation as filtered through a different set of legal, political and moral traditions with often serious consequences, as Borrows and others point out. Engaging in public reasoning requires an openness to one's worldviews and claims being tested and re-translated back to you; there is no escaping mediation and thus cultural change. But the ideal of mutual justification places a premium on each and every person subject to the coercive power of the state being able to contest those norms and rules which affect their fundamental interests. And here the problem is that by domesticating their claims, by 'continuing to enfold Aboriginal peoples tightly within the existing federal fabric … without changing that weave to accommodate them significantly', those capacities for contestation and for the equal pursuit of their ways of life are considerably weakened.[82]

Since power is ubiquitous there is no way of completely insulating any set of norms or practices from the kinds of distortions that Borrows and others identify. But the point here has been to emphasize the potential for a *critical* use of the capabilities approach, as applied to the justification of Aboriginal rights in liberal democratic societies. The emphasis on the contestable and deliberative nature of the basic threshold it identifies for human well-being, the multiple realizability of basic capabilities as opposed to mandated functionings, and a practice-oriented account of human freedom, all place an emphasis on the continual contestability of the means used to make interpersonal comparisons for the purpose of equality. At the very least, the capabilities approach asks the right kinds of questions about the institutional arrangements and policies in place: How do they actually enable people to realize their valued functionings? What kinds of conflicts might emerge between securing one kind of capability as opposed to another? How has the authoritative description of the capabilities to be promoted and secured been arrived at in the first place? Finally, it leaves open the possibility – something postcolonial liberalism expects and welcomes – of the creative adaptation by indigenous and non-indigenous institutions in meeting the demands of both 'cultural appropriateness' and fairness and equity. If Aboriginal cultural and political life is internally differentiated and dynamic rather than static, then we should expect to see some *reverse domestication* occurring as well. Liberal modalities of government can be turned around and used to protect or promote valued forms of indigenous functioning. Thus different forms of negotiated coexistence between liberal and indigenous norms and social orders may emerge in unexpected ways.

## Conclusion

A sympathetic reader might, at this point, be willing to grant something along these lines: Aboriginal rights promote the central capabilities of

Aboriginal people by helping to secure their important and distinctive interests in relation to land, culture and self-government, interests they have in addition to those associated with basic citizenship rights. Securing these interests helps to secure and promote the equality of effective social freedom. The capabilities approach, suitably adapted, directs us to the right kinds of question here: what can people actually achieve with the resources they have? How do current land rights regimes actually help secure their interests in property? How does enabling Aboriginal groups to reproduce their cultural practices over time protect and promote the basic interests and capabilities of their members? How do self-governing institutions actually improve Aboriginal peoples' material and social conditions? However, the reader might continue, since (as we have claimed) power is ubiquitous and the presence of arbitrary and unjustified arrangements inevitable, the same reasons which lead us to see the reasonableness of Aboriginal rights should lead us to seek reasonable cross-cultural norms for evaluating and correcting such asymmetries between and *within* these different normative orders as well. Does not a reliance upon the capabilities approach warrant intrusive and imperial interference in the affairs of Aboriginal self-governing societies on the grounds of securing the central capabilities of all of its members? And if it does not, how will the interests and capabilities of the most vulnerable be protected?

These kinds of questions are difficult to answer in the abstract, because a suitable answer requires as much attention to context – to historical, social, cultural and political contexts – as it does to fundamental normative issues. Neither liberal nor Aboriginal practices are inherently unjust, but neither are they immune from injustice either. The ideal of complex mutual coexistence is intended to acknowledge the ways in which people are subject to multiple cultural, social and political allegiances often simultaneously, and the need for negotiated ways of managing the conflicts that can emerge in relation to them. But what about the conflicts that inevitably emerge between the different values and interests being deliberated and balanced in these processes, including between the powerful and the more vulnerable members of the different communities?[83] How should conflicts between Aboriginal rights and liberal rights be resolved? I have offered some general principles above and in previous chapters; we should seek discursively ligitimated *modus vivendi* agreements on constitutional essentials that secure and promote people's basic capabilities (where what counts as a basic capability is itself subject to processes of discursive legitimation). But how would this actually work on the ground? How does it address the fears of the Aboriginal reader, that her interests are always subject to certain pre-established liberal conditions she cannot question but which 'modify, infringe or extinguish' her distinctive rights? And how does it address the fears of the liberal reader, that what the localization or customization of liberalism ultimately amounts to is a relativization of it, and thus to endorsing rather than challenging illiberal relations of power?

# 7    Land, law and governance

> In discharging its duty to declare the common law of Australia, this
> Court is not free to adopt rules that accord with contemporary notions
> of justice and human rights if their adoption would fracture the skele-
> ton of principle which gives the body of law its shape and internal con-
> sistency ... Whenever such a question arises, it is necessary to assess
> whether the particular rule is an essential doctrine of our legal system
> and whether, if the rule were to be overturned, the disturbance to be
> apprehended would be disproportionate to the benefit flowing from
> the overturning.[1]

We have an outline now of the normative shape of postcolonial liberalism: complex mutual coexistence between indigenous peoples and the
state, grounded in a discursively legitimated sets of dynamic *modi
vivendi* on constitutional essentials and institutional arrangements that
help to secure and promote people's basic capabilities. Aboriginal rights
are a crucial aspect of this kind of liberalism. They embody both temporal and normative dimensions. They are a product not only of the distinctive customs and practices of indigenous peoples that existed long
before the arrival of European nations and continue today, but also of
the complex interactions and negotiations that subsequently arose
between them. And they are a means to securing their equality and
freedom. Aboriginal rights protect indigenous peoples' distinctive and
valuable interests in land, culture and self-government, and in so doing
they secure crucial opportunities and freedoms – real freedoms – for
them to construct and pursue meaningful lives according to their own
laws, customs and practices.

But what about the inevitable conflicts between these different normative orders? Whose norms should take priority when they conflict: the
group's or the state's? Liberals tend to focus on the voluntariness or
involuntariness of one's membership in an association in order to guide
the evaluation of the costs associated with it, and whether the state can
and should act to compensate for them. The greater the degree of non-

voluntariness, the greater the scope for public intervention, and vice-versa.[2] The suggestion here is that there are fundamental trade-offs that cannot be avoided; *either* self-government *or* assimilation into the wider community; *either* the applicability of general laws to all *or* an unworkable and inequitable patchwork of cultural and customary exemptions; *either* the application of basic human rights norms to all *or* the abandonment of the vulnerable and disempowered to oppressive cultural norms and elites; *either* the promotion of capabilities that secure equality and freedom, *or* cultural autonomy that may threaten it. But as Ayelet Shachar and others have argued recently, it is precisely this 'either–or' dichotomy that needs to be challenged. For it ignores the way situated individuals are subject to *concurrent* and *simultaneous* multiple affiliations—to their cultural group, gender, religion, family, class, and state—which can both overlap and conflict at different points in time.[3] This is particularly true of indigenous peoples. For they are both citizens of the wider state and yet also members of particular, internally differentiated indigenous communities, with specific norms, rules and laws inherent to them. They make claims based on their own customs and laws, as well as with reference to liberal-democratic legal and political instruments. So how should these different normative orders be managed and arranged?

## Three models

Consider three models applied to the basic premises of the overlapping and concurrent modes of multicultural and multinational affiliation discussed above.

First, we might try to fix certain basic priority rules in advance, and then calibrate departures from that baseline in relation to that conception. Call this the *core-periphery* approach. It involves identifying a core of basic rights (or interests, or capabilities) in advance of public deliberations, or at least as structuring those deliberations, and allowing exemptions from or variations to generally applicable laws and institutions only insofar as they do not adversely affect those core basic rights and the rule of law. So: does this law/practice/institution create not simply a burden on the claimant, but one meriting some form of exemption from or variation to the generally applicable law or institutional set-up? Is there *room* for such an exemption or variation? Would any such exemption/variation affect the core rights of those affected by the exemption/variation (including third parties)?[4] Is it fair to assign the benefit of the exemption/variation to this particular claimant? According to the core-periphery approach, it will only be fair to assign room for an exemption or variation where the general law or institution has a special kind of impact on the claimant which it does not have on others. It will only be fair to assign the exemption or variation in relation to someone or some group, if the requirements of state law are burdensome in the sense of preventing members of the group from reproducing valuable constitutive aspects of their non-public identities. But not just any identity. Judgments about the nature of the burden imposed will require the various parties making reasonable arguments, either in supporting exemptions or alternative arrangements, or in rejecting them. The core-periphery approach suggests that there may be a set of basic rights or capabilities tied to state law (or international law) that can never be breached, no matter how genuinely torn someone was between the authoritative norms of one way of life and those promoted by the state. No one, as Jeremy Waldron argues, thinks that respect for cultural diversity would require us to stand back and allow a man to batter his wife to death for adultery (or for anything else for that matter). And even where there is some leeway for a cultural defence or exemption in the criminal law (to be discussed in greater detail below), it might still be the case that respect for the basic rights of the victim trump such considerations.

The second approach tries to avoid any pre-loaded conception of core and periphery, and instead focuses on the conditions in which the claims are heard and discussed; call this the *deliberative approach*. If the aim is to produce legitimate political principles and policies that govern the exercise of social and political power, then they must meet with the ongoing endorsement of those subject to them. But since legitimacy is based upon the authority of reasons, and these reasons are in turn grounded in aspects of citizens' multiple identities affiliations, then it remains something of an open question as to which policies or institutions, exactly, will be endorsable on these grounds. Citizens must offer public reasons and be open to compromise, and to having their minds changed or different public reasons prevailing in the end. Still, there are constraints, and these flow from the demands of thinking of legitimacy in this way. They might flow from the nature of communicative reason itself, from the formal features of citizenship, or from an ideal of democratic freedom to question and challenge prevailing norms of recognition and distribution.[5] The point is not to identify in advance a core set of rights from which no deviation can ever occur, but instead to ask how various claims for exemptions or variations to existing laws and institutions can be squared with the conditions required for discursive legitimacy. Being committed to the practice of public reason-giving in the first place goes a long way towards creating the conditions for reconciling the group seeking exemptions or variations to existing laws and institutions, and the state concerned with enforcing general standards.

The third approach has a more legal-institutional focus. It asks: what incentives can be provided that reduce the likelihood of harm that undermines people's basic rights or capabilities, whilst at the same time allowing people to realize and protect their commitments to particular social and cultural groups?[6] Call this the *institutional design approach*. A good example of this approach can be found in Ayelet Shachar's conception of 'transformative accommodation'. Here the aim is not so much to establish an order of precedence between the different and competing sources of authority, but rather 'an ongoing dialogue' between them. The aim is to create a 'circulation of power between authorities, rather than allowing its systematic unequal accumulation'.[7] So instead of authority and jurisdiction always being a matter of belonging to either the state or the group, the institutional design approach accepts the multiplicity of possible jurisdictional lines and the need for coordination and interaction between them. Jurisdiction, where possible, can be allocated along different 'sub-matter lines' (for example, between status and property matters in family law; or conviction and sentencing matters in the criminal law). Neither the group nor the state should ever acquire a monopoly of control over a contested social arena that 'affects individuals both as group members and citizens' (the 'no-monopoly restraint').[8] And finally, members and citizens must be provided with clear options which enable them to actually choose between these different jurisdictions, up to and including opting out of the relevant jurisdiction and choosing another.[9]

These measures, suggests Shachar, are particularly valuable for ensuring that members are not locked into asymmetric distributions of power and goods, as well as generating incentives for change to occur from within the group. Delegating power down to the individual member to switch from one jurisdiction to another with regard to a specific 'sub-matter', at least where a meaningful remedy is not forthcoming for 'the plight of the individual', provides each jurisdictional authority (i.e. the state and the group) with incentives to 'serve their citizenry better'.[10] The threat of selective exit forces leaders to be more accountable for the interests of all of the members they serve, since it raises the costs of not responding to their constituents' needs and concerns (by potentially strengthening alternative sources of authority, or losing their self-regulating power piecemeal). It thus provides more vulnerable members of the group with the capacity, Shachar suggests, to argue for changes within the group, without necessarily being forced to consider the often unrealistic prospect of complete exit from it.

Each of these approaches – the core-periphery, deliberative and institutional design models – offer valuable insights into the best way of handling the complex intersection between liberal-democratic and indigenous normative orders that postcolonial liberalism addresses. In fact, they are complementary in many ways. Without being subject to proper deliberation and thus legitimation, the core set of rights (and institutions meant to enforce them) in the core-periphery model, and the legal-institutional mechanisms outlined in the institutional design model, risk being seen as arbitrary by those subject to them, and thus unable to generate the kind of reasoned support required to be effective. And without at least *some* account of the formal features of liberal citizenship, or of an ideal of democratic freedom – i.e. the preconditions that enable reasonable political deliberation to occur in the first place – too much can be left up for grabs. This can leave not only groups vulnerable to majoritarian decision-making within the state, but also particular individuals vulnerable within the group. Ruling out in advance what arguments can or cannot enter the public sphere is a common strategy in liberal accounts of deliberative democracy.[11] But since the range of issues amenable to deliberation changes over time, any set of preconditions to deliberation must be seen as equally dynamic, and thus subject to deliberative scrutiny. The activity of deliberation itself contains built-in 'domain restriction mechanisms'[12] that can work against the entrenchment of arbitrary or 'external' preferences in public arguments. Deliberative liberals reject the social choice assumption that preferences remain static or unaffected by political processes.

At this stage, rather than working through the theoretical advantages and disadvantages of each model from the perspective of postcolonial liberalism, I would like to turn to some concrete examples. These will enable us to put the various models to work in evaluating the extent to which liberal and indigenous normative orders intersect, and the difficulties such intersections can create.

## Indigenous law: recognition or incorporation?

A belief in the rule of law usually means that we want the law to be the same for everyone. Governments and citizens should be governed by laws which are general, knowable and performable. Generality is the key, if ultimately controversial, characteristic. It appeals to a sense of impartiality. Rule by law presumes to exclude arbitrary exercises of power, or at least fickle and particularistic exercises of power which favour narrow interests over general ones, and discretionary privileges over rights. Lawful political power is a capacity limited in its action by general rules.

But in conditions of 'deep diversity'[13] and complexity, that is, not only a diversity of cultural, religious, ethnic and racial groups, but also of the ways in which members of these groups belong to the larger polity, governments are forced to govern in a myriad of particularistic and indirect ways which often violate strict notions of generality. Legal institutions are meant to establish and set limits upon the common standards to which everyone must conform, but they are often called upon to adjudicate between a huge variety of divergent interests, cultures and groups. 'A key task for a legal system', writes Cass Sunstein, 'is to enable people who disagree on first principles to converge on outcomes in particular cases ... to produce judgments on relative particulars amidst conflict on relative abstractions'.[14]

This is especially true in the case of indigenous peoples living in liberal democratic states. Aboriginal and non-Aboriginal people may share a general notion of law as such, perhaps even 'the rule of law', but not necessarily similar conceptions of what it requires.[15] To complicate matters, these legal systems have intersected frequently over time, usually to the detriment of Aboriginal peoples. The importance of seeing the relational character of these systems of law cannot be underestimated. Indeed the common law can and does host and/or frame indigenous systems it runs up against in being carried to new domains.[16] Careful scholarship has shown that there was a form of 'imperial constitutional law' which governed the acquisition of Crown sovereignty in settler states such as Australia and Canada. This was part of a body of fundamental constitutional law that was logically *prior* to the introduction of common law, that is, it conditioned the introduction of English common law to settler states.[17] It included the presumptive legal structure applicable to settler–'native' relations, in addition to establishing the rights to property and sovereignty with respect to the exclusion of other *European* nations.[18] The crucial point – summarizing much complex historical literature – is that Aboriginal societies retain rights to land as well as a degree of autonomy in relation to the Crown according to the introduced common law as conditioned by the imperial constitutional norms. An assertion of sovereignty over a territory, according to this doctrine, does not automatically extinguish Aboriginal rights. The common law, in other words, can recognize alternative sources of law.[19] But what does this mean?

Jacob Levy has suggested that the danger of recognizing or incorporating Aboriginal law is that it may undermine the virtues of transparency, simplicity, mobility and clarity in the legal system – 'it multiplies the fundamental legal philosophies as well as multiplying jurisdictions and interpreters'.[20] Moreover, as jurisdictions and legal concepts multiply, comprehensibility becomes more difficult and transaction costs increased; those bound by a 'customary' system of law will be much less likely to invest the time 'to learn about the law of the wider state, their rights under that law, and the possibility of using it rather than customary law for some purposes'. Hence they become more vulnerable to potential abuses of the their basic rights or capabilities.[21]

Not recognizing or incorporating Aboriginal law also has serious consequences. Doing so may deny equality before the law to indigenous peoples with respect to their property rights. Denying them self-government rights may undermine not only their equal standing as (in principle) self-governing peoples, but also their capacities for addressing the social and economic disadvantage blighting many of their communities (see below). The way in which incorporation occurs also matters. One form of incorporation may bolster common citizenship rights at the expense of their distinctive circumstances. But this may, in turn, undermine the goal of forging social unity through citizenship if it makes the form and content of that citizenship particularly burdensome for indigenous people.

Let me turn to an example from Australia to flesh these general remarks out. In 1992, a majority of the High Court of Australia in *Mabo v State of Queensland (No. 2)*[22] held that the Meriam people of the Murray Islands retained native title to their land which was not extinguished by the annexation of the islands to the colony of Queensland in 1879, nor by subsequent legislation. The Crown held radical title to land in the territory, which allowed it to grant various interests, but 'it is not a corollary of the Crown's acquisition of radical title to land in an occupied territory that the Crown has acquired absolute beneficial ownership of that land to the exclusion of the indigenous inhabitants'. 'Native title' was thus part of the common law of the settled territory of Australia. This form of title is also recognized as existing in terms of the 'traditional laws acknowledged by and the traditional customs observed by the indigenous inhabitants', and 'the nature and incidents of native title must be ascertained as a matter of fact by reference to those laws and customs'.[23] Among the crucial questions the decision raised was this: What does it mean for indigenous law be 'part of' the common law of Australia?

One of the most interesting answers was provided by Noel Pearson, an influential indigenous lawyer and political leader. He argued that native title constitutes the 'recognition space between the common law and the Aboriginal law'.[24] Thus native title is recognized but not created by the common law. But what kind of space is this? There are a number of different possibilities.[25] Indigenous law could be seen as ultimately subsumed or incorporated into the common law, but allowed a certain room for manoeuvre. Or it might be considered a system parallel to the common law, not subsumed within it, but perhaps sharing some of the same goals of the general legal system. There are dangers and costs associated with each possibility. Simply incorporating indigenous law into the common law raises complex questions about the translation between the two systems, and the difficult issue of using Anglo-European courts to determine and enforce Aboriginal standards. On the other hand, by being subsumed into the common law, indigenous people might gain access to the protection it offers, but at the cost of any acknowledgment of the autonomous nature of their legal systems. They might even fail to gain the advantages the common law is said to provide, depending on how incorporation into the common law is carried out and upon what grounds.

For example, in *Mabo*, the Court made clear that native title was vulnerable to extinguishment by sovereign acts with a 'clear and plain intention' to do so, as opposed to mere regulation, and where there has been a loss of connection with the land.[26] Interests granted that are wholly or partially inconsistent with a continuing right to enjoy native title extinguish it to the extent of the inconsistency, subject now to the constraints of the *Racial Discrimination Act 1975 (Cth)*.[27] So Aboriginal rights and interests were not 'stripped away' by the common law at the point of settlement, but through the acts of sovereign governments (state and federal).[28] The Court split on whether extinguishments in the absence of clear and plain legislative intent required either consent or compensation, a requirement one would normally expect in the case of a common law proprietary interest.

The political response to *Mabo* is interesting to consider at this point. Some suggested that people's backyards were now under threat, which was of course absurd. As *Mabo* made clear, native title was almost certainly to have been extinguished in the more settled urban areas of Australia. The requirements imposed for making a valid claim meant that the chances of urban Aboriginal groups meeting the burden of proof were, as Richard Bartlett puts it, exceedingly 'dim'. In fact, the dispossession of those lands was *validated* by *Mabo*, not put into question by it.[29] The legislative response to *Mabo*, the *Native Title Act 1993 (Cth)*, validated Crown grants up to 1994 without any prior consent or compensation required for those potential native title holders (despite the Racial Discrimination Act being in force since 1975). Instead, an *Indigenous Land Corporation* was established, to help purchase lands on the open market for dispossessed indigenous groups who were unable to meet the new criteria for registering native title claims. The Act created a limited 'right to negotiate' for registered native title claimants and holders, which imposed a duty on governments and grantees to seek agreement with regard to various kinds of grants (including mining tenements). It also created a Native Title Tribunal to help settle native title claims, where possible, by agreement and conciliation. The Federal Court, however, was empowered to make determinations of native title in case of disagreement.

In a subsequent decision, *Wik Peoples v Queensland (1996)*,[30] the High Court held that native title could, in fact, survive on pastoral leases, and that an inconsistent grant could only extinguish native title if legislation manifested a clear and plain intention that it should, as per a general rule applicable 'to *all* interests imposing a presumption against [the] expropriation of existing rights, in particular without compensation'.[31] Nevertheless, in the case of pastoral leases, where the rights of the grantee and those of the native title holder were in conflict, the former prevailed.[32] The decision concerning pastoral leases was significant, since large portions of Western Australia, South Australia, Queensland, the Northern Territory and New South Wales contain areas of pastoral tenure. Significant mining and petroleum exploration activities take place on these lands. Worries about the security of existing leases and titles, the complexity caused by concurrent native title rights, as well as the scope of potential compensation payments, became prominent. State and territory governments were forced to review many of their procedures in light of the decision, and this caused delays in the processing of mining, mineral and exploration titles. All of this stoked a charged atmosphere in which powerful economic and political interests saw native title as undermining economic and social development.

Unfortunately, instead of seeking a mutually acceptable set of arrangements between *all* of the parties, especially the indigenous ones, what resulted was a shameless exploitation of the uncertainties thrown up by *Wik*. In the end, the government of the day responded with a *Native Title Amendment Bill 1998 (Cth)*. What this did, among other things, was to severely reduce the (already circumscribed) 'right to negotiate' recognized in the *Native Title Act 1993*, and tip the balance strongly in favour of non-native title holders.[33] As Murrandoo Yanner put it:

The farmers in their hysteria think they're going to lose their land. Our people in their error think they're going to get their land. They're both wrong. So you win native title on a pastoral lease, and then what happens? The pastoralist opens the gate and says, 'Murrandoo, go do your dance and song and catch a turtle – and close the gate when you leave tommorrow'. Native title is not sovereignty. It's not land rights ... it gets us to the table, that's all'.[34]

It is striking that although various gestures were made by the government justifying the amendments with regard to substantive and formal notions of equality, the only real argument towards that end was that it had the 'discretion in fashioning appropriate measures' to promote such equality, including the application of the right to negotiate.[35] But the changes proposed for that right were so far-reaching that it arguably gutted it, and thus failed to provide what was called for even according to a principle of formal equality, let alone substantial equality.

This story raises worries about the common law mode of incorporation. On the one hand, making native title rights more like familiar common law property rights might strengthen their proprietary content, as well as make them clearer and easier to work with, hence more efficient.[36] But at what cost? It leaves behind the governmental relationship to land, which is potentially a significant one. To begin with, such an approach seems to assume that native title is simply 'another kind of interest affecting land [that] can be slipped into the structure of [existing] property law'.[37] Although there is no necessary logical connection between the recognition of interests in land and recognizing a form of inherent sovereignty, the two are difficult to keep apart for very long.[38] As *Mabo* made clear, not only the origin but the *content* of native title is given by the traditional laws and customs observed by the inhabitants of the territory *today*, not only in the past.[39] This means that what is being recognized is not simply a discrete or 'confined set of rights' but the capacities of a legal and normative order for determining the evolution of its law according to its own self-understandings and practices, albeit always in (an uneasy) relation to the wider legal regime. Although the Australian High Court has been leery about explicitly acknowledging any residual sovereignty on the part of indigenous peoples,[40] it has, in fact, refrained from trying to determine the nature of entitlements within indigenous law, because it really is not any of its business to do so.[41]

Another way of putting this is to say that insofar as native title is reduced to a question of ownership, it misses the territorial dimension of those interests implied in the collective nature of Aboriginal title.[42] One only has to listen to indigenous accounts of the nature of the relationship to their lands to notice how it is not merely about ownership, and especially in terms of the way western political and legal theory understands property ownership.[43] The value of these territorial or governmental interests is not merely symbolic: faced with the need to negotiate with powerful state and federal governments, as well as large multinational corporations, the narrower the legal/political protection for their interests the more vulnerable they become. Giving up on these governmental interests means native title holders must place all of their faith in the existing statutes governing native title, as well as the legislative and judicial bodies charged with applying and interpreting them. No doubt this is unavoidable whatever legal or political regime is in place. But to forfeit their sovereign interests means that indigenous peoples potentially miss out on a valuable reversal point from common law incorporation, especially when it becomes bogged down in the judicial and political machinations of the day. One example of such a reversal point in Australia stems from an interesting unintended effect of the *Native Title Act* making provision for 'Indigenous Land Use Agreements' outside of the machinery of the Act. These tailor-made agreements can be struck with governments (federal, state, regional, local), public bodies (such as the Cattlemen's Union, Farmers' Union, the Conservation Foundation, and so on[44]) and multinational corporations. In a country without an extensive history of treaty-making, these 'regional agreements' present an opportunity to build, step-by-step and from the ground-up, forms of settlement by agreement that come very close to the ideal of complex mutual coexistence. The agreements can be tailored to provide for the certainty of native title, for the maintenance of traditional rights on lands subject to development, and participation in (including beneficial entitlement from) decisions concerning the nature of the development and its effects on the local indigenous communities. There can be common interests between developers and indigenous people, as the Canadian experience makes clear. And these kinds of agreements are no less likely – in fact, probably more likely – to address concerns about the promotion of efficiency expressed by those who would subsume all of the interests of indigenous peoples to the common law.

So the governmental relationship to land is an important bulwark against the slow grinding away of native title rights cut loose from the laws that give them their content and meaning. This is only slowly being acknowledged in Australia, as new indigenous administrative and political institutions spring up, mainly in response to the legislative framework put in place since *Mabo*. There are tensions within these bodies between the requirements of modern liberal democratic governance on the one hand, and those of the particular indigenous communities they are meant to serve.[45] And there are further tensions between certain indigenous bodies corporate, such as Land Councils, which fit unevenly into existing indigenous authority relations, and particular groups of native title claimants or holders. But overall, these developments symbolize an evolving new set of political and governmental relationships – admittedly imperfect and unequal – both within indigenous communities and between them and the state.

If 'common law incorporation' is problematic for various reasons, then the alternative idea of two parallel systems, if taken literally, is also fraught with difficulty. It cannot simply mean the continuation of indigenous law as it was before, since it has been, and continues to be, unavoidably shaped by its encounter with non-indigenous institutions and discourses. The fact that both indigenous and non-indigenous people refer to their interests as *rights* is significant in this sense, as Jeremy Webber points out; 'interests that are recognized are expressed in a form that involves some accommodation to the need for the rights to be intelligible within the broader legal framework ... [hence] there is ... a measure of translation and adjustment in the very act of recognition, and this process may well be unequal'.[46] This is an important point. Even if we acknowledge the autonomous reality of indigenous legal and normative orders, the interests related to and emerging from them will inevitably be mediated (always awkwardly and unevenly) by non-indigenous processes of recognition. This is another risk associated with relying solely upon common law incorporation. It does not provide indigenous people with enough room to contest and reshape the social, cultural, political, and economic forces acting on them. But since inter-action with the wider legal and political sphere is unavoidable, especially as the demographic shape and geographical spread of indigenous peoples change, the need to develop mutually acceptable points of accommodation and integration between the different orders is also important.

Thus postcolonial liberalism makes a descriptive and normative claim. First, the sovereignty of Canada, the US and Australia is more complicated than usually assumed. There is a kind of *coordinate sovereignty* which exists between Aboriginal people and the Crown.[47] By coordinate sovereignty I mean the coordination, usually through negotiation, of these different sources of law. Perhaps the most striking examples of this are the Marshall decisions in the United States (1823–32), and to a lesser extent, Canada's *Royal Proclamation* of 1763 (upon which the Marshall doctrines are partly built).[48] These – and the many hundreds of treaties signed between indigenous peoples and settlers between 1600 and 1900 – are good examples of the complex *inter-societal* character of the constitutional structures of North America. Canada and the United States partly came into being through these interchanges between aboriginal nations and settlers, both peaceful and violent. Though almost no such similar declarations have occurred in Australia, there was clearly an awareness, from the time of settlement onwards, that this kind of doctrine was intended to apply to its circumstances as well.

Second, the governmental relationship between indigenous peoples and the liberal state must be justified normatively as well. Self-government rights relate to certain crucial interests of Aboriginal people, in at least three ways. First, they acknowledge the equal standing of indigenous nations as peoples equal to those European nations who first landed on their shores. Second, they provide the means not only for protecting their culture (given the differential costs of reproducing it compared to other citizens), but also for addressing some of the severe social and economic disadvantages their members face. It does not follow that these interests are best protected *in every instance* through self-government. Different contexts, and more importantly the different choices indigenous peoples make, will ultimately determine that. But self-government, in general, is directly related to successful social and economic development. In fact, recent research in the United States has shown that 'in every case ... of sustained economic development on Indian reservations ... the primary economic decisions are being made by the tribe, not by outsiders'.[49] The underlying logic is clear enough. The more communities take responsibility for their social and economic decisions, the more they reflect the goals of the community; and 'when outsiders make bad decisions, they don't pay the price of those decisions ... As long as the outside decision maker doesn't pay the price of bad decisions, there's no incentive for that decision maker to make better decisions'.[50] Finally, self-government rights also provide a means of securing and promoting Aboriginal perspectives in relation to the larger political system, ones that have been ignored or distorted within it.[51] The harm caused by not securing an effective voice for Aboriginal communities is evident from the history of liberal-democratic governments' paternalistic relations with them. Given the disadvantages that follow from these interests not being protected, claims for self-government should be taken as relevant to considerations of what it means to treat Aboriginal people fairly and equally, and to ensure their effective social freedom to contest those norms and processes that act on them.

Securing self-government rights then is about securing space apart from, and yet at the same time alongside of, the wider legal and political system within which indigenous peoples live. But since postcolonial liberalism acknowledges that cultural practices can be both freedom-enhancing and oppressive, it is also concerned with minimizing domination and protecting the basic capabilities of everyone. So how does it envisage the scope of jurisdiction that self-governing indigenous communities would exercise? What happens when the need to preserve a set of cultural, territorial, and governmental interests conflicts with the basic interests of some members of that group? Between the interests of Yvonne Bedard, for example, in being able to live in her family home on the Six Nations Reserve in Southern Ontario, and the right of the Band Council to decide on who is and who is not a member of their community and thus eligible for the benefits attached to membership?[52] Or between the protection of basic freedoms, including the freedom to purchase and drink alcohol, and the need to preserve social order from the ravages of alcohol-related violence and abuse?[53] Postcolonial liberalism seems caught between its desire, on the one hand, to make room for the normative and legal reality of indigenous peoples, and on the other hand, to promote each and every citizen's basic capabilities. I have already argued that we should see Aboriginal rights as constituting a distinctive capability set for indigenous peoples, one that protects and promotes certain crucial interests they have in relation to land, culture and self-government. But now we are confronted with a potential conflict between protecting one set of capabilities at the expense of another. How are these conflicts best handled?

Return for a moment to the discussion above concerning the core-periphery, deliberative and institutional-design models. According to postcolonial liberalism, the ideal of mutual coexistence applies both *between* and *within* the different parties, along with the ideal of public reason that accompanies it. So already, both the particular group and the state will have to ensure that *all* of the relevant parties are able to genuinely contest and contribute to the reshaping of the rules of recognition and distribution governing their interactions. But context and historical circumstances are also important here. The aim should be to try and custom-fit the rules of recognition and distribution to suit the particular circumstances of indigenous peoples and the state within which they live. And that means we cannot say in advance that one model is best suited for each and every circumstance; the particular history of colonization and interaction, the existing social and political institutions, and the nature and diversity of the various indigenous groups making claims all need to be taken into consideration in deciding on which model is most appropriate for each particular situation.

For example, the core-periphery model suggests that the best way to protect the basic interests of indigenous peoples, as well as everyone else's for that matter, is to identify, in advance, a set of basic rights or capabilities that are to be protected, no matter what the particular cultural or political situation of the group asserting rights of self-government. Thus in the US, tribes and tribal courts are subject to a kind of 'Indian Bill of Rights', but only to limited judicial review.[54] In Canada, the situation is complex. The Canadian Constitution contains a Charter of Rights, but it also recognizes existing Aboriginal and Treaty rights, including an inherent right to self-government.[55] There is some dispute, then, over the extent to which the Charter applies to that right (affirmed in Section 35).[56] Some argue that it does not apply and that it should not, since it involves imposing non-Aboriginal values and interests onto Aboriginal governments and communities. Instead, the kinds of concerns embodied in the Charter should be allowed to emerge from within those indigenous societies in more culturally appropriate ways, including the possibility of developing Aboriginal Charters of Rights as part of the constitutions of the various First Nation, Metis and Inuit nations, that would not displace but exist alongside the Canadian Charter.[57] Others have argued that the Charter does and should apply, because it offers protection for the more vulnerable members of Aboriginal societies, especially women,[58] as well as helping with the difficult transition from colonial rule to self-government. Still others have argued that although the Charter might apply to Aboriginal governments, it should only be applied – through a subtle interplay of its various components– in such a way so as to minimize its potentially corrosive effects on Aboriginal governmental authority without minimizing the protection it offers to less powerful individual members.[59]

In Australia, on the other hand, the constitution offers very little by way of institutional possibilities for complex mutual coexistence. In fact, as it currently stands, it is ill-suited to recognizing or promoting indigenous interests.[60] Hence the focus, by and large, in Australia, on the common law and legislation. Predictably, however, agitation for constitutional change (and more specifically for treaties) has been an important feature of past and more recent campaigns. The general thrust of postcolonial liberalism supports such developments.

## Membership and punishment

What is striking at this point is how the three models begin to interact and overlap. A constitutional scheme that contains both a commitment to recognizing Aboriginal rights as well as certain basic rights and freedoms guaranteed to all, needs mechanisms for arbitrating between these interests when they conflict. Hence the institutional design approach, which focuses on the institutional incentives that can be created for ensuring that both the state and the group do not ignore or violate the basic capabilities of their constituent members. The pressure here is 'on the group to transform its laws from within' – to give them the authority to decide on a crucial 'sub-matter' – but then to provide 'reversal points' whereby vulnerable members can seek a remedy from another jurisdiction in case of situations where threats to their basic rights or capabilities fail to be addressed. However, the allocation of sub-matter authority, and the viability of any set of reversal points, will depend crucially on the forms of recognition the group claiming that authority and subject to those reversal points receives. In the case of indigenous peoples, it is unlikely that these kinds of processes will work if their authority is premised on being a delegation from the Crown, as opposed to being recognized as inherent. Or, where the reversal points are simply imposed rather than negotiated. Hence the main lesson of the deliberative approach also needs to be heeded: any rules or norms of recognition and distribution proposed must be discursively legitimated, which in turn means that the conditions for reasonable deliberation be secured both within and between the state and the group.

Consider the case of a clash between the membership rules of an Aboriginal community and the basic freedoms and capacities of citizens. The aim should be to '[maximize] the opportunity to air and accommodate the competing interests at stake'.[61] Membership rules should be evaluated not only in light of the legitimate interests the Aboriginal group has in controlling those rules (given the cultural, political and economic resources at stake), but also the basic interests and capacities of those adversely affected by those rules as well. Can the objective of preserving control over membership be achieved in a less discriminatory manner? Is there room for accommodation and compromise between the parties within the group, as well as between the group and the state?[62]

Similarly, if Aboriginal law is to be recognized and accommodated not just in land law, but in the criminal justice system, does this mean its distinctive approach to breaches of Aboriginal law, including spearing or stabbing (at least in the Australian context), should be tolerated? The whole question of dispute resolution in Aboriginal law is handled very differently than in Anglo-European law, with great variations between different indigenous groups. Disputes and breaches of the law are supposed to be resolved with a view to re-balancing relations upset by the offence or dispute. Failing to resolve these legal breaches can mean a dispute not being 'closed off', and thus perpetuate the conflict and sense of injustice felt by the victim, the families involved and the community as a whole.[63] In Australia, at least, the purpose of indigenous 'punishment' is to do with controlled retribution and the restoration and repair of social order. And the means of doing so range from duelling, shaming, compensation, dispersion, banishment, up to and including spearing, stabbing and other forms of corporal punishment.

Many of these practices, and certainly the beliefs underpinning them, continue to be relevant to a number of Aboriginal communities in Australia today. Perhaps the most controversial of these has been spearing, and other forms of corporal punishment. Spearing involves the offender being speared, usually in the leg, in relatively controlled circumstances (i.e. in a supposedly non-lethal and non-permanently disabling manner). It has been made even more controversial given the fact that Aboriginal law does not always recognize that it is only the offender who should be punished, but sometimes the various kin relations as well (although not necessarily by spearing). Thus blame and responsibility may be distributed differently than in European systems.

The justification for a parallel or separate system of criminal justice usually combines a mixture of arguments.[64] On the sovereignty argument, the authority to deal with criminal justice and social control more generally, is simply an extension of the claim to inherent rights of self-government. Other kinds of justifications are available too. Aboriginal legal remedies are said to provide more appropriate treatment for offenders (in some but not all circumstances) compared to non-Aboriginal ones, especially imprisonment. This is said to follow from the importance Aboriginal people place upon the socializing and re-integrative effects of clan and/or kin networks, and from the vast over-representation of Aboriginal people in Australian prisons, and the terrible consequences many have suffered as a result of this.[65] In other words, many of the retributivist and instrumental ends of the mainstream criminal justice system would be just as well served – even better served – in a parallel Aboriginal criminal justice system, or at least through a significant recognition of Aboriginal law within the existing criminal law.

There are at least two major problems confronting these arguments. The first is a consequence of the 'authority vacuums' that can arise in many Aboriginal communities today, at least as reported by anthropologists, to do with the consequences of colonial rule. This makes the reassertion of these older forms of dispute resolution extremely difficult to accomplish.[66] Talk of recognizing Aboriginal law in these circumstances may be much more complicated than originally thought. Second, just how would the recognition of Aboriginal law actually work; should it be narrow and selective, or broad ranging and systematic? In Australia, explicit and systematic recognition of Aboriginal law, at least beyond land law, has yet to occur.[67] Any leeway has been given at the discretion of particular judges and magistrates, thus engendering considerable uncertainty and confusion about its use in relation to the criminal law.[68] Courts in the Northern Territory, for example (where Aborigines make up close to one third of the general population), have taken into account the probability of traditional punishments in the sentencing orders of Aboriginal offenders.[69] But even this has proved deeply problematic, since they have tended to incorporate the relevance of indigenous law into their proceedings in a very unsystematic way, often without much expert advice or input from a wide range of indigenous participants. Much therefore depends on who is providing the evidence concerning Aboriginal law – usually non-indigenous lawyers (especially defence lawyers) – which is then interpreted by non-indigenous magistrates. One recent study has shown how this has resulted in some worrying developments, especially with regard to the interests of Aboriginal women as victims of violence.[70] In these circumstances, some indigenous people might seek a *greater* not a lesser role for the application of Australian law. And the explicit toleration of practices like non-lethal spearing might be something questioned not only by the wider community, but by indigenous people as well.[71]

As we have seen, recognition is always in part a process of construction; it elicits and reshapes interests as much as it acknowledges them. This is unavoidable. But the process of recognition and (re)construction can proceed in better and worse ways. Aboriginal law, like any law, is never simply 'read off' a statute book, or a set of social, political and cultural practices, but interpreted and constructed by a range of different actors, Aboriginal and non-Aboriginal, for better or worse. The danger is always that those excluded from or marginalised within that domain are not allowed to participate in interpreting and shaping those interests and laws equally, and suffer adversely as a result. This is true of Aboriginal people generally within the mainstream legal system, and of various groups within Aboriginal societies as well, especially Aboriginal women.

So once again, the lesson from these practical examples is that no one size-fits-all solution is available. Where a membership rule adversely affects the basic capabilities or interests of vulnerable members of the group, everything possible should be done to ensure those affected have the opportunity to change and reshape the rule in question. If that fails, and the consequences are serious enough – as in the case of many women on Canadian reserves and elsewhere – a reversal point should be on offer, whereby an appeal can be made to another authority for a more appropriate remedy. But who that authority should be, and what kind of remedy should be applied, requires further negotiation and accommodation. Should it be a mainstream court guided by a mixture of liberal and indigenous norms and values deciding on the merits of the case, or a tribal court or council guided exclusively by indigenous law? Should it be a Treaty Commission composed of both Aboriginal and non-Aboriginal members? Or should it be an international body, made up of both state and non-state members? All of this remains to be negotiated and deliberated between the various parties.[72]

Similarly, in the case of Aboriginal forms of retribution or punishment that seem to fall far outside the bounds of Anglo-European law, explicit toleration may be difficult to accommodate. It may be something many indigenous people are unhappy to continue with too, given the changing nature of indigenous societies. But where the beliefs underpinning these practices are still highly relevant, more explicit and systematic guidance on the admission of evidence and sentencing guidelines, worked out between indigenous and non-indigenous legal experts, may promote a proper consideration of all the interests at stake in its application to a particular case. This in turn may promote innovative modes of 'transformative accommodation', in Shachar's phrase. For example, spearing may not be banned outright, but a reversal point negotiated whereby the option of appealing to a non-Aboriginal magistrate or judge is provided, if the offender thinks the punishment too severe, or the victim (or his or her family) is dissatisfied with the processes of Aboriginal law. Non-Aboriginal legal instruments, such as community service-orders, could be applied to promoting indigenous legal ends, just as Aboriginal legal principles and philosophies may be put to work within the Anglo-European legal system.[73] But none of these negotiated accommodation points can be reached if the normative reality and complexity of indigenous social and legal orders are ignored by non-indigenous actors, or over-simplified by both non-indigenous and indigenous ones.

## Social breakdown and 'welfare poison'

Finally, what if the situation of some Aboriginal communities is so bad – racked by unemployment, alcoholism, petrol-sniffing and violence – that all this talk of self-government and autonomous legal and normative orders is moot? The reality is actually much worse: that in many instances, social order – indigenous or otherwise – has simply broken down, irreparably, under the weight of both external and self-inflicted problems. Talk of Aboriginal rights in these contexts, so this argument goes, is therefore the worst kind of liberal indulgence. The focus should instead be on the raw essentials, delivered by any means necessary: protecting women from the horrendous toll of abuse they have suffered and continue to suffer; getting alcohol out of remote communities and alcoholics and other drug abusers away from the source of their and their families' and community's misery; and finding meaningful employment, education and training for indigenous people, especially young people, rather than perpetuating welfare dependency and work for the dole. More controversially, Aboriginal cultural and political practices themselves may need radical reshaping, from within.

These arguments are driven by the recognition of a paradox, put most forcefully in Australia by Noel Pearson, amongst others, who has been challenging both conservative critics and liberal supporters of Aboriginal rights to confront these realities. He asks:

why has a social breakdown accompanied this advancement in the formal rights of our people, not the least the recognition and restoration of our homelands ...

Aboriginal families and communities now often live on their homelands, in very much flashier housing and infrastructure than decades ago – but at a much diminished quality of life, such that commentators familiar with these remote communities often call them 'outback ghettoes' ... [W]hy during the period of indigenous policy enlightenment and recognition and despite billions of dollars of much improved housing and infrastructure and government services, has there been a corresponding social deterioration? ... Why are my people disintegrating and why are we unable to do anything about it?[74]

For Pearson, the basic cause is the reliance on passive welfare and the lack of a real economic base for most Aboriginal communities. As a result, addiction and substance abuse take root and become almost impossible to eradicate, contributing to the terrible scourge of crime and violence committed against vulnerable members of these communities. It is important to point out that not *all* indigenous communities suffer from these difficulties – the complexity, diversity and particularity of Aboriginal communities must always be acknowledged, and there are just as many success stories too. But Pearson's point is that too many are suffering from these problems. What makes matters worse, argues Pearson, is that both the left and the right get their analysis of the issues wrong. The right seeks to undermine land rights, which are one of the few genuine sources of potential wealth creation and development that indigenous people have. But the left fails to see the connection between passive welfare, substance abuse and social order. The trauma of colonialism and dispossession, no matter how recent, argues Pearson, may make communities susceptible to 'grog and drug epidemics', but they do not automatically cause the abusive behaviour that follows. Once entrenched in a community, abusive behaviour perpetuates itself, whatever the historical legacy of colonialism. For Pearson this is as much a political question as it is a health or moral one; it is the struggle to 'prevent the final establishment of new abuse epidemics, and to limit by means of restrictions the damage done by the endemic addictions of Australian society such as alcohol and gambling'. He recommends tough medicine. No more unconditional support for addicts who do not change, and a rejection of abusive behaviour by the community in material, social and emotional terms. There should be enforced treatment, including the 'absolute intolerance of illicit drugs, absolute enforcement of social order, and mandatory and humane treatment of people who are engaged in abuse'. And finally, an end to passive welfare: '[this] explains the phenomenon that even as our material condition improved over recent decades, our social condition deteriorated. The lack of purpose and meaning passive welfare generates in people's lives compounds the effects of dispossession and makes people susceptible to drug and alcohol abuse'. These two problems 'feed off one another'.[75]

This is a powerful and provocative analysis, crafted to gain maximum political impact in a political culture dominated by moral individualism and an emphasis on personal responsibility. Note immediately, however, that postcolonial liberalism's focus on seeing Aboriginal rights as best understood as effective capabilities – or real freedoms, in Sen's evocative phrase – draws our attention to precisely the kinds of concerns Pearson raises so forcefully: What are the factors that 'make [indigenous people] unable to benefit from the money that has been transferred to us and the infrastructure, services and health care that has already been provided'? According to the capabilities approach, as we saw in Chapter 6, it is not just a question of the transfer of resources that matters in promoting equality, but of providing the means for the effective conversion of those resources into valuable human functionings. Pearson provides one set of answers to the problems he outlines, but there are others too, and his analysis has been challenged on many fronts.[76] But note that the solutions he and others envisage hardly entail giving up on Aboriginal rights, quite the contrary. Instead, they involve challenging and stretching existing understandings of rights on the part of *both* indigenous and non-indigenous people. The proposals make demands on the non-indigenous community to support land rights, but at the same time to revisit their attitudes, for example, towards drug and alcohol abuse and to remain open to accommodating indigenous choices about ways to address these problems that might clash with wider liberal norms (for example, banning the sale of alcohol in some instances, or changing the way some resources, including welfare payments, are distributed within communities and families). But they also involve challenging indigenous values and practices.[77] In Pearson's case, it involves challenging the way indigenous familial and local authority is distributed, and reshaping indigenous domains in which authority structures are 'diffuse, fractured and highly contested'.[78] Similarly, in the case of more urban-based Aborigines, not only do their unique circumstances place demands on the delivery of basic health, education and employment services, but also on indigenous modes of governance and social and political organization.[79] And in both cases, greater economic independence and development will require targeted engagement with the wider economy, and thus developing the skills, capacities and knowledge required for such participation.

It is this dual process of accommodation and change between and within indigenous and non-indigenous normative orders and institutions that postcolonial liberalism seeks to acknowledge, encourage and learn from. But it also highlights the inherent complexity and difficulty of developing appropriate forms of recognition and accommodation. These points of accommodation and recognition can not be prescribed or pre-determined in advance of the understandings and choices of indigenous people themselves. And yet these forms of self-understanding and the choices they make cannot help but be shaped by the wider legal and political system in which they are located.

## Conclusion

Norms, rules, practices or policies that adversely affect the basic capabilities and interests of especially vulnerable individuals trigger the need to ensure the conditions in which they can be contested and reshaped are provided to every citizen, whatever their cultural, social, political or economic situation. But since individuals are situated in a range of different social, political and cultural contexts, some with significant moral and normative effects, these contexts must also be acknowledged and accommodated. Aboriginal rights are thus a complex bundle of capacities, both collective and individual, that enable indigenous people to live, as much as is possible, according to their own customs and practices, and especially to negotiate the always-evolving interface between indigenous and non-indigenous worlds. What counts as a basic capability or right is always contestable, always susceptible to challenges between indigenous peoples and the state, and within indigenous communities themselves.

That it is the *state*, in every case, which should intervene to protect the basic capabilities of individuals is ultimately a pragmatic question. The point should be to ensure people are able to effectively convert the resources they have, whether via the 'real economy' or the welfare system, into effective and valuable human functionings – to achieve real freedoms – and minimize relations of domination. The difficulty is that modern liberal states often lack the moral authority and legitimacy amongst indigenous people to promote effective change, and this means the local institutions they help to create (through incorporation acts and other forms of legislation), however much intended to be 'culturally appropriate', often lack the requisite authority within indigenous communities. Change has to come from within, but sometimes the conditions for engendering change are absent, or severely constrained. States, in general, are often clumsy at intervening in the associational life of complex cultural groups. But the state also has a duty to protect and secure the basic interests of all. Thus postcolonial liberalism aims to multiply the points of accommodation that provide indigenous societies with the room to evolve and adapt to the particular circumstances they face. Multiplying them reduces the risk (never wholly eliminated) of asymmetric distributions of constructive social power, since it reduces the opportunities for one particular group or institution holding a monopoly of 'recognitive' or distributive power. But this inevitably involves more than simply recognizing indigenous legal and normative orders. Hence the need for a negotiated and always contestable set of entry, exit and reversal points between liberal and indigenous normative orders that can help structure these interactions, extended along both domestic and possibly international lines.[80] The three models discussed above offer various possibilities, which then need to be tailored to the specific social, cultural, political and historical circumstances of each particular group and their relation to the state.

# Conclusion

If this is meant to be an argument about *postcolonial* liberalism, then where are all the Aboriginal concepts and conceptual schemes? Why have I not outlined more precisely how liberal political thought can be transformed by indigenous political theories and worldviews, and the possible fusions between different liberal and indigenous concepts? These are good questions. But as I made clear in the Introduction, my task in this book has been to try and provide, from a non-indigenous perspective, an account of how liberalism needs to be rethought as a first step towards the kind of two-way learning process envisaged in the ideal of mutual coexistence. Which transitive concepts or mutually acceptable authoritative reasons will actually emerge cannot be settled here, but only in the actual deliberations between indigenous and non-indigenous peoples. The crucial thing is that there be a genuine 'multi-logue' not just between the state and indigenous peoples, but between them and other cultural and national groups, and between individuals outside and within those groups as well. A postcolonial liberal order does not yet exist, but among the conditions required for its emergence will be this context-sensitive and embedded form of public dialogue and deliberation.

But having said all this, there are interesting possibilities at hand. John Borrows, for example, suggests that since national and international forces influence even the most remote indigenous communities, Aboriginal traditions and philosophies must engage with the outside world in order to have any chance of promoting their own interests and ends. 'Aboriginal control of Canadian affairs', he writes, 'could change contemporary notions of Canadian citizenship', for example, by gener-ating a 'greater attentiveness to land uses and cultural practices that are preferred by many Aboriginal peoples .... and further reduce tolerance for land uses which extirpate these pursuits'. Thus Aboriginal values concerning land could become 'entrenched in Canada's governing ideas and institutions, and help to reconfigure Canada in an important way'.[1] Similar suggestions have been linked to the impact of *Mabo* in Australia.[2] In fact, the concept of 'Aboriginal rights', in general, offers a potential form of intercultural common ground upon which the diverse array of indigenous concepts and world views can hook into more general principles of justice, equality and freedom that circulate in the public sphere of liberal democracies. How could the accumulated 'insider's knowledge' and 'metis' of peoples who have lived for thousands of years on the territories now occupied by states such as Canada and Australia *not* have something important to contribute to the way all of us grapple with our complex relations to these lands?

So the forms of intercultural conceptual schemes and public reasons that might emerge from the engagement of indigenous and non-indigenous peoples in the public sphere are many, and rich in potential. But for this potential to become realizable, non-indigenous citizens have to be willing to negotiate in good faith about the many ways in which the consequences of indigenous claims for land and self-government might be implemented. Without effective 'Aboriginal control over Aboriginal affairs', to the extent that this is possible, the potential for genuine cross-cultural engagement and interaction is severely limited.

In order to foster the conditions in which such a genuine multilogue might occur, I suggested two things needed to happen. First, we need to envision a liberal political order that is attuned to the inevitable spill-overs between liberal and non-liberal ways of life and associations, and between practices of public and non-public reasoning. The ideal of complex mutual coexistence is meant to capture at least one possible version of this kind of liberal political order. Second, since rights ultimately rest on controversial moral beliefs, and only make sense if there are effective mechanisms for enforcing them, it is perhaps more helpful to talk about the capabilities we want individuals or groups to have – as opposed to the rights they apparently already possess – and then of the mechanisms and institutions required for their effective exercise. 'Aboriginal rights' therefore, represent a bundle of arguments – a normative thesis – about the distinctive interests indigenous people have in relation to land, culture and sovereignty (in addition to the basic interests they share with other human beings), and a claim that these interests ought to be acknowledged by others.

Tying indigenous peoples' claims to the language of rights is a historically contingent relation, but then so is the relation between the language of rights and liberalism.[3] Indigenous scholars such as Robert Williams, Dale Turner and Taiaiake Alfred are absolutely correct to point out how Western discourses of rights and sovereignty have been used to dominate indigenous peoples as much as to liberate them. But it is perhaps not surprising, given the prevalence of rights-language in politics today, that indigenous peoples – amongst others – have reached for it to press their claims. The success of this strategy, however, will depend on the development of effective mechanisms to enforce and pro-mote the interests to which their rights refer. Thus it makes perfect sense that so much effort has been put into the legal struggle over native title in Australia, for example, since the legal system offers – albeit always limited and imperfect– possibilities for actually enforcing the protection of those interests. But precisely because those legal possibilities are tightly constrained, efforts at asserting self-government rights will also persist, and rightly so. These arguments face difficult challenges, how-ever, because although it is increasingly accepted that the legal and moral claims for self-government are independent of any delegation from the Crown, in reality, indigenous peoples face great difficulties in developing the institutions and mechanisms required to effectively exer-cise and enforce their self-governing rights. As much as it is ultimately up to them to take responsibility for re-developing and reasserting these capacities, and adjusting and acting creatively in the face of the econom-ic, social, political and cultural realities they face, non-indigenous insti-tutions will be required to help too. In both Australia and Canada then, various models and arrangements have been proposed that tend to involve a slow, gradual, evolution from discrete and domain-specific powers (for the delivery of services to do with health, employment, education, policing and resource development, etc.) up to wider and more diffuse powers.[4] This seems right, since it offers the opportunity for innovative institutional design and policy initiatives focused on local and manageable problems, the effective handling of which builds confidence on all sides. And it offers a framework for handling the disagreements and diversity of views about the value and meaning of self-government within indigenous communities as much as outside of them. But the ultimate path of development is, of course, up to indige-nous people themselves. Non-indigenous people have a duty to negoti-ate in good faith about the implementation of the arrangements they choose to pursue.

It is frequently suggested in public debates over Aboriginal rights that, aside from violating common understandings of equality – a charge we have considered in detail and rejected – they are divisive and under-mine social and national unity. Of course they *do* undermine the exist-ing bases of social unity, but then they are precisely what is at issue. There is no returning the national unity genie once it is out of the bottle. Successful liberal societies are ones in which people are willing to settle their disagreements through peaceful means rather than violent ones; to make some sacrifices for the sake of the common good; and to be will-ing to participate, to some degree, in public discourse and deliberations. What then will motivate citizens of multinational states to do these kinds of things? First of all, we should not overestimate the bonds of social unity that exist in even the most stable and peaceful states. Most citizens of the industrially advanced liberal democracies in the world today do not share a comprehensive conception of the good, or even a comprehensive conception of right. They might share a very broad set of general notions to do with the basic grammar of justice, but only that.[5] Instead, states usually forge some kind of national identity over time that draws on a range of different sources: a language or set of languages, a shared public culture, political institutions or history. But in multinational states – in states where there is more than one 'people' – these can be as much a source of division and disagreement as social unity.

So what binds multinational societies together, if anything? In the end, nothing less than a commitment to that multinational identity; to the ideal of a political order in which different national groups, with different modes of belonging and different conceptions of the good and the right, nevertheless share a willingness to live under political arrangements that reflect this plurality.[6] The difficulty with this ideal is that it cannot fall back on some supposedly objective property or characteristic – such as a language, common culture, history, religion, set of shared values or 'homeland' – to thicken out this common identity, but instead must construct it out of the various forms of practical accommodations and negotiations that emerge over time between the different peoples who share that territory. 'Diversity awareness', on the part of citizens, must somehow become transformed into 'diversity attachment', as they slowly (perhaps even unwittingly) come to value the framework within which these struggles over recognition and distribution take place, and which provide them with the freedom for contesting and reshaping the rules and norms that act on them.[7] There is no guarantee that they will. And it is a precarious thread upon which to hang one's hopes for a mutually acceptable set of political arrangements, especially if you are a small minority up against the still considerable powers of the state and increasingly the imperatives of the global market. So it is *right*, in both the strategic and objective sense of the word, that indigenous peoples seek to secure their interests in their traditional lands, protect and adapt their cultural practices to the world as it is now, and exercise their rights of self-government wherever they can. The benefits of doing so accrue not simply to them, and the duties to help realize the values and institutions required to secure those interests are not solely theirs. These benefits and duties fall upon all of us, whether indigenous or non-indigenous, and especially upon those who aspire to create a genuinely postcolonial liberal political order.

# Notes

## Introduction

1 In the book I use the expressions 'indigenous peoples' and 'Aboriginal peoples' interchangeably and very widely to distinguish between them and non-indigenous peoples. But there are significant differences of identity, culture and collective life among those who count as Aboriginal. In Canada, for example, there are First Nations, Inuit and Metis; in Australia, Aboriginal and Torres Strait Islanders. Within these, there are those who live on traditional lands and those who do not; those who identify primarily with a particular people or nation, and those who do not, or do so in different ways. These differences will become increasingly important as the argument of the book progresses.

2 This notion of liberalism 'going local' has been drawn from a number of sources, including: James Scott *Domination and the Arts of Resistance* (New Haven, Yale University Press, 1990); *Seeing Like a State: How certain schemes to improve the human condition have failed* (New Haven, Yale University Press, 1998); Will Kymlicka, *Multicultural Citizenship* (Oxford, Oxford University Press, 1995) pp. 164–172; Michael Ignatieff, 'Human rights', in Carla Hesse and Robert Post (eds), *Human Rights in Political Transitions: Gettysburg to Bosnia* (New York, Zone Books, 1999), pp. 313–342. The argument also builds on the general approach of John Rawls in *Political Liberalism* (New York, Columbia University Press, 1993), but departs from it in a number of important ways, as will become clear in Chapters 2–4.

3 The classic discussion is by Hohfeld, who identified four kinds of rights: privileges or liberties, claim rights, powers and immunities. All of these feature in the concept of 'Aboriginal rights'. See W. Hohfeld, *Fundamental Legal Conceptions as Applied to Judicial Reasoning* (New Haven, Yale University Press, 1923). The most important discussion of interest-based rights is provided by Joseph Raz, *The Morality of Freedom* (Oxford, Clarendon Press, 1986), pp. 166ff.

4 See for further discussion Brian Barry, *Political Argument: A Reissue With a New Introduction* (Hemel Hempstead, Harvester Wheatsheaf, 1990), p. lv.

5 Raz, *The Morality of Freedom*, pp. 166ff.

6 Dale Turner, 'Vision: towards an understanding of Aboriginal sovereignty', in Ronald Beiner and Wayne Norman (eds), *Canadian Political Philosophy* (Toronto, Oxford University Press, 2001), p. 325.

7  Taiaiake Alfred, *Peace, Power, Righteousness: an indigenous manifesto* (Don Mills, Oxford University Press, 1999) p. 140; see also pp. 57–58.
8  On the strategic nature of rights claims see my 'The Disciplinary Moment: Foucault, Law and the Reinscription of Rights', in Jeremy Moss (ed.), *The Later Foucault* (London, Sage, 1998), pp. 129–148; and Geuss, *History and Illusion in Politics* (Cambridge, Cambridge University Press, 2001) pp. 149–150.
9  *Report of the Royal Commission on Aboriginal Peoples, Vol 2: Reconstructing the Relationship*, (Ottawa, Ministry of Supply and Services, 1996). sec. 2.3 Chapter 3. Important expressions of Aboriginal rights in Australia in the modern era include the *Yirrkala Bark Petition* (1963), the *Barunga Statement* (1988), the *Eva Valley Statement* (1993) and Patrick Dodson's lecture, 'Lingari: Until the Chains are broken', reprinted in Michelle Grattan (ed.), *Essays on Australian Reconciliation* (Melbourne, Bookman Press, 2000), pp. 264–274. Both the *Yirrkala Bark Petition* and *Barunga Statement* provoked government responses. In the case of the former, an inquiry into the decision to mine traditional lands which originally provoked the petition, but which turned out to be only the first step in a long fight for land rights. And in the latter a promise by Prime Minister Hawke to negotiate a treaty with Aboriginal people (which subsequently never occurred).
10 Michael Sandel, *Liberalism and the Limits of Justice* (Cambridge, Cambridge University Press, 1982), pp. 31–33; for a response see Allen Buchanan, 'Assessing the Communitarian Critique of Liberalism', *Ethics* 99, 4 (1989), pp. 852–882.
11 Brian Barry, *Culture & Equality: An Egalitarian Critique of Multiculturalism* (Cambridge, Polity Press, 2001), p. 326.
12 The notion of a 'conditioning good' is from Ian Shapiro, *Democratic Justice* (New Haven, Yale University Press, 1999).
13 I attempted to tackle this question in broader historical terms in *The Self at Liberty: Political Argument and the Arts of Government* (Ithaca, Cornell University Press, 1997). See also John Tomasi, *Liberalism beyond Justice: Citizens, Society and the Boundaries of Political Theory* (Princeton, Princeton University Press, 2001).
14 G. W. F. Hegel, *Philosophy of Right*, ed. Allen W. Wood (Cambridge, Cambridge University Press) §268, §260. For further discussion see Michael Hardimon, *Hegel's Social Philosophy: The Project of Reconciliation* (New York, Cambridge University Press, 1994), pp. 95–96.
15 See Hardimon, *Hegel's Social Philosophy*, passim; Raymond Plant, *Hegel* (London, Allen & Unwin, 1973), Chapter 6.
16 There are good discussions of this complex Hegelian idea in Hardimon, *Hegel's Social Philosophy*, pp. 99–108; and Charles Taylor, *Hegel* (New York, Cambridge University Press, 1975), pp. 381–388; 411–416. Bernard Williams suggests that this Hegelian vision involves the idea that the relations of 'human beings to society and to each other, if properly enacted, can realise a harmonious identity that involves no real loss', *Shame and Necessity* (Berkeley, University of California Press, 1989), p. 162. But compare Hardimon, *Hegel's Social Philosophy*, pp. 39–40.
17 Taylor, *Hegel*, p. 383.

18 The relevant discussions are in the 'Preface' to the *Philosophy of Right*; and *Lectures on the Philosophy of World History* ed. H. B. Nisbet (Cambridge, Cambridge University Press, 1975).

19 John Rawls, *Political Liberalism* (New York, Columbia University Press, 1993). This distinction will be discussed in detail below. For a helpful discussion of what I am calling a weaker sense of reconciliation see Andrew Mason, 'Political Community, Liberal-Nationalism, and the Ethics of Assimilation', *Ethics* 109, 9 (1999), pp. 261–286.

20 *Political Liberalism*, p. 137.

21 'Justice as Fairness: Political Not Metaphysical', *Philosophy and Public Affairs*, 14 (1985), p. 230. See other references to reconciliation by reason in *A Theory of Justice* (Cambridge Mass., Harvard University Press, 1972) p. 580; *Political Liberalism*, pp. lx–lxii, 157–158; *Justice as Fairness: A Restatement*, ed. Erin Kelly (Cambridge Mass., Harvard University Press, 2001), pp. 3–4. See also Hardimon, *Hegel's Social Philosophy*, pp. 6, 128–129; Frederick Neuhoser, *Foundations of Hegel's Social Theory: Actualizing Freedom* (Cambridge Mass., Harvard University Press, 2000); and Anthony Simon Laden, *Reasonably Radical: Deliberative Liberalism and the Politics of Identity* (Ithaca, Cornell University Press, 2001), pp. 207–210.

22 *Political Liberalism*, p. lx.

23 Rawls, *Justice as Fairness*, p. 3.

24 See Williams, *Shame and Necessity*.

25 Hardimon, *Hegel's Social Philosophy*, pp. 120–121.

26 See, for example, David Miller, *On Nationality* (Oxford, Oxford University Press, 1995); Yael Tamir, *Liberal Nationalism* (Princeton, Princeton University Press, 1993); Will Kymlicka, *Liberalism, Community, Culture* (Oxford, Oxford University Press, 1989); Maurizio Viroli, *For Love of Country: An Essay on Patriotism and Nationalism* (Oxford, Oxford University Press, 1995).

27 See David Laitin, 'Political Cultural and Political Preferences', *American Political Science Review*, 82 (1988), 589–590; 'Liberal Theory and the Nation', *Political Theory* 26 (1998), 228–229.

28 By domination I mean: a set of conditions in which people, whether individually or collectively, are prevented from acting in such a way so as to modify the actions that act on them. Relations of domination exist when relations of power become fixed or stable such that, whether directly or indirectly, some are able to control – arbitrarily, and with relative certainty and without reciprocation – the conduct of others. An important consequence of this account of domination is that responses to it often entail going beyond strictly distributional notions of justice, since the norms, practices, institutions and history of a particular society shape distributional patterns. In other words, the 'what' of justice is often deeply influenced by the 'how'. The conception of domination I develop here and below is indebted to: Michel Foucault, 'The Subject and Power', in Hubert L. Dreyfus and Paul Rabinow, *Michel Foucault: Beyond Structuralism and Hermeneutics* (Chicago, University of Chicago Press, 1983), pp. 208–226; Iris Young, *Justice and the Politics of Difference*, Chapters 1–2; Ian Shapiro, *Democratic Justice*; Philip Pettit, *Republicanism: A Theory of Freedom and Government* (Oxford, Oxford University Press, 1997); and Scott, *Domination and the Arts of Resistance*.

29  The theme is prominent in the work of Ian Shapiro and Joseph Carens, but also in that of James Tully, Michel Foucault, and Quentin Skinner. For a systematic statement see Joseph Carens, *Culture, Citizenship and Community: A Contextual Exploration of Justice as Evenhandedness* (Oxford, Oxford University Press, 2000), pp. 1–20.

## 1  The liberal justificatory ideal

1  'Isaiah Berlin in conversation with Steven Lukes', *Salmagundi*, 120 (1998), pp. 121–122.
2  Stephen Macedo, *Liberal Virtues* (Oxford, Clarendon Press, 1990) calls it the 'moral lodestar of liberalism', p. 78.
3  In Australia, for example, at the time of the 1996 Census, they made up 2.1 per cent of the general population; in Canada they make up almost 5 per cent (*Report of the Royal Commission on Aboriginal Peoples 1: Looking Forward, Looking Back* (Ottawa, Ministry of Supply and Services, 1996), p. 14.
4  See Ross Poole, *Nation and Identity* (London, Routledge, 1999), p. 138.
5  See Ted Robert Gurr and Barbara Harff, *Ethnic Conflict in World Politics* (Boulder, Co., Westview Press, 1994); Walker Connor, 'National Self-Determination and Tomorrow's Political Map', in Alan Cairns et al (eds), *Citizenship, Pluralism* (Montreal, Kingston, McGill-Queens University Press, 1999).
6  See for example Yael Tamir, *Liberal Nationalism* (Princeton, Princeton University Press, 1993).
7  Raymond Guess, *History and Illusion in Politics* (Cambridge, Cambridge University Press, 2001), p. 69; echoing the Nietzschean dictum that only that which has no history can be defined.
8  Here I follow Charles Larmore, 'Political Liberalism', *Political Theory* 18 (1990), 339–360; Foucault, 'On Governmentality'; and Rawls, *Political Liberalism*; compare Geuss, *History and Illusion*, pp. 69–73.
9  Barry, 'How not to defend liberal institutions', in Brian Barry, *Liberty and Justice: Essays in Political Theory 2* (Oxford, Clarendon Press, 1991) pp. 23–39; but compare now *Justice as Impartiality* (Oxford, Clarendon Press, 1995); and Ronald Beiner,*What's wrong with liberalism* (Berkeley, University of California Press, 1992).
10  Rawls, *Political Liberalism*, pp. 191–194. For a defence of 'neutrality of effect' from the perspective of political liberalism, see John Tomasi, *Liberalism beyond justice* (Princeton, Princeton University Press, 2001).
11  For example, Joseph Raz, *The Morality of Freedom* (Oxford, Clarendon Press, 1986).
12  Charles Taylor, 'Legitimation Crisis', in *Philosophy and Human Sciences: Philosophical Papers 2* (Cambridge, Cambridge University Press, 1985), pp. 248–288.
13  For the distinction between an 'interactionist' and 'institutional' approach to questions of justice see Thomas Pogge, 'Three Problems with Contractarian-Consequentialist Ways of Assessing Social Institutions', *Social Philosophy and Policy*, 12 (1995), 241–266.
14  Amy Gutmann and Dennis Thompson, *Democracy and Disagreement*, p. 52; Joshua Cohen, 'Deliberation and Democratic Legitimacy', in Alan Hamlin

and Philip Pettit (eds), *The Good Polity: Normative Analyses of the State* (Oxford, Basil Blackwell, 1989); Seyla Benhabib, 'Deliberative Rationality and Models of deliberative democracy', *Constellations*, 1 (1994), 26–52; Jan Elster (ed.), *Deliberative Democracy* (New York, Cambridge University Press, 1998).

15  Gutmann and Thompson, *Democracy and Disagreement*, p. 55.

16  Jean Hampton, 'The Common Faith of Liberalism', *Pacific Philosophical Quarterly*, 75 (1994), p. 193; and 'The Moral Commitments of Liberalism', in David Copp, Jean Hampton and John Roemer (eds), *The Idea of Democracy* (New York, Cambridge University Press, 1993), pp. 292–313.

17  Hampton, 'The Common Faith of Liberalism', p. 212.

18  Rawls, *Political Liberalism*, p. 61 on the burdens of judgment setting limits to what can be reasonably justified to others.

19  For the former see Joseph Raz, 'Facing Diversity: The Case of Epistemic Abstinence', *Philosophy and Public Affairs* (1990), 19, 1, pp. 3–46; and for the latter, Richard Rorty, 'The Priority of Democracy to Philosophy', in *Objectivity, Relativism and Truth* (Cambridge, Cambridge University Press, 1991), pp. 175–196.

20  Hampton, 'The Common Faith of Liberalism'.

21  John Rawls, 'The Domain of the Political and Overlapping Consensus', *New York University Law Review*, 654, 2 (1989), p. 250.

22  Foucault, 'Space, Knowledge, Power', in *Foucault Reader*, ed. Paul Rabinow (New York, Vintage Books, 1984), p. 249. He goes on: 'if it is extremely dangerous to say that Reason is the enemy that should be eliminated, it is just as dangerous to say that any critical questioning of this rationality risks sending us into irrationality'.

23  The phrase is taken from Hampton, 'The moral commitments of liberalism', p. 306.

24  On objectivity in the social contract tradition see Barry, *Theories of Justice*, (Hemel Hempstead, Harvesten-Wheatsheaf, 1989) pp. 264–271.

25  Jeremy Waldron, 'The Philosophical Foundations of Liberalism', in *Liberal Rights* (Cambridge, Cambridge University Press, 1993), p. 58.

26  The phrase 'registers of justice/injustice' is from Connolly, *Ethos of Pluralization* (Minneapolis, University of Minnesota Press, 1995); but my thoughts here also draw heavily on the work of Quentin Skinner: see especially 'Reply to my Critics', in Tully (ed) *Meaning and Context* (Cambridge, Polity Press, 1988). I take up some of the normative questions this raises in Chapter 4.

27  Alasdair MacIntyre, *After Virtue* (London, Duckworth, 1981); John Gray *Enlightenment's Wake: politics and culture at the close of the modern age* (London, Routledge, 1995), especially pp. 131–184. Gray argues that contemporary Anglo-American liberalism 'trivializes' late-modern value pluralism and should be abandoned for a pragmatic, culturally specific form of *modus-vivendi* pluralism. My defence of a discursive and dynamic *modus-vivendi* liberalism is distinct from Gray's in a number of ways, as will hopefully become clear. For a more detailed discussion of Gray's specific argument see my 'Pluralism and the Hobbesian logic of negative constitutionalism', *Political Studies*, 47 (1999), 83–99.

28  As does Gray, *Enlightenment's Wake*, p. 156.
29  Claude Lefort, cited in Robert Post, *Constitutional Domains: Democracy, Community Management* (Cambridge, Mass., Harvard University Press, 1995), pp. 23, 188.
30  William Galston, 'Two Concepts of Liberalism', *Ethics*, 105 (1995), 516–534; and Will Kymlicka, *Liberalism, Community and Culture* (Oxford, Clarendon Press, 1989).
31  See Charles Beitz, *Political Equality* (Princeton, Princeton University Press, 1989), pp. 75–96.
32  The importance of a loyal opposition in relation to democratic theory is central to Ian Shapiro's argument in *Democratic Justice*.
33  I am indebted here to the discussion in Waldron, *The Dignity of Legislation* (Cambridge, Cambridge University Press, 1999), pp. 160–162.
34  Charles W. Mills, *The Racial Contract* (Ithaca, Cornell University Press, 1997), pp. 16–17. Importantly these assumptions also entail that whites benefit materially as well. The economic imperatives of imperial expansion are a major theme of the historical literature on 'New World' colonialism; see for a sample and references V. G. Kiernan, *Imperialism and its Contradictions* (London, Routledge, 1995); and Anthony Pagden, *Lords of all the World* (New Haven, Yale University Press, 1995). There have been intense debates within postcolonial theory as to the need for re-emphasizing the centrality of the economic aspects of 'first' and 'third' world relations over and above the questions of cultural or national identity. See, for example, A. Ahmad, *In Theory: nations, classes, literature* (London, Verso, 1991); and Gayatri Chakravorty Spivak, *A Critique of Post-Colonial Reason: Toward a History of the Vanishing Present* (Cambridge, Mass., Harvard University Press, 1999).
35  Robert A. Williams Jr, 'The Algebra of Federal Indian Law: The Hard Trail of Decolonization and Americanizing the White Man's Indian Jurisprudence', *Wisconsin Law Review* (1986), p. 229 (emphasis added); *The American Indian in Western Legal Thought: The Discourse of Conquest* (New York, Oxford University Press, 1990); see also James Anaya, *Indigenous Peoples in International Law* (New York, Oxford University Press, 1996); Henry Reynolds, *The Law of the Land* (Melbourne, Penguin, 1987). Compare Pagden, *The Fall of Natural Man* (Cambridge, Cambridge University Press, 1982; second edn 1986); David Armitage, *The Ideological Origins of the British Empire* (Cambridge, Cambridge University Press, 2000).
36  Spivak, *A Critique of Postcolonial Reason*, pp. 3, 71, 89, 361.
37  Notably Charles Beitz, *Political Theory and International Relations* (Princeton, Princeton University Press, 1979); Onora O'Neill, *Towards Justice and Virtue* (Cambridge, Cambridge University Press, 1996); *Faces of Hunger* (London, Allen & Unwin, 1986); Thomas Pogge, 'Cosmopolitanism and Sovereignty', *Ethics*, 103 (1992), 48–75; D. Mapel and T. Nardin (eds), *International Society: Diverse Ethical Perspectives* (Princeton, Princeton University Press, 1998); David Held, *Democracy and the Global Order* (Cambridge, Polity Press, 1995); Charles Jones, *Global Justice: defending cosmopolitanism* (Oxford, Clarendon Press, 1999).

38  For a good overview of this history see Will Kymlicka, 'American Multiculturalism and the "Nations Within" ', in Duncan Ivison, Paul Patton and Will Sanders (eds), *Political Theory and the Rights of Indigenous Peoples* (Cambridge, Cambridge University Press, 2000), pp. 216–236.

39  For three striking examples of this history see Richard White, *The Middle Ground: Indians, Empires and Republics in the Great Lakes Region 1650–1815* (New York, Cambridge University Press, 1991); Nicholas Thomas, *Possessions: Indigenous Art/Colonial Culture* (London, Thames and Hudson, 1999); and Robert Williams, *Visions of Law and Peace 1600–1800* (New York, Oxford University Press, 1997). Iris Young and James Tully have drawn on this material to construct contemporary normative frameworks for considering Indigenous claims; see Tully, *Strange Multiplicity: Constitutionalism in an age of diversity* (Cambridge, Cambridge University Press, 1995); and Young, 'Hybrid Democracy: Iroquois Federalism and the Postcolonial Project', in Ivison, Patton and Sanders (eds) *Political Theory and the Rights of Indigenous Peoples*, pp. 237–258.

40  James Clifford, *The Predicament of Culture* (Cambridge, Mass., Harvard University Press, 1988), pp. 19, 342–343, 338.

41  White, *The Middle Ground*, pp. x; 52–53.

42  As White brilliantly shows, such 'strange proximity' often involved an unstable mixture of political and economic exchange and violence. See, for example, the differences in the way French and English colonial authorities managed their relations with the various Indian nations; *The Middle Ground*, pp. 223–365.

43  On the uneasiness of colonists see Andrew Fitzmaurice, 'The civic solution to the crisis of English colonization 1609–25', *Historical Journal* 42 (1999) 25–51; and Armitage, *The Ideological Origins of British Empire*, Chapter 1; for a discussion of humanitarian activists in nineteenth and early twentieth century Australia, see Henry Reynolds, *This Whispering in Our Hearts* (Sydney, Allen & Unwin, 1998); also White, *The Middle Ground*, pp. 469–517.

44  See, for example, Claus Offe, 'Homogeneity and Constitutional Democracy: Coping with Identity Conflicts through Group Rights', *Journal of Political Philosophy*, 6 (1998), 113–141; Robert Post, 'Constitutionalism and Cultural Heterogeneity', *Australian Journal of Legal Philosophy*, 25, 2 (2000), 65–84.

45  See Chapter 5 for further discussion.

46  Spivak warns of a too uncritical 'celebration of the "hybrid" which can inadvertently legitimate the "pure" by reversal': *A Critique of Postcolonial Reason*, p. 65; see also the comments on 'colonialism/nationalism', pp. 60–62.

47  See, for example, Stephen White, *Sustaining Affirmation: the Strengths of Weak Ontology in Political Theory* (Princeton, Princeton University Press, 2000).

48  O'Neill, *Faces of Hunger*, pp. 27–51.

49  O'Neill, *Faces of Hunger*, p. 41; also Michelle Moody-Adams, *Fieldwork in Familiar Places: Morality, Culture and Philosophy* (Cambridge, Mass., Harvard University Press, 1997).

50  Brian Barry, *Justice as Impartiality*, p. 145. This openness to the heterogeneity of public reason seems to have vanished in his more recent *Culture & Equality: An Egalitarian Critique of Multiculturalism* (Cambridge, Polity Press, 2001).

## 2 The postcolonial challenge

1 Clifford Geertz, 'The Uses of Diversity and the Future of Ethnocentrism', *Michigan Quarterly Review* 25, (1985) p. 112.

2 Dipesh Chakrabarty, *Provincializing Europe* (Princeton, Princeton University Press, 2000), p. 17.

3 G. Spivak, *A Critique of Postcolonial Reason: toward a history of the vanishing present* (Cambridge, Mass., Harvard University Press, 1999).

4 See for example Brian Barry, 'International Society from a Cosmopolitan Perspective', in David Mapel and Terry Nardin (eds), *International Society: Diverse Perspectives* (Princeton, Princeton University Press, 1998); Charles Beitz, 'Cosmopolitan liberalism and the states system', in Chris Brown (ed.), *Political Restructuring in Europe: Ethical Perspectives* (London, Routledge 1994); Charles Jones, *Global justice: defending cosmopolitanism* (Oxford, Oxford University Press, 1999).

5 Marx presents the classic critique of liberalism as a handmaiden of capitalist power: see *On the Jewish Question* (1844). Postcolonial liberalism thus appeals to those aspects of the liberal tradition that are critical of not only state power, but of unregulated capitalist power as well. Arguably Rawls falls into the latter camp. For debate over this question see G. A. Cohen, 'Where the action is: On the Site of Distributive Justice', *Philosophy and Public Affairs*, 26 (1997), 3–30; David Estlund, 'Liberalism, Equality and Fraternity in Cohen's critique of Rawls', *Journal of Political Philosophy*, 6 (1998), 99–112.

6 See Taiaiake Alfred, *Peace, Power, Righteousness: an indigenous manifesto* (Don Mills, Oxford University Press, 1999), pp. 140–141: 'The concept of "rights", especially in the common Western sense, leads nowhere for indigenous peoples, because it alienates the individual from the group'.

7 Thomas Nagel, 'The Fragmentation of Value', in *Mortal Questions* (Cambridge, Cambridge University Press, 1979), pp. 128–141; also Michelle Moody-Adams, *Fieldwork in Familiar Places: Morality, Culture and Philosophy* (Cambridge, Mass., Harvard University Press, 1997), Chapter 3.

8 See Michael Walzer, *Thick and Thin: Moral Argument at Home and Abroad* (Notre Dame, Notre Dame University Press, 1994), pp. 203–205.

9 Or as William Galston puts it, 'The most difficult political choices are not between good and bad but good and good': 'Value Pluralism and Liberal Political Theory', *American Political Science Review*, 93 (1999), p. 771.

10 Alasdair MacIntyre, 'Toleration and the Goods of Conflict', Morrell Lecture on Toleration, University of York, 1998, unpublished.

11 Michel Foucault, 'Governmentality', in James D. Faubion (ed.), *Michel Foucault: The Essential Works, 3: Power* (London, Allen Lane, 2001), pp. 201–222.

12 Edward Said, *Culture and Imperialism* (New York, Vintage Books, 1994) , p. 81.

13 Said, *Culture and Imperialism*, p. 81.

14 The link between the Enlightenment and colonialism has been explored most recently by Anthony Pagden, *Lords of all the World: Ideologies of Empire in Spain, Britain and France c1500–c1800* (New Haven, Yale University

Press, 1995); Richard Tuck, *The rights of war and peace: political thought and international order from Grotius to Kant* (Oxford, Oxford University Press, 1999); David Armitage, *The Ideological Origins of British Empire* (Cambridge, Cambridge University Press, 2000)

15  Armitage, *Ideological Origins of British Empire*, p. 15.
16  Armitage, *Ideological Origins of British Empire*, p. 23.
17  See Uday Mehta, *Liberalism and Empire: A study in nineteenth century British liberal thought* (Chicago, University of Chicago Press, 1999).
18  Daniel Weinstock, 'How can collective rights and liberalism be reconciled', p. 296; also implied in John Tomasi, 'Kymlicka: Liberalism and Respect for Minorities', *Ethics*, 105 (1995), 580–603.
19  Istvan Hont, 'The language of sociability and commerce: Samuel Pufendorf and the theoretical foundations of the "Four–Stages Theory" ', in Anthony Pagden (ed), *The Languages of Early Modern Political Thought* (Cambridge, Cambridge University Press, 1987), pp. 253–276.
20  Pagden, *The Fall of Natural Man* (Cambridge, Cambridge University Press, 1982) p. 2.
21  Anthony Pagden, 'The "defence of civilization" in eighteenth century social theory', *History of the Human Sciences*, 1, 1 (1988), 33–43.
22  See Pagden, *The Fall of Natural Man;* for a contemporary discussion linking anthropology to central questions of moral philosophy see Moody Adams, *Fieldwork in Familiar Places.*
23  Ruth Benedict, *Patterns of Culture* (Boston: Houghton Mifflin, 1934), p. 46.
24  Clifford, *The Predicament of Culture*, p. 235.
25  Clifford, *The Predicament of Culture*, p. 338.
26  See the discussion in Moody Adams, *Fieldwork in Familiar Places.*
27  Clifford, *The Predicament of Culture*, p. 14. This open–textured account of culture is suggested by a number of anthropologists and cultural theorists; see, for example, Clifford Geertz, *The Interpretation of Cultures* (New York, Basic Books, 1973); Michael Carrithers, *Why Humans Have Cultures* (Oxford, Oxford University Press, 1992); Terence Turner, 'Anthropology and Multculturalism: What is Anthropology that Multiculturalists Should be Mindful of?', *Cultural Anthropology*, 8 (1993), 411–429.
28  Clifford, *The Predicament of Culture*, p. 344.
29  Clifford Geertz, 'The Uses of Diversity and the Future of Ethnocentrism', p. 120.
30  This is an important point to note in relation to indigenous cultures; See Alfred, *Peace, power, righteousness*, pp. 147, 80–88.
31  Geertz, *The Interpretation of Cultures*, pp. 44–45. See also Bikuh Parekh, *Rethinking Multiculturalism* (London, Macmillan, 2000), p. 143; culture is a 'historically created system of meaning and significance ... a system of beliefs and practices in terms of which a group of human beings understand, regulate and structure their individual and collective lives'.
32  Geertz, *The Interpretation of Cultures*, p. 45.
33  Homi K. Bhabha, 'Cultural Choice and the Revision of Freedom', in Austin Sarat and Thomas R. Kearns (eds) *Human Rights: Concepts, Contests, Contingencies* (Ann Arbor, The University of Michigan Press, 2001), p. 57.
34  Joseph Raz, 'Multiculturalism: A Liberal Perspective', in *Ethics in the Public Domain* (Oxford, Clarendon Press, 1994), p. 162.

35  See for more discussion Moody Adams, *Fieldwork in Familiar Places*, pp. 168–169; Ross Poole, *Nation and Identity* (London and New York, Routledge, 1999), pp. 14–15, 34–35.

36  Philippe Van Parijs, 'Must Europe be Belgian?' in Iain Hampsher-Monk, Catriona McKinnon (eds), *The Demands of Citizenship* (London, Continuum, 2000), pp. 235–253; Will Kymlicka, 'Citizenship in an era of globalization: comment on Held' in Ian Shapiro and Casiano Hacker-Cordon (eds), *Democracy's Edges* (Cambridge, Cambridge University Press, 1999), pp. 112–126.

37  Jeremy Waldron, 'What is Cosmopolitan', *Journal of Political Philosophy* 8, 2 (2000), 235–236.

38  David Laitain, 'Political Culture and Political Preference', *American Political Science Review*, 82 (1988), 589–592.

39  For a somewhat one–sided argument to this end see Russell Hardin, *One For All: The Logic of Group Conflict* (Princeton, Princeton University Press, 1995); David Laitain, 'National revivals and violence', *Archive European de Sociologie*, XXXVI (1995), 3–43; and more generally, *Identity in Formation*.

40  See Homi Bhabha, *The Location of Culture* (New York and London, Routledge, 1994); Nicolas Thomas, *Colonialism's Culture: Anthropology, Travel and Government* (Cambridge, Polity Press, 1994); R. Guha and G. Spivak, *Selected Subaltern Studies* (New York, Oxford University Press, 1988); Gyan Prakash, 'Writing Post-Orientalist Histories of the Third World: Perspectives from Indian Historiography', *Comparative Studies in Society and History*, 32 (1990), 383–408. Dipesh Chakrabarty, *Provincializing Europe*; G. Spivak, *The Critique of Postcolonial Reason*; and Ranjit Guha, 'The Migrant's Time', *Postcolonial Studies*, 1, 2 (1998), 155–160; Partha Chatterjee, *The Nation and its Fragments: Colonial and Postcolonial Histories* (Princeton, Princeton University Press, 1993).

41  Foundationalism refers to the claim that knowledge be structured upon secure foundations usually found in some combination of reason and exprience. Anti–foundationalism thus refers to a rejection of the need for such foundations; however there are different ways of formulating its consequences for knowledge. Postcolonial theorists tend to associate foundationalism with essentialism, the view that we can distinguish between the properties of a thing that are essential to it, and those which are merely contingent or accidental to it. Essentialism is thought to be particularly problematical, according to postcolonial writers, when associated with claims about the nature of persons, as well as cultures and social and political processes generally. Hence postcolonial theory tends to be anti–foundationalist in its epistemology and anti–essentialist in its ontology.

42  Prakash, 'Writing Post–Orientalist Histories', p. 383.

43  Prakash, 'Writing Post–Orientalist Histories', p. 384.

44  Prakash, 'Postcolonial Criticism and Indian Historiography', *Social Text*, 10 (1992), p. 8.

45  Chakrabarty, *Provincializing Europe*, p. 16.

46  Prakash, 'Writing Post–Orientalist Histories', p. 397; Bhabha, *Locations of Culture*, p. 59.

47  Dipesh Chakrabarty 'Postcoloniality and the artifice of history', *Representations*, 37 (1992), 10–12; reprinted (abridged) in *Provincializing Europe*, pp. 27–46 (with a short postscript at p. 46); compare Bhabha, *Locations of Culture*, p. 6; Chaterjee, *The Nation and its Fragments*, p. 11.

48  Parekh, *Rethinking Multiculturalism*, Chapter 1.

49  Bhabha, *Locations of Culture*, p. 2. For criticisms of the descriptive and normative limits of this notion of hybridity see Aijaz. Ahmed, *In Theory: Classes, Nations, Literatures* (London, Verso, 1992); and Gillian Cowlishaw, *Rednecks, Eggheads and Blackfellas: A Study of Racial Power and Intimacy in Australia* (Sydney, Allen and Unwin, 1999); and Pratap Bhanu Mehta, 'Cosmopolitanism and the Circle of Reason', *Political Theory* 28, 5 (2000) 619–639.

50  Homi K. Bhabha, 'On minorities: cultural rights', *Radical Philosophy*, 100 (March/April 2000), p. 4.

51  Bhabha, 'Cultural Choice and the Revision of Freedom', p. 46.

52  *Locations of Culture*, p. 4.

53  *Locations of Culture*, p. 175. The affinity with feminist critiques of liberalism is striking; see *Locations of Culture*, p. 10 and Chakrabarty 'Postcoloniality', p. 20.

54  Bhabha, 'On minorities: cultural rights', p. 4.

55  Bhabha, 'On minorities: cultural rights', p. 6.

56  Chakrabarty 'Postcoloniality', p. 20; *Provincializing Europe*, p. 42.

57  Chakrabarty 'Postcoloniality', p. 23.

58  Chakrabarty 'Postcoloniality', p. 23; *Provincializing Europe*, p. 46; compare Bhabha's discussion of a 'postcolonial contra-modernity', in *Locations of Culture*, p. 6.

59  *Provincializing Europe*, pp. 42–43.

60  For a very clear statement of this charge see A. Stoler and F. Cooper (eds), 'Introduction' in *Tensions of Empire: Colonial Cultures in a Bourgeois World* (Berkeley, University of California Press, 1997), pp. 35–37.

61  See Duncan Ivison, *The Self at Liberty; Political Argument and the Arts of Government* (Ithaca and London, Cornell University Press, 1997).

62  See James Tully, 'The Struggle of Indigenous Peoples for and of Freedom', in Duncan Ivison, Paul Patton and Will Sanders (eds), *Political Theory and the Rights of Indigenous Peoples* (Cambridge, Cambridge University Press, 2000), pp. 36–59; Alfred, *Peace, Power Righteousness*, pp. 40–95.

63  For an historical overview of modern pluralist approaches to this problem see David Runciman, *Pluralism and the personality of the state* (Cambridge, Cambridge University Press, 1997).

64  E. Povinelli, 'Settler Modernity and the Quest for an Indigenous Tradition', *Public Culture*, 11, 1 (1999), p. 23.

65  Povinelli, 'Settler Modernity', p. 45.

66  Where it is acknowledged, it is limited to those peoples who were subject to colonization from overseas, as opposed to national minorities within a territorially contiguous state (the so–called 'saltwater thesis'). For a critique see Tully, 'Indigenous Peoples' struggles for and of freedom', pp. 54–57.

67  Will Kymlicka, 'Theorizing indigenous rights', *University of Toronto Law Review*, 49 (1999), p. 284.

68  Cited in Bhabha, 'On minorities: cultural rights', p. 4.

69 Will Kymlicka, 'Human Rights and Ethnocultural Justice', *Review of Constitutional Studies*, 24 (1994), p. 213; 'Theorizing indigenous rights', pp. 284–285.

70 Note that they represent two very different periods in the history of the British Empire; the first empire, associated with early modern Britain and its territories in the West Indies and North America, and the second empire, beginning in the second half of the eighteenth century and encompassing South Asia, Australasia, Africa and parts of the Americas respectively.

71 Bikhu Parekh, 'Liberalism and Colonialism; a critique of Locke and Mill', in Jan Nederveen Pieterse and Bhikhu Parekh (eds), *The Decolonization of Imagination: Culture, Knowledge, Power* (London and New Jersey, Zed Books, 1995) pp. 81–98. Uday Mehta, *Liberalism and Empire: a study in nineteenth century British liberal thought* (Chicago, University of Chicago Press, 1999); Tully, 'The Two Treatises and aboriginal rights', in *Locke in contexts: an approach to political philosophy* (Cambridge, Cambridge University Press, 1993), pp. 137–176; Robert A. Williams, *The American Indian in western legal thought: the discourses of conquest* (New York, Oxford University Press, 1990); Armitage, *Ideological Origins of the British Empire*, pp. 93–99. See also Andrew Fitzmaurice, 'The civic solution to the crisis of English colonization 1609–1625', *Historical Journal*, 42, 1 (1999), 25–52 and 'The Machiavellian argument for colonial possession', forthcoming.

72 J. S. Mill, *Considerations on Representative Government* (Oxford, Oxford University Press, 1975), pp. 386–387; Chatterjee calls this the 'rule of colonial difference', *Nation and Fragments*, p. 18.

73 Judith Butler, 'Universality in Culture', in Joshua Cohen (ed.), *For Love of Country: Debating the Limits of Patriotism* (Boston, Beacon Press, 1996), p. 52.

74 See for example Butler, 'Universality in Culture' passim; Bhabha, 'On minorities: cultural rights', p. 6. The analogy with translation has also been emphasized by Chakrabarty, *Provincializing Europe*, pp. 17–20 and passim; and specifically in relation to indigenous peoples' claims by Paul Patton, 'The translation of indigenous land into property: the mere analogy of English jurisprudence …', *parallax*, 6 (2000), 25–38.

75 See Patton, 'The translation of indigenous land into property' and Jeremy Webber, 'Beyond Regret: Mabo's Implications for Australian Constitutionalism', in Ivison, Patton and Sanders (eds), *Political Theory and the Rights of Indigenous Peoples*, especially pp. 63–70.

76 William Connolly, *The Ethos of Pluralization* (Minneapolis, University of Minnesota Press, 1995), pp. 181ff.

77 Connolly, *The Ethos of Pluralization*, pp. 181–187.

78 William Connolly, 'Rethinking the Ethos of Pluralization', *Philosophy and Social Criticism*, 24 (1998), p. 85.

79 Connolly, 'Rethinking the Ethos of Pluralization', p. 95; also *The Ethos of Pluralization*, pp. 184–186.

80 The phrase is from Moira Gatens and Genevieve Lloyd, *Collective Imaginings: Spinoza, Past and Present* (New York and London, Routledge, 1999), p. 65.

## 3  Reason and community

1  Michel Foucault, *Dits et Ecrits IV* (Paris, Gallimard, 1994), p. 707.
2  David Copp, 'Democracy and Communal Self-Determination', in Robert McKim and Jeff McMahan (eds), *The Morality of Nationalism* (Oxford, Oxford University Press, 1997), p. 277.
3  See Alan Buchanan, 'Self-Determination, Secession and the Rule of Law', in McKim and McMahan (eds), *The Morality of Nationalism*, p. 306.
4  Brian Barry, *Culture and Equality: An Egalitarian Critique of Multiculturalism* (Cambridge, Polity Press, 2001) p. 138.
5  See the discussion in Joseph Raz, *The Morality of Freedom* (Oxford, Oxford University Press, 1986), pp. 17–18; and Charles Taylor, 'Cross-purposes: The Liberal-Communitarian Debate', in *Philosophical Arguments* (Cambridge, Mass., Harvard University Press, 1995), pp. 181–203.
6  John Rawls, *Justice as Fairness: A Restatement*, ed. Erin Kelly (Cambridge, Mass., Harvard University Press, 2001), pp. 199–200.
7  Taylor, 'Cross-purposes', pp. 189ff.
8  The notion of freedom at work here is closer to a 'state' rather than a voluntarist account, to borrow a distinction from Robert Pippen: 'Naturalness and Mindedness: Hegel's Compatibilism', *European Journal of Philosophy*, 7 (1999), 194–212. According to a voluntarist notion of freedom, I am free when I possess some causal power to initiate an action by an act of will independent of any antecedent causal conditions. According to 'state' notion of freedom, I am free to the extent that I act in a certain way distinguished as 'free' not by having some special causal origin, but by being undertaken in a certain way (for example as for Hegel, when I act 'self-consciously' or in such a way that I can 'identify' with my projects and activities).
9  See Foucault, 'Space, Knowledge, Power', in Paul Rabinow (ed.), *The Foucault Reader* (New York, Pantheon, 1984).
10  Robert E. Goodin, 'Communities of Enlightenment', *British Journal of Political Science*, 28 (1998), 531–558.
11  Russell Hardin, *One for All: The Logic of Group Conflict* (Princeton, Princeton University Press, 1995), p. 69; also Chapter 7 passim.
12  Hardin, *One For All*, p. 77.
13  As Goodin puts it, here we slip from the 'decently encumbered self' to the 'fanatically immersed self'; 'Communities of Enlightenment', p. 554.
14  Hardin, *One for All*, pp. 209–210.
15  See Shane O'Neill, *Impartiality in Context: Grounding Justice in a Pluralist World* (Albany, State University of New York Press, 1997), Chapter 4.
16  Michael Walzer, *Spheres of Justice: A Defence of Pluralism and Equality* (New York, Basic Books, 1983), p. xiii.
17  Hardin, *One for All*, pp. 204–206.
18  See Robert Goodin, 'Conventions and Conversions, or, Why is Nationalism Sometimes So Nasty?', in McKim and McMahan (eds), *The Morality of Nationalism*, pp. 94–98.
19  On the circularity and yet influential provenance of this argument, see Tom Baldwin, 'The Territorial State', in H. Gross and R. Harrison (eds), *Jurisprudence: Cambridge Essays* (Oxford, Clarendon Press, 1992), pp. 207–230.

20  David Copp, 'Democracy and Communal Self-Determination' in McKim and McMahan (eds), *The Morality of Nationalism*, pp. 281–282.

21  See Alan Buchanan, 'Self-Determination, Secession and the Rule of Law', in McKim and McMahan (eds), *The Morality of Nationalism*, pp. 316–317; and 'Theories of Succession', *Philosophy and Public Affairs*, 26 (1997), 31–61.

22  Walzer, *Thick and Thin: Moral Argument at Home and Abroad* (Notre Dame, University of Notre Dame Press, 1994), p. 79; 'Nation and Universe', in Grethe B. Peterson (ed), *Tanner Lectures on Human Values XI* (Salt Lake City, Utah University Press, 1990), p. 544.

23  See *Spheres of Justice*, p. 28; for discussions of the problem this raises for divided societies, and minority rights in particular see O'Neill, *Impartiality in Context*, Chapter 8 (using the case of Northern Ireland); and Will Kymlicka, *Liberalism, Community and Culture* (Oxford, Clarendon Press, 1989), pp. 220–236.

24  O'Neill, *Impartiality in Context*, p. 183.

25  *Spheres of Justice*, p. 29; my emphasis.

26  Kymlicka, *Liberalism, Community and Culture*, pp. 223, 227.

27  *Thick and Thin*, pp. 73–81.

28  *Thick and Thin*, pp. 74–75; my emphasis.

29  *Report of the Royal Commission on Aboriginal Peoples* (5 vols, Ottawa, Ministry of Supply and Services, 1996).

30  For a discussion of one instance of treaty making in early colonial Australia, see Henry Reynolds, *Fate of a Free People* (Ringwood, Vic., Penguin, 1995); for a history of more recent attempts, see John Chesterman and Brian Galligan, *Citizens Without Rights: Aborigines and Australian Citizenship* (Cambridge, Cambridge University Press, 1998).

31  Taylor, 'Irreducibly Social Goods', in *Philosophical Arguments*, pp. 127–145.

32  Thomas Hurka, 'The Justification of National Partiality', pp. 144–146; and Jeff McMahan, 'The Limits of National Partiality', pp. 123–124; both in McKim and McMahan (eds), *The Morality of Nationalism*.

33  Hurka, 'The Justification of National Partiality', p. 145.

34  Charles Taylor, 'Multiculturalism and the "Politics of Recognition" ' , p. 58; 'Irreducibly Social Goods', in *Philosophical Arguments*, passim. For criticism see Hardin, *One for All*, pp. 66–70.

35  Compare the discussions in Will Kymlicka, *Multicultural Citizenship: A Liberal Theory of Minority Rights* (Oxford, Clarendon Press, 1995), pp. 161ff; and Barry, *Culture and Equality*, pp. 162–193.

36  Applying religious criteria for ordination or leadership in a church is obviously justifiable, but should a church be able to restrict such offices to men? Should it be able to demand of teachers in a religious school, for example, a declaration of faith or standard of conduct with reference to a particular religious ethos? Should a religious-based university be allowed to prohibit inter-racial dating on the basis of its creed or governing ethos? There is disagreement about these examples amongst liberals, not surprisingly, because there is disagreement about the consequences of these policies for the basic interests of the individuals involved and for the wider interests of society. Compare Nancy Rosenblum, *Membership and Morals: The Personal Use of Pluralism in America* (Princeton, Princeton University Press, 1999); Denis

Rheaume, 'Common-law construction of group autonomy: A Case Study' in Ian Shapiro and Will Kymlicka (eds), *Ethnicity and Group Rights* (New York, New York University Press, 1997), pp. 257–289; and Barry, *Culture and Equality*, pp. 165–193.

37  Barry, *Culture and Equality*, p. 171.

38  Barry, *Culture and Equality*, p. 175.

39  I am grateful to Robert Fullinwider for discussion on this point.

40  Jacob T. Levy, 'Classifying Cultural Rights' in Shapiro and Kymlicka (eds), *Ethnicity and Group Rights*, pp. 22–66.

41  Drawing the appropriate boundaries to identify relevant groups for political purposes is subject to all kinds of problems. Who draws the boundaries – the group or the state? If the boundaries are drawn too narrowly, this creates opportunities for discriminating against dissidents or minorities within that group. If they are drawn too broadly, then some people might be included who do not want to be, or who do not identify with the group in the same way as those drawing the boundary. For a critical discussion see Claus Offe, '"Homogeneity" and Constitutional Democracy: Coping with Identity Conflicts through Group Rights', *Journal of Political Philosophy*, 6 (1998), 126–30; on the complexity of group identification see Brian Slattery, 'The Paradoxes of National Self-Determination', *Osgoode Hall Law Journal*, 32 (1994), 703–733. Self-identification by the group is also vulnerable to the 'fallacy of the doctrine of real group personality': i.e. the confusion of the belief that groups have a real personality with the ability of groups to actually decide that personality for themselves; see David Runciman, *Pluralism and the Personality of the State* (Cambridge, Cambridge University Press, 1997), Chapters 12–14.

42  Bhikhu Parekh, *Rethinking Multiculturalism: Cultural Diversity and Political Theory* (London, Macmillan, 2000).

43  Parekh, *Rethinking Multiculturalism*, pp. 165–172.

44  One of the main points of Rawls's argument in *Political Liberalism* is to enable citizens to endorse the political conception of justice from within their own partially comprehensive world view.

45  Jeremy Waldron, 'Superseding Historical Injustice', *Ethics*, 103 (1992), 4–28; Levy, 'Classifying Cultural Rights', p. 36; Offe, '"Homogeneity" and Constitutional Democracy', pp. 129–130; Buchanan, 'Liberalism and Group Rights', p. 10.

46  See Joseph Raz and Avishai Margalit, 'National Self-Determination', *Journal of Philosophy*, 87 (1990), especially pp. 442–447, 457; for a critical discussion of their argument see Slattery, 'Paradoxes of National Self-Determination', pp. 716–733.

47  Kymlicka, *Liberalism, Community and Culture*, especially Chapter 9; *Multicultural Citizenship*, pp. 83–92.

48  *Multicultural Citizenship*, pp. 76–80.

49  *Liberalism, Community and Culture*, pp. 170–173; *Multicultural Citizenship*, pp. 153, 202 n. 1.

50  Levy's eight-fold classification is useful here ('Classifying Cultural Rights'), for it is clear that the forms of accommodation claimed will depend on the nature of the group and the purpose of the right. Claims for exemptions are not the same as claims for assistance or recognition, which in turn are not

necessarily justified in the same way as self-government rights. In fact, not all of these claims are necessarily about culture either, as we shall see in the case of indigenous peoples.

51  'American Multiculturalism and the "Nations Within"', in Ivison, Patton and Sanders (eds), *Political Theory and the Rights of Indigenous Peoples*, pp. 230–231.

52  Will Kymlicka, *Finding Our Way: Rethinking Ethnocultural Relations in Canada* (Don Mills, Oxford University Press, 1998), pp. 144–146: there he writes that one of the most 'urgent obligations of justice' is that Canadians 'recognize the principle of the inherent right of self-government and negotiate in good faith about its appropriate implementation' (p. 145).

53  The phrase 'prescriptive rights' is Buchanan's; see 'Liberalism and Group Rights', pp. 9–11.

54  *Multicultural Citizenship*, p. 92.

55  *Liberalism, Community and Culture*, pp. 165–171.

56  For example, in *Multicultural Citizenship*, Kymlicka writes: 'I have defended the right of national minorities to maintain their culturally distinct societies, but only if, and in so far as, they are themselves governed by liberal principles' (p. 153).

57  Susan Mellor Okin, 'Feminism and Multiculturalism: Some Tensions', *Ethics*, 108 (1998), especially pp. 679–680: 'it is not enough, for one to be able to "question one's inherited roles" and to have the capacity to make choices about one's life one wants to lead, that one's culture be protected. At least as important ... is one's place within that culture ... [and the capacity to question] whether one's culture instills in and enforces on one particular social roles'.

58  See Chandran Kukathas, 'Are there any Cultural Rights?', *Political Theory*, 20 (1992), 105–139; 'Liberalism, Multiculturalism and Oppression' in Andrew Vincent (ed), *Political Theory: tradition and diversity* (Cambridge, Cambridge University Press, 1997), pp. 132–153; and 'Cultural Toleration' in Shapiro and Kymlicka (eds), *Ethnicity and Group Rights*, pp. 69–104.

59  E.g. Barry, *Culture and Equality*, pp. 308–309; Joseph Carens, *Culture, Citizenship and Community: A Contextual Exploration of Justice as Even-handedness* (Oxford, Oxford University Press, 2000), Chapter 3.

60  John Tomasi, 'Kymlicka, Liberalism and Respect for Cultural Minorities', *Ethics*, 105 (1995), 580–603; James Nickel, 'The Value of Cultural Belonging: Expanding Kymlicka's Theory', *Dialogue*, XXXIII (1994), 635–642; Alan Patten, 'Liberal Egalitarianism and the Case for Supporting National Cultures', *The Monist*, 82 (1999), 387–410.

61  *Multicultural Citizenship*, pp. 53–56, 76.

62  Carens, *Culture, Citizenship and Community*, p. 63.

63  Barry, *Culture and Equality*, p. 326; see also p. 21; and pp. 257–258.

64  Offe, ' "Homogeneity" and Constitutional Democracy', passim; see also Barry's *Culture and Equality*; and Hardin, *One For All*.

65  The importance of these two dimensions of multiculturalism has been emphasized especially by James Tully throughout his work; see for example 'Introduction', in Alain G. Gagnon, *Multinational Democracies* (Cambridge, Cambridge University Press, 2001), pp. 1–37.

66  Shapiro, *Democracy's Place*, Chapter 5.

67 Philip Pettit, 'Minority claims under two conceptions of democracy', in Ivison, Patton and Sanders (eds), *Political Theory and the Rights of Indigenous Peoples*, pp. 199–215.
68 Shapiro, *Democracy's Place*, pp. 115–116;
69 'Qu'est-ce que la critique?', *Bulletin de la Société Francaise de Philosophie*, 84 (1990), pp. 35–63.
70 Shapiro, *Democratic Justice*, Chapter 1; also Tully, 'Introduction', p. 28.

## 4 Disagreement and public reason

1 Oral submission of the Attorney General of Saskatchewan cited in *Reference re Secession of Quebec* (1998), 2 *SCR* at paragraph 96.
2 'Religious Minorities and the secular state: Reflections on an Indian impasse', *Public Culture*, 8 (1995), p. 30.
3 Michel Foucault, *Power: Essential Works Volume 3*, ed. James D. Faubion (London, The Penguin Press, 2001); James Scott, *Domination and the Arts of Resistance* (New Haven, Yale University Press, 1990).
4 This point should not be underestimated. For example, in Canada, the *Indian Act* imposed membership rules on Indian nations which relied on racialist criteria as to who was to be counted as an 'Indian', and thus be eligible for various rights and benefits tied to being a 'Status Indian'. In response, some Indian governments have adapted racialist criteria themselves to re-assert control over membership, despite being traditionally and historically receptive to the integration of outsiders, including non-Natives. These moves have attracted a barrage of criticism. But it is important to understand the context in which such rules have emerged as a response to circumstances in which the community felt its very ability to survive was under threat. For more specific discussions of the 'blood quantum' rule see Audra Simpson, 'Paths towards a Mohawk Nation', in Duncan Ivison, Paul Patton and Will Sanders (eds), *Political Theory and the Rights of Indigenous Peoples* (Cambridge, Cambridge University Press, 2000) pp. 128–129; Gerald Alfred, *Heeding the Voices of our Ancestors* (Toronto, Oxford University Press, 1995), pp. 163–177; see also Partha Chatterjee's remarks on 'fuzzy' and 'enumerated' communities in *The Nation and its Fragments*, pp. 220–239.
5 See for example Seyla Benhabib, 'Communicative ethics and contemporary controversies in political philosophy in S. Benhabib and F. Dallmayr (eds), *The Communicative Ethics Controversy* (Cambridge, Mass., MIT Press, 1990); James Bohman, 'Public Reason and Cultural Pluralism: Political Liberalism and the Problem of Moral Conflict', *Political Theory*, 23 (1995), 253–279; John Dryzek, 'Legitimacy and Economy in Deliberative Democracy', *Political Theory*, 29 (2001), 651–669.
6 See classically Joseph Schumpeter, *Capitalism, Socialism and Democracy* (London, Allen & Unwin, 1943); also the essays by Ian Shapiro and Michael Walzer in Stephen Macedo (ed.), *Deliberative Politics: Essays on Democracy and Disagreement* (New York, Oxford University Press, 1999).
7 On discursive democracy see John Dryzek, *Deliberative Democracy and Beyond: Liberals, Critics, Contestations* (Oxford, Oxford University Press, 2000); on 'incompletely theorized agreements' see Cass Sunstein,

'Incompletely Theorized Agreements', *Harvard Law Review*, 108 (1995), 1735–1736. I am particularly indebted to Dryzek's discussion in this chapter.

8 Stanley Fish, 'Mutual Respect as a Device for Exclusion', in Macedo (ed), *Deliberative Politics*, p. 96.

9 Povinelli, 'Settler Modernity', pp. 35–36; see the whole run of argument between especially pp. 29–38; the liberal state is castigated for its 'own continuing intolerance, its own failures to achieve a *truly* multicultural formation without recourse to discipline and repression' (p. 36, my emphasis).

10 Fish, 'Mutual Respect as a Device for Exclusion', p. 98.

11 Brian Barry, *Justice as Impartiality* (Oxford, Oxford University Press, 1995) p. 77.

12 Barry, *Justice as Impartiality*, pp. 205–207.

13 John Rawls, *Political Liberalism* (New York, Columbia University Press, 1993) pp. 214, 224; 'Lecture VI', passim.

14 The terms are adapted from Fred D'Agostino, 'Some Modes of Public Justification', *Australasian Journal of Philosophy*, 69 (1991), 390–414; and Gerald Postema, 'Public Practical Reason: an Archaeology', *Social Philosophy and Policy*, 12, (1995) pp. 64–73; and 'Public Practical Reason: Political Practice', in Ian Shapiro and Judith Wagner Delew (eds) *Theory and Practice*, (New York, New York University Press, 1995), pp. 348–352.

15 Robert Goodin, 'Laundering Preferences' in J. Elster and J. Hylland (eds), *Foundations of Social Choice Theory* (New York, Cambridge University Press, 1986), pp. 75–102.

16 David Gauthier, 'Moral Artifice', *Canadian Journal of Philosophy*, 18, (1988). 385–418; and *Morals by Agreement* (Oxford, Oxford University Press, 1986).

17 David Gauthier, 'Mutual Advantage and Impartiality', in Paul Kelly (ed.), *Impartiality, Neutrality and Justice: Re–Reading Brian Barry's* Justice as Impartiality (Edinburgh, Edinburgh University Press, 1998), pp. 121–122.

18 Rawls, *A Theory of Justice*, p. 4, cited in David Gauthier, 'Constituting democracy', in David Copp, Jean Hampton and John Roemer (eds), *The Idea of Democracy* (New York, Cambridge University Press, 1993), p. 317.

19 John Rawls, *A Theory of Justice* (Cambridge, Mass., Harvard University Press, 1972), p. 134.

20 David Gauthier 'Political Contractarianism', *Journal of Political Philosophy*, 5 (1997), p. 134.

21 David Gauthier 'Public Reason', *Social Philosophy and Policy*, 12 (1995), p. 37; and 'Constituting Democracy', pp. 320–321, 326.

22 Gauthier, 'Constituting Democracy', p. 320.

23 Gauthier, 'Constituting Democracy', p. 321.

24 Gauthier, 'Constituting Democracy', p. 321.

25 Gauthier, 'Constituting Democracy', p. 318.

26 Gauthier, 'Constituting Democracy', p. 318.

27 Compare Gauthier and Rawls on the function of 'civic friendship': 'Constituting Democracy', p. 321 n. 4; p. 332; Rawls, 'The Idea of Public Reason Revisited', in Samuel Freeman (ed.), *John Rawls: Collected Papers* (Cambridge, Mass., Harvard University Press, 1999), p. 579.

28 I owe this formulation to Matt Matravers.

29 'We regard each bargainer as serving as an ideal representative of the particular person he will be in the social world to be shaped by the constitution on which all agree', Gauthier, 'Constituting Democracy', p. 324.

30 Gauthier, 'Constituting Democracy', p. 333 n. 12; *Morals by Agreement*, pp. 155–156, 201–205.

31 See especially Gauthier, 'Constituting Democracy', p. 332 n. 4 and p. 333 n. 12.

32 *Political Liberalism*, p. 137.

33 *Political Liberalism*, pp. 212–214.

34 *Political Liberalism*, p. 217.

35 *Political Liberalism*, p. 218

36 *Political Liberalism*, pp. 250–254.

37 Rawls now thinks that when debating fundamental political questions we can introduce comprehensive doctrines into political discussions provided that, 'in due course, we give properly public reasons to support the principles and policies our comprehensive doctrine is said to support' ('The Idea of Public Reason Revisited', pp. 584, 591–594; see the definition of the reasonable citizen at p. 578).

38 Rawls at one point insists in *Political Liberalism* that there is 'but one public reason' (p. 220), but that '[a]ccepting the idea of public reason and its principle of legitimacy emphatically does not mean ... accepting a particular liberal conception of justice down to the last details ...' (p. 226). He takes this one step further in 'The Idea of Public Reason': 'the forms of permissible public reason are always several' (p. 583).

39 I am indebted here to Anthony Simon Laden's excellent discussion in *Reasonably Radical; Deliberative Liberalism and the Politics of Identity* (Ithaca and London, Cornell University Press, 2001), especially at pp. 116–126.

40 Note that for Rawls, the 'depth and breadth' of an overlapping consensus extends not only to the *principles* of justice but 'goes down to the fundamental ideas within which justice as fairness is worked out' (*Political Liberalism*, p. 149). But compare now 'The Idea of Public Reason Revisited' (pp. 581–588, 592–593), where room is given for the development of new and changing political conceptions of justice through public reason, as well as varying interpretations of them (see especially pp. 586–587 n. 35), within a family of conceptions rather than just one. But to be admissible, conceptions must still meet two sets of criteria, and these criteria are essentially those originally laid out in *Political Liberalism* (see pp. 581–585).

41 *Political Liberalism*, pp. 39–40.

42 *Political Liberalism*, pp. 147, 158–168.

43 *Political Liberalism*, p. 30; compare p. 148: 'No sensible view can possibly get by without the reasonable and rational as I use them'.

44 *Political Liberalism*, pp. 139–140.

45 On this point see Richard Arneson, 'The Priority of the Right over the Good Rides Again', *Ethics*, 108 (1997), 187–188; and Michael Sandel, 'Political Liberalism', *Harvard Law Review*, 107 (1994), 1782–1789.

46 But for a notable exception see Laden, *Reasonably Radical*.

47 *Strange Multiplicity*; 'Wittgenstein and Political Philosophy; Understanding Practices of Critical Reflection', *Political Theory*, 17 (1989), 172–204.

48 *Strange Multiplicity*, pp. 115–116.

49 *Strange Multiplicity*, pp. 116, 181.

50  *Strange Multiplicity*, pp. 116ff.

51  *Strange Multiplicity*, pp. 138–139.

52  On the analogy between the stochastic nature of the processes of language acquisition and a more context–sensitive approach to politics see James C. Scott, *Seeing Like a State: How Certain Schemes to Improve the Human Condition Have Failed* (New Haven, Yale University Press, 1998), pp. 318–320.

53  Scott, *Domination and the Arts of Resistance*; Focault, *Power*.

54  *Strange Multiplicity*, pp. 165–182.

55  See especially *Strange Multiplicity*, p. 211: 'on these conventions we ... stand fast, for they are the rules of the common ground on which we stand. Even transgressions by Locke, Kant, Herder, Publius and Mill are not tolerated'.

56  *Strange Multiplicity*, p. 173. Tully acknowledges the importance of principles such as 'mutual respect for individuals and minorities, toleration, freedom, equality of peoples, autonomy, community [and] international human rights' in work since *Strange Multiplicity*. His point now seems to be that the parties in struggles over recognition often do share a set of common principles, but that a maximum amount of room must be left open to allow for varying interpretations of them by the parties themselves according to their particular circumstances. See 'The Challenge of Reimagining Citizenship and Belonging in Multicultural and Multinational Societies', in Catriona McKinnon and Iain Hampsher-Monk (eds), *The Demands of Citizenship* (London, Continuum, 2000), pp. 212–234.

57  Claus Offe and Ulrich Preuss, 'Democratic Institutions and Moral Resources', in D. Held (ed.), *Political Theory Today* (Cambridge, Polity Press, 1991), pp. 143–171.

58  My point is that a static *modus vivendi* may evolve into a discursive *modus vivendi*, but not necessarily in the way described by Rawls. Hence I also mean to distinguish my discussion from that of Charles Larmore in *Patterns of Moral Complexity* (New York: Cambridge University Press, 1987), especially at pp. 122–130. Rather confusingly, at least for my purposes, he endorses a view of liberalism 'as modus vivendi' by which he means the view Rawls has now developed more explicitly in *Political Liberalism* (New York, Columbia University Press, 1993).

59  Gauthier, 'Constituting Democracy'.

60  William E. Connolly *Identity/Difference: Democratic Negotiations of Political Paradox* (Ithaca and London, Cornell University Press, 1991), especially pp. 64–68.

61  William E. Connolly, *The Ethos of Pluralization* (Minneapolis, University of Minnesota Press, 1995).

62  William E. Connolly, *Why I am not a Secularist* (Minneapolis, University of Minnesota Press, 1999), p. 23.

63  See Connolly's discussion of Kant and Habermas in this regard; *Why I am not a Secularist*, pp. 29–46; and Stephen White, *Affirmation: The Strengths of Weak Ontology in Political Theory* (Princeton, Princeton University Press, 2000).

64  Cass Sunstein, 'Incompletely Theorized Agreements', pp. 1735–1736.

65  Larmore, *Patterns of Moral Complexity*, pp. 64–65; Barry, *Justice as Impartiality*, pp. 175–176.

66  See White, *Affirmation*, passim. On the importance of micro-political 'practices of the self' see Connolly, *Why I am not a Secularist*, pp. 146–148; 174–176.

67  I am grateful to Fiona Jenkins for pressing this criticism on me and for discussions with her about it. Note that there are other kinds of arguments about the importance of affect in public reason that I do not discuss here. A particularly interesting and valuable discussion, from a Spinozist perspective, can be found in Moira Gatens and Genevieve Lloyd, *Collective Imaginings: Spinoza and the Present* (London and New York, Routledge, 1999).

68  This is an ideal present in recent work by Jacques Derrida; see for example, *Politics of Friendship*, tr. G. Collins (London and New York, Verso, 1997).

69  Simon Critchley, 'Remarks on Derrida and Habermas', *Constellations*, 7, 4 (2000), p. 462.

70  In Derrida's work, at least according to Simon Critchley, justice is a moment of 'formal universality', of making explicit what is implicit in the performative structure of speech acts; see Critchley, 'Remarks on Derrida and Habermas', pp. 455–465.

71  The idea of a constellation of discourses occupying the public sphere is nicely described in John Dryzek, *Deliberative Democracy and Beyond: Liberals, Critics, Contestations*, pp. 74–80; and in Nancy Fraser's 'Rethinking the Public Sphere: A Contribution to the Critique of Actually Existing Democracies', in Craig Calhoun (ed.), *Habermas and the Public Sphere* (Cambridge, Mass., MIT Press, 1992), pp. 109–142.

72  John Dryzek, 'Legitimacy and Economy in Deliberative Democracy', *Political Theory*, 29, 5 (2001), p. 660.

73  'Legitimacy and Economy', p. 659.

74  Arguments about the benefits of conflict have a long lineage in the history of political thought: see Duncan Ivison, *The Self at Liberty: Political Argument and the Arts of Government* (Ithaca, Cornell University Press, 1997), Chapter 3 and Chapter 6; also John P. McCormick, 'Machiavellian Democracy: Controlling Elites with Ferocious Populism', *American Political Science Review*, 95, 2 (2001), 301–303; Albert O. Hirschman, 'Social Conflicts as Pillars of Democratic Market Societies', in his *A Propensity to Self-Subversion* (Cambridge, Mass., Harvard University Press, 1995), pp. 231–247.

75  Stephen Holmes, *Passions & Constraint: On the Theory of Liberal Democracy* (Chicago, University of Chicago Press, 1995).

76  Adam Przeworski, 'Minimalist conception of democracy: a defence', in Ian Shapiro and Casiano Hacker-Cordon (eds), *Democracy's Value* (New York, Cambridge University Press, 1999), pp. 30–31; see also Ian Shapiro, 'Enough of Deliberation: Politics is about Interests and Power', in Macedo (ed.), *Deliberative Politics*, p. 31.

77  J. G. A Pocock, *Politics, Langauge and Time* (Chicago, University of Chicago Press, 1989); Stuart Hampshire, *Justice is Conflict* (London, Duckworth, 1999), p. 34; Lloyd and Gatens, *Collective Imaginings*, pp. 58–83, 136–149.

## 5 Historical injustice

1 Aristotle, *The Politics*, ed. Trevor J. Saunders (Harmondsworth, Penguin, 1979), 1276a, 17–34.

2 The idea of the 'circumstances of politics' is from Jeremy Waldron, *The Dignity of Legislation* (Cambridge, Cambridge University Press, 1999), pp. 154–155.

3 In Australia, the national reconciliation debate quickly became bogged down over the appropriateness of the national government apologizing for some of the consequences of past racialist policies, in particular the removal of indigenous children from their families. The Prime Minister, John Howard, refused to apologize on behalf of the nation to families of what is known as the 'Stolen Generation', on the grounds that people should not be held collectively responsible for past actions they did not carry out, and that were moreover, at the time, part of official government policy. Parliament did eventually pass a Howard-sponsored motion of 'sincere regret', but which again resiled from any commitment to a notion of collective responsibility.

4 The phrase is from James Booth, 'Communities of Memory', in Ronald Beiner and Wayne Norman (eds), *Canadian Political Philosophy: contemporary reflections* (Don Mills, Oxford University Press, 2001), p. 264.

5 For two thoughtful discussions of this good see James Tully, *Strange Multiplicity: Constitutionalism in an Age of Diversity* (Cambridge, Cambridge University Press, 1995), pp. 202–203; and Michael Hardimon, *Hegel's Social Philosophy: The Project of Reconciliation* (New York, Cambridge University Press, 1975), pp. 15–41. See also Andrew Mason, 'Political Community, Liberal-Nationalism, and the Ethics of Assimilation', *Ethics*, 109 (1999), 261–286.

6 On 'metis' see James Scott, *Seeing Like a State: How Certain Schemes to Improve the Human Condition Have Failed* (New Haven, Yale University Press, 1998), pp. 6–7, 311–316, 340–341.

7 Gopal Sreenivasan, 'Interpretation and Reason', *Philosophy and Public Affairs*, 27 (1998), 144–145.

8 Michael Walzer, *Spheres of Justice: A Defence of Pluralism and Equality* (New York, Basic Books, 1983), p. 29.

9 Walzer is aware of this: see his 'Nation and Universe', in Grethe B. Peterson (ed.), *Tanner Lectures on Human Values XI* (Salt Lake City, Utah University Press, 1990), pp. 528–529.

10 Note that many of these policies continued well into the twentieth century, and from the perspective of some indigenous people, continue today.

11 A considerable part of the philosophical literature focuses on the problems with entitlement theories of justice in general. This debate is not the main focus of this chapter. For further discussion see Peter Laslett and James Fishkin (eds), *Justice between groups and generations* (New Haven, Yale University Press, 1992; George Sher, 'Ancient Wrongs, Modern Rights', *Philosophy and Public Affairs*, 19 (1981), 3–17; David Lyons, 'The new Indian claims and original rights to land', *Social Theory and Practice*, 4 (1977), 249–272. Christine Korsgaard, 'Kant on the right to revolution' in Andrews Reath et al (eds), *Reclaiming the History of Ethics: Essays for John*

*Rawls* (New York, Cambridge University Press, 1997), p. 306; Andrew Sharp, *Justice and the Maori*, Second Edition (Auckland, Oxford University Press, 1997), pp. 125–177; A. John Simmons, 'Historical Rights and Fair Shares', *Law and Philosophy*, 14 (1995), 149–184; Onora O'Neill, 'Rights to Compensation', *Social Philosophy and Policy*, 5 (1989), 149–184.

12  'Superseding Historic Injustice', pp. 4–28. See also Melissa Williams, *Voice, Trust, Memory: Marginalized Groups and the Failings of Liberal Representation* (Princeton, Princeton University Press, 1998), especially pp. 191–192.

13  Waldron, 'Superseding Historic Injustice', pp. 13–19.

14  Waldron, 'Superseding Historic Injustice', p. 7. Waldron is mistaken to suggest that the choice is between 'full' reparations and 'symbolic' payments; there are surely options in between. Furthermore, it is not clear why forms of compensation that do not involve transfers of land suffer from the same problems Waldron identifies. Moreover, if he thinks the historical injustice 'superseded', why is an apology required?

15  Waldron, 'Superseding Historic Injustice', p. 27.

16  Tully, *Strange Multiplicity*; Susan Dodds, 'Justice and Indigenous Land Rights', *Inquiry*, 41 (1998), 187–205.

17  Arguably, liberals implicitly appeal to historical arguments anyway when justifying special treatment for minorities, including indigenous peoples; see George Sher, 'Diversity', *Philosophy and Public Affairs*, 28 (1999), 85–104.

18  Waldron, 'Superseding Historic Injustice', p. 6.

19  Bernard Williams, *Shame and Necessity* (Berkeley, University of California Press, 1993), pp. 92–93.

20  As Williams puts it, 'the internalization of shame does not simply internalize an other who is representative of the neighbours. The internalized "other" is conceived of as one whose reactions I would respect, and one would respect the same reactions if directed at him', *Shame and Necessity*, p. 83.

21  This phrase is from Charles Taylor, *Sources of the Self: The Making of the Modern Identity* (Cambridge, Mass., Harvard University Press, 1989), pp. 26–30.

22  Bernard Williams, *Moral Luck* (Cambridge, Cambridge University Press, 1981), pp. 29–30.

23  See Anthony W. Marx, *Making Race and Nation: A comparison of South Africa, the United States and Brazil* (New York, Cambridge University Press, 1998); Charles Mills, *The Racial Contract* (Ithaca, Cornell University Press, 1997); Rogers M. Smith, *Civic Ideals: Visions of Citizenship in US History* (New Haven, Yale University Press, 1997); John Chesterman and Brian Galligan, *Citizens Without Rights: Aborigines and Australian Citizenship* (Cambridge, Cambridge University Press, 1997).

24  For a version of this argument see Jeff McMahan, 'The Limits of National Partiality', in Robert McKim and Jeff McMahan (eds), *The Morality of Nationalism* (New York, Oxford University Press, 1997), pp. 107–138.

25  For further discussion see Williams, *Shame and Necessity*, Chapter 5.

26  That is, when citizens have 'adopted a way of resolving conflicts, making decisions, interacting with other states, and planning together for an ongo-

ing future', Christine Korsgaard, *Creating the Kingdom of Ends* (New York, Cambridge University Press, 1996), p. 373.

27  Jeremy Webber, 'The Jurisprudence of Regret: The Search for Standards of Justice in Mabo', *Sydney Law Review*, 17 (1995), p. 11; see also Gerald Postema 'On the Moral Presence of our Past', *McGill Law Journal*, 36 (1991), 1178–1180; 'Collective Evils, Harms and the Law', *Ethics*, 97 (1987), 414–440.

28  Yael Tamir, *Liberal Nationalism* (Princeton, Princeton University Press, 1993), pp. 95–116, 134–139.

29  Postema, 'Collective Evils, Harms and the Law', pp. 426–427.

30  The phrase is from Alasdair MacIntyre, *After Virtue* (London, Duckworth, 1981), p. 207. For an interesting development of this theme see Jeremy Webber, *Reimagining Canada* (Montreal, McGill-Queens Press, 1994).

31  People usually have a much more acute sense of what is unjust than of what is just in politics; see the discussion in Ian Shapiro, *Democratic Justice* (New Haven, Yale University Press, 1999) pp. 19–20. See also Stuart Hampshire, *Justice is Conflict* (London, Duckworth, 1999).

32  Samuel Scheffler, 'Relationships and Responsibilities', *Philosophy and Public Affairs*, 26 (1998), 191–192, 202.

33  Thomas Hurka, 'The Justification of National Partiality', in McKim and McMahan (eds), *The Morality of Nationalism*, p. 151.

34  There is a crucial ambiguity here in talking about 'political membership'. Do we mean all citizens or all residents? Do refugees or landed immigrants, for example, who do not have a right to vote or even to various social services, have these responsibilities as well? On the face of it, no.

35  See the discussion in Tamir, *Liberal Nationalism*, pp. 101–102; William E. Connolly, *The Ethos of Pluralization* (Minneapolis, University of Minnesota Press, 1995) pp. 41–74. An interesting example of this dilemma is discussed by David Dyzenhaus, *Judging the Judges: Judging Ourselves: Truth, Reconciliation and the Apartheid Legal Order* (Oxford, Hart Publishing, 1998).

36  There is considerable debate as to whether special obligations, if they are merely derivative of general obligations of fairness or impartiality, are all that special after all. On the other hand, 'associative obligations' are often implicitly appealed to anyway by liberals, given the need to explain why we owe the bulk of our duties of justice to our fellow citizens as opposed to anyone else. My point is that the tension between these two views is built into any plausible account of political obligation, and cannot be easily dissolved. See Yael Tamir, *Liberal Nationalism* (Princeton, Princeton University Press, 1993), pp. 95–116; and Samuel Scheffler, 'Liberalism, Nationalism and Egalitarianism', in McKim and McMahan (eds), *The Morality of Nationalism*, pp. 204–205.

37  These two goods are discussed in Tully, *Strange Multiplicity*, pp. 31–2.

38  See Jeremy Webber, 'Beyond Regret: Mabo's Implications for Australian Constitutionalism', in Duncan Ivison, Paul Patton and Will Sanders (eds), *Political Theory and the Rights of Indigenous Peoples* (Cambridge, Cambridge University Press, 2000), pp. 60–88.

39  For a defence of the epistemic gains of an inclusive theory of public deliberation which is contrasted with a 'juridical' model (i.e., Rawls's), see

Melissa Williams, 'Justice towards Groups: Political not Juridical', *Political Theory*, 23 (1995), 80–81.

40 Compare Bonnie Honig, *Political Theory and the Displacement of Politics* (Ithaca, Cornell University Press, 1993). But it does mean being suspicious of attempts to impose solutions from above, or to achieve desirable outcomes without attention to local contexts and circumstances.

41 Margaret Levi, 'Death and taxes: extractive equality and the development of democratic institutions', in Ian Shapiro and Casiano Hacker-Cordon (eds), *Democracy's Value* (Cambridge, Cambridge University Press, 1999), p. 124.

42 Compare Arthur Ripstein, 'Context, Continuity, and Fairness', in McKim and McMahan (eds), *The Morality of Nationalism*, pp. 217–223.

43 John Dryzek, *Deliberative Democracy and Beyond: Liberals, Critics, Contestations* (Oxford, Oxford University Press, 2000), pp. 76–77.

## 6 The postcolonial state

1 Michel Foucault, 'What is Enlightenment', in Paul Rabinow (ed.), *The Foucault Reader* (New York, Vintage, 1984).

2 James Tully, 'Struggles for and of freedom', in Duncan Ivison, Paul Patton and Will Sanders (eds), *Political Theory and the Rights of Indigenous Peoples* (Cambridge, Cambridge University Press, 2000), p. 58.

3 Taiaiake Alfred, *Peace, Power, Righteousness: an indigenous manifesto* (Don Mills, Oxford University Press, 1999); Tully, 'The Struggles of indigenous peoples for and of freedom'; Macklem, *Indigenous Difference*.

4 See the excellent discussion in Patrick Macklem, *Indigenous Difference and the Canadian Constitution* (Toronto, University of Toronto Press, 2001), Chapters 1–4.

5 James Tully, 'Struggles over Recognition and Distribution', *Constellations*, 7, 4 (2000), p. 469.

6 It should also be concerned with not undermining, at the very least, the basic interests and well-being of those people who are not citizens – whether refugees or asylum seekers arriving on its territories – and those suffering from severe deprivation and harm elsewhere in the world.

7 William Jonas and Margaret Donaldson, 'The Legitimacy of Special Measures' in Sam Garkaw, Loretta Kelly and Warwick Fisher (eds), *Indigenous Human Rights* (Sydney, Sydney Institute of Criminology, 2001), p. 11.

8 Max Weber, 'The Profession and Vocation of Politics' in Peter Lassman, Ronald Spiers (eds) *Weber: Political Writings* (Cambridge, Cambridge University Press, 1994), pp. 310–11.

9 D. Held, 'The transformation of political community', in Ian Shapiro and Casiano Hacker-Cordon (eds), *Democracy's Edges* (New York, Cambridge University Press, 1999), p. 92.

10 David Held et al, *Global Transformations* (Cambridge, Polity Press, 1999); James Tully, 'Democracy and Globalization: A Defeasible Sketch', in Ronald Beiner and Wayne Norman (eds), *Canadian Political Philosophy* (Don Mills, Oxford University Press, 2001) pp. 36–62; William E. Connolly, *The Ethos of Pluralization* (Minneapolis, University of Minnesota

Press, 1995). On the internationalization of the indigenous rights movement see James Anaya, *Indigenous Peoples in International Law* (Oxford, Oxford University Press, 1996).

11  One of the most notorious examples of this was the Canadian government's 1969 White Paper on Indian Policy, which proposed doing away with any special treatment for Aboriginal people, including abandoning treaty negotiations, on the grounds of it being 'antithetical to Canadian political traditions' and to protecting individual rights.

12  M. Boldt, *Surviving as Indians: The Challenge of Self-Government* (Toronto, University of Toronto Press, 1993).

13  Joseph Carens, *Culture, Citizenship and Community: A Contextual Exploration of Justice as Evenhandedness* (Oxford, Oxford University Press, 2000), p. 190.

14  Charles Larmore, *Patterns of Moral Complexity* (New York, Cambridge University Press, 1987) pp. 64–65.

15  Arthur Ripstein, 'Coercion and Disagreement', in Beiner and Norman (eds), *Canadian Political Philosophy*, p. 352; see also Larmore, *Patterns of Moral Complexity*, pp. 62–66.

16  Ripstein, 'Coercion and Disagreement', p. 354–355.

17  Stanley Fish, 'Mutual Respect as a Device for Exclusion' in Stephen Macedo (ed.), *Deliberative Politics: Essays on Democracy and Disagreement* (New York, Oxford University Press, 1999).

18  John Rawls, *Political Liberalism* (New York, Columbia University Press, 1993); Jurgen Habermas, *Between Facts and Norms: Contributions to a Discourse Theory of Law and Democracy* (Cambridge, Mass., MIT Press, 1996).

19  For example: Brian Barry, *Culture and Equality: An Egalitarian Critique of Multiculturalism* (Cambridge, Polity Press, 2001)

20  Iris Marion Young, 'Equality of Whom? Social Groups and Judgements of Injustice', *Journal of Political Philosophy*, 9 (2001), 1–18; Elizabeth Anderson, 'What is the point of equality?' *Ethics* 109 (1999), 287–337.

21  See Melissa Williams, *Voice, Trust, Memory: marginalised groups and the failings of liberal representation* (Princeton, Princeton University Press, 1998).

22  For an excellent survey of these argument, see M. Clayton and A. Williams 'Egalitarian Justice and Interpersonal Comparison', *European Journal of Political Research*, 35 (1999), 445–464.

23  Ronald Dworkin, 'What is Equality? Part 2: equality of resources', *Philosophy and Public Affairs*, 10 (1981), 283–345; Richard Arneson, 'Equality' in Philip Pettit and Robert Goodin (eds), *A Companion to Contemporary Political Philosophy* (Oxford, Blackwell, 1995), pp. 489–507.

24  John Rawls, *A Theory of Justice* (Cambridge, Mass., Harvard University Press, 1972) pp. 101–104.

25  Crucially, Rawls thinks these are key indicators for determining who is worst off; see *A Theory of Justice*, p. 97; but also pp. 396–397.

26  *A Theory of Justice*, p. 396; also pp. 178–179, 440–441; *Political Liberalism*, p. 181.

27  *Political Liberalism*, pp. 178–190.

28  Ronald Dworkin, 'What is Equality? Part 1: equality of welfare', *Philosophy and Public Affairs*, 10 (1981), 300–301.

29  See Will Kymlicka, *Contemporary Political Philosophy: An Introduction* (Oxford, Clarendon Press, 1990), pp. 81–90 and references therein; also Arneson, 'Equality'.

30  'Equality of Resources', pp. 311–313.
31  See the excellent discussion in Ian Shapiro, *Democratic Justice* (New Haven, Yale University Press, 1999), pp. 154–155.
32  Amartya Sen, *Inequality Reexamined* (Oxford, Oxford University Press, 1992), pp. 81–82.
33  *Women and Human Development: The Capabilities Approach* (Cambridge, Cambridge University Press, 2000). See also the helpful discussion of her and Sen's arguments in David A. Crocker, 'Functioning and Capability: The Foundations of Sen's and Nussbaum's Development Ethic, Part 2' in Martha C. Nussbaum and Jonathan Glover (eds), *Women, Culture, and Development* (Oxford, Oxford University Press, 1995), pp. 153–198; and the symposium on her work in *Ethics*, 111 (2000), 8–140.
34  Nussbaum admits there will be some instances where we might want to mandate certain functionings, for example in relation to the interests of children; see 'Aristotle, Politics, and Human Capabilities: A Response to Antony, Arneson, Charlesworth, and Mulgan', *Ethics*, 111 (2000), p. 131.
35  Will Kymlicka, *Liberalism, Community and Culture* (Oxford, Clarendon Press, 1989) p. 183.
36  For this point see James Nickel, 'The Value of Cultural Belonging: Expanding Kymlicka's Theory', *Dialogue* XXXIII (1994), 635–642; John Tomasi, 'Kymlicka, Liberalism and Respect for Cultural Minorities', *Ethics*, 105 (1995), 580–603; Alan Patten, 'Liberal Egalitarianism and the Case for Supporting National Cultures', *The Monist*, 82, 3 (1999), 387–410.
37  Nickel, 'The Value of Cultural Belonging', pp. 639–640.
38  For this argument see Alan Patten, 'Liberal Egalitarianism', pp. 404–405. See also the discussion in Barry, *Culture & Equality*, pp. 36–37.
39  Patten, 'Liberal Egalitarianism', p. 398.
40  This is objection is elaborated in Dworkin, 'What is Equality? Part 1: Equality of Welfare', pp. 185–246.
41  *Liberalism, Community, Culture*, p. 187.
42  On the argument from burdensomeness Jeremy Waldron, 'The Logic of Cultural Accommodation', paper presented to the American Political Science Association, September 2001; and Anthony Simon Laden, *Reasonably Radical: Deliberative Liberalism and the Politics of Identity* (Ithaca and London, Cornell Univesrity Press, 2001), pp. 173–180.
43  Barry, *Culture & Equality*, p. 150.
44  See the discussion in Laden, *Reasonably Radical*, pp. 175–178.
45  See for example P. P. McGuinness, 'Assimilation, Christians, and the Vicar of Bray', *Quadrant* (June 2000), 2–4; Roger Sandall, 'Romancing the Stone Age', *Sydney Morning Herald* (Spectrum), 12/13 May 2001, pp. 2ff.
46  Will Kymlicka, *Multicultural Citizenship* (Oxford, Oxford University Press, 1995), pp. 85–86.
47  Clayton and Williams, 'Egalitarian Justice and Interpersonal Comparison', p. 448. The relevant discussion in Rawls is at *Theory of Justice*, pp. 396–397, 440; *Political Liberalism*, pp. 179–190.
48  *Women and Human Development*, p. 68. See also Sen, 'Gender Inequality and Theories of Justice', pp. 264–266; and *Inequality Reexamined*, passim. Note that Rawls now accepts that his primary goods metric is incomplete and proposes a supplement to meet some of Sen's objections; *Political Liberalism*, pp. 178–190.

49 What is a capability? A capability is a kind of power to do or be something. It can be more or less developed and more or less feasible, in relation to both internal factors with regard to the agent and external factors to do with the context in which the agent acts. For a close discussion of the differences between Sen and Nussbaum on the notion of a capabaility see Crocker, 'Foundations', pp. 157–164.

50 Nussbaum, *Women and Human Development*, pp. 74–75; Sen is more circumspect about Rawls's recent reformulation; see 'Gender Inequality', p. 266.

51 These kinds of criticisms are developed in Arneson, 'Perfectionism and Politics', *Ethics*, 111 (2000), pp. 37–63; Crocker, 'Foundations', especially pp. 178–196; and Clayton and Williams, 'Egalitarian Justice', pp. 453–456.

52 The price of this indeterminancy, at this stage, is that we do not get a clear sense of the kinds of inequalities above the threshold that our theory would find problematic.

53 Nussbaum, *Women and Human Development*, p. 77.

54 See Onora O'Neill's 'Justice, Capabilities and Vulnerabilities' in Nussbaum, in Glover (ed.), *Women, Capabilities, Development*, pp. 140–152.

55 'Capabilities theory would be a prescription for tyranny if it bypassed the nation' (*Women and Human Development*, p. 104). This must apply within multinational states as much as it does between them.

56 *Women and Human Development*, pp. 101–102.

57 This is discussed by Nussbaum, *Women and Human Development*, pp. 96–101; see the critical discussion of rights by Raymond Guess, *History and Illusion in Politics* (Cambridge, Cambridge University Press) pp. 138–152.

58 Bernard Williams, 'The Standard of Living: Interests and Capabilities', cited by Nussbaum, *Women and Human Development*, p. 98.

59 *Women and Human Development*, pp. 84–85.

60 Shapiro, *Democratic Justice*, p. 160.

61 The phrase is from Laden, *Reasonably Radical*, pp. 152–158. I am indebted to his discussion in general here.

62 Amartya Sen, 'The moral standing of markets', *Social Philosophy and Policy*, 2 (1985), p. 208.

63 There are liberal, republican, Hegelian and poststructuralist variations of this practice-dependent conception of freedom; see for example Joseph Raz, *The Morality of Freedom* (Oxford, Clarendon Press, 1986); Quentin Skinner, *Liberty before Liberalism* (Cambridge, Cambridge University Press, 1998); Frederick Neuhouser, *Foundations of Hegel's Social Theory; Actualizing Freedom* (Cambridge, Mass., Harvard University Press, 2000); Paul Patton, *Deleuze and the Political* (London, Routledge, 2000).

64 Rawls, *Political Liberalism*, p. 186; Shapiro, *Democratic Justice*, p. 85.

65 Notice how the capabilities approach provides significant critical bite for evaluating the real freedoms of contemporary indigenous peoples. In Australia, for example, the life expectancy of Aboriginal people is 20 years below that of non-Aborigines. Black death rates between the ages of 25 and 54 are five to eight times those of whites. Suicide rates among Aboriginal males in remote communities are almost five time higher than state-wide rates. Aboriginal women are 45 times more likely to experience violence than non-indigenous women, and ten times more likely to die as a result.

Indigenous children in Queensland (between 1999–2000) were nearly six times more likely than non-indigenous children to be under protective orders (because of neglect, or physical, emotional and sexual abuse). Figures are from *Cape York Justice Study* (Advance copy, available from http://www.premiers.qld.gov.au/about/community/studies.htm), Volume 1, pp. 9, 19–20.

66 For Rawls, once a society instantiates the two principles of justice, that is, when the material and social guarantees provided by them are publicly affirmed as expressing each citizen's understanding of the just terms of cooperation and hence as publicly affirming the worth of each other, it has done most of what is necessary to ensure the appropriate distribution of the social bases of self–respect. See *A Theory of Justice*, pp. 179, 440–441.

67 Shapiro, *Democratic Justice*, pp. 87–89. Aboriginal people who live in remote locations will probably enjoy lesser opportunities for greater economic participation than those closer to economic centres (due to the lack of access to labour markets, vocational training etc.), and as a result, may be more reliant upon state-provided benefits. It does not follow that they should be penalized for this by the withdrawal of benefits. In Australia, for example, social security arrangements have been modified to address these particular circumstances through 'Community Development Employment Projects', where unemployment benefits are tied to participation in community-run development projects, for which participants are paid a wage. There are now over 300 of these schemes in operation, with over 30,000 participants. See Will Sanders, *Unemployment payments, the activity test and Indigenous Australian: understanding breach rates* (Canberra, CAEPR Research Monograph no. 15, 2000) Note that 26 per cent of indigenous people in Australia live in 'remote' or 'highly remote' areas. However both urban and remote indigenous people suffer from high rates of unemployment compared with the non-indigenous population: *Commonwealth Grants Commission: Report on Indigenous Funding vol. 1* (Canberra, CanPrint Communications, 2001) Chapter 2, p. 8.

68 The conception of freedom underlying this discussion is generally a compatibilist one, accepting as it does the socialization of capacities thesis. But as T.M. Scanlon argues, to attribute moral responsibility to someone in the sense of their being open to moral criticism for their actions, is not the same thing as holding them responsible in the 'substantive' sense, i.e. that they are not entitled to any assistance in dealing with the problems that contributed to their actions. In other words, we should not rush to infer liability from culpability (as conservatives tend to do), nor claim that individuals are never really blameworthy (as some liberals tend to do). If someone is unemployable in part because of generally horrible treatment as a child, and as a result is undisciplined and unreliable, he can be properly criticized for his actions and attitudes, but 'he cannot simply be left to bear the consequences, since he has not had adequate opportunity to avoid being subject to them'. See the discussion in T. M. Scanlon, *What We Owe To Each Other* (Cambridge, Mass., Harvard University Press, 1998), pp. 250–294.

69 Sen, 'Gender Inequality', p. 267; *Inequality Reexamined*, passim.

70 The main reason for denying their sovereign interests was that European nations considered Aboriginal peoples racially and culturally inferior. That

justification no longer stands. If the claim is now that Aboriginal nations have been legitimately subsumed under the sovereignty of the existing nation state, then reasons have to be provided for this claim. An appeal to consent, as we have seen, is dubious. If the main justification is a pragmatic one – that acknowledging indigenous sovereignty undermines national unity or the territorial integrity of the state – then that claim is vulnerable to all kinds of normative and empirical rebuttals. For one thing, sovereignty itself is increasingly conceptualized (in both international law and political theory), in less absolutist terms and compatible with being distributed across multiple and discrete units of governance within a nation-state. See the lucid discussion in Macklem, *Indigenous Difference*, pp. 120–131, 288.

71  On the costs of inclusion more generally for non-state actors in liberal democracies, see the discussion in Dryzek, *Deliberative Democracy and Beyond*, pp. 81–114.

72  The phrase is from Tomasi, *Liberalism Beyond Justice* (Princeton, Princeton University Press, 2001), p. 33.

73  James Bohman, 'Deliberative Democracy and Effective Social Freedom', in James Bohman and William Rehg (eds), *Deliberative Democracy: Essays on Reason and Politics* (Cambridge, Mass., MIT Press, 1997), pp. 322–325.

74  Needless to say, there is no need for Aboriginal peoples to use this approach to justify their rights to themselves; they are justified according to their own self–understandings. But these internal reasons will have only limited purchase in practices of public reasoning with others. Hence the need for transitive arguments that link the distinctive historical and social bases of indigenous difference to normative claims in the public sphere that can become the object of collective will formation between both indigenous and non-indigenous peoples.

75  A valuable byproduct of this approach is that it minimizes the language of special measures, which tends to reinforce the sense of departures from a baseline of 'equal treatment = identical 'treatment' are in need of special justification.

76  Another way of putting this is to say it translates 'difference-blindness' into 'diversity awareness'; for this argument see James Tully, *Strange Multiplicity: constitutionalism in an age of diversity* (Cambridge, Cambridge University Press, 1995). Cf. Amy Gutmann's discussion of the relation between 'color consciousness' and a 'color-blind' principle of fairness in Amy Gutmann and K. Anthony Appiah, *Color Conscious: The Political Morality of Race* (Princeton, Princeton University Press, 1996), p. 174.

77  Tim Rowse, 'Indigenous citizenship: the politics of communal capacities', unpublished paper, p. 13.

78  Rowse, 'Indigenous citizenship', p. 14.

79  See Tim Rowse, 'Culturally appropriate Indigenous accountability', *American Behavioural Scientist*, 43 (2000), 1514–1532.

80  John Borrows, 'Domesticating Doctrines: Aboriginal Peoples after the Royal Commission', *McGill Law Journal*, 46, 3, (2001), 615–661; T. Alfred, *Peace, power, righteousness*; Menno Boldt and J. Anthony Long 'Tribal Traditions and European-Western Political Ideologies: The Dilemma of Canada's Native Indians', in Boldt and Long (eds), *The Quest for Justice: Aboriginal People and Aboriginal Rights* (Toronto, University of Toronto Press, 1985), p. 333; Sue Dodds and John Bern, 'On the Plurality of Interests: Aboriginal

Self–Government and Land Rights', in Ivison, Patton and Sanders (eds), *Political Theory and the Rights of Indigenous Peoples*; Povinelli, 'Settler Modernity'.

81  Borrows, 'Domesticating Doctrines', p. 618.

82  Borrows, 'Domesticating Doctrines', p. 660.

83  The problem of the comparative value of different capabilities and functionings afflicts the capabilities approach in general, as we shall see in Chapter 7.


## 7  Land, law and governance

1  *Mabo v the State of Queensland (No. 2) (1992), ALJR* 66, p. 416.

2  Brian Barry, *Culture & Equality: An Egalitarian Critique of Multiculturalism* (Cambridge, Polity Press, 2001), pp. 150–154.

3  Ayelet Shachar, *Multicultural Jurisdictions: Cultural Differences and Women's Rights* (Cambridge, Cambridge University Press, 2001), pp. 5, 70–71, 86–87. I am indebted to Shachar's valuable discussion here. A similar focus can also be found in the work of Joseph Carens, Patrick Macklem, James Tully and Anthony Laden.

4  See Jeremy Waldron, 'The logic of Cultural Accommodation', paper presented to the American Political Science Association Meeting, September 2001.

5  These refer to the arguments of Habermas, Laden, and Tully respectively.

6  See Shachar, *Multicultural Jurisdictions*: basic capabilities for her include: bodily integrity, access to education, vocational training, and control over some independent means of livelihood; see pp. 4–5, 20, 27–28, 112–130. The language of 'nomos' as applied to religious and cultural groups within the state has been made famous by Robert Cover, 'The Supreme Court 1982 Term, Forward: Nomos and Narrative', *Harvard Law Review*, 97 (1983), 4–68; I have made use of his work in 'Decolonizing the rule of law: Mabo's case and postcolonial constitutionalism', *Oxford Journal of Legal Studies*, 17 (1997), pp. 253–279.

7  *Multicultural Jurisdictions*, p. 119.

8  *Multicultural Jurisdictions*, p. 121.

9  On the importance of 'exit' as a tool of institutional design see the classic discussion in A. O. Hirschmann, *Exit, Voice and Loyalty: responses to decline in firms, organizations and states* (Cambridge, Mass., Harvard University Press, 1970); also Susan Mellor-Okin, 'Inequalities between the sexes in different cultural contexts', in Martha C. Nussbaum, Jonathan Glover (eds), *Women, Culture and Development* (Oxford, Oxford University Press, 1995), pp. 286–291; Shachar, *Multicultural Jurisdictions*, pp. 122–123; Barry, *Culture & Equality*, pp. 150–154; Tim Rowse, 'Culturally appropriate indigenous accountability', *American Behavioural Scientist* 43 (2000), 1514-1532.

10  *Multicultural Jurisdictions*, p. 122. Note that this entails establishing clear 'reversal points' through negotiation between the state and the group as a precondition for establishing a legitimate joint governance regime in the first place (p. 124).

198 Notes (pages 144-146)

11 See for example Amy Gutmann and Dennis Thompson, *Democracy and Disagreement*: (Cambridge, Mass., Harvard University Press, 1996). On the way in which preconditions for admissibility into public reason can change over time, see Rawls's discussion of the 'proviso' in the 'Ideal of Public Reason Re-visited', in Samuel Freeman (ed.), *John Rawls: Collected Papers* (Cambridge, Mass., Harvard University Press, 1999), pp. 591–594.

12 The phrase is from John Dryzek, *Deliberative Democracy and Beyond; Liberals, Critics, Contestations* (Oxford, Oxford University Press, 2000), pp. 45–46.

13 Charles Taylor, 'Shared and Divergent Values', in Ronald Watts and D. Brown (eds), *Options for a New Canada* (Toronto: University of Toronto Press, 1991), pp. 53–76.

14 Cass Sunstein, 'Incompletely Theorized Agreements', *Harvard Law Review*, 108 (1995), p. 1171.

15 Compare James Youngblood Henderson, 'The Doctrine of Aboriginal Rights in Western Legal Tradition', in Menno Boldt and J. Anthony Long (eds), *The Quest for Justice* (Toronto, University of Toronto Press, 1985), p. 220; Robert Williams, *The American Indian in Western Legal Thought* (Oxford: Oxford University Press, 1990); also Waldron, 'The Logic of Cultural Accommodation'.

16 Kent McNeil, *Common Law Aboriginal Title* (Oxford, Clarendon Press, 1989), pp. 110–116, 181–183.

17 Brian Slattery, 'Understanding Aboriginal Rights' *Canadian Bar Review*, 66 (1987), 737–738; 'Aboriginal Sovereignty and Imperial Claims' *Osgoode Hall Law Journal*, 29 (1991), 681–703; McNeil, *Common Law Aboriginal Title*, passim; Henry Reynolds, *The Law of the Land* (Ringwood, Penguin, 1992); John Hookey, 'Settlement and Sovereignty', in Peter Hanks and Bryan Keon-Cohen (eds), *Aborigines and the Law* (Sydney, Allen & Unwin, 1984), pp. 1–18; Peter Kulchyski (ed.), *Unjust Relations: Aboriginal Rights in Canadian Courts* (Toronto, Oxford University Press, 1994); James Tully, 'Aboriginal Property and Western Theory: Recovering the Middle Ground', *Social Philosophy and Policy*, 11 (1994), 153–180.

18 See Tully, 'Aboriginal Property', p. 172.

19 Slattery, 'Understanding Aboriginal Rights', p. 738.

20 Jacob Levy, 'Three modes of Incorporating Indigenous Law', in Will Kymlicka and Wayne Norman (eds), *Citizenship in Diverse Societies* (Oxford, Oxford University Press, 2000). Although I take a different line on some of these issues to Levy, I am still indebted to his discussion.

21 Levy, 'Three modes', pp. 319–320, 322.

22 *Mabo v State of Queensland [No. 2]* (1992) *ALJR* 66, p. 408. Page references are to the *ALJR*. There is now a massive literature originating in Australia on this case and its consequences. Some helpful collections of essays include; M. A. Stephenson and Suri Ratnapala (eds) *Mabo: A Judicial Revolution?* (St Lucia, University of Queensland Press, 1993); Murray Goot and Tim Rowse (eds), *Make a Better Offer: The Politics of Mabo* (Sydney, Pluto Press, 1994); Will Sanders (ed.), *Mabo and Native Title: Origins and Institutional Implications* (Canberra, CAEPR, 1994); Bain Attwood (ed.), *In the Age of Mabo: History, Aborigines and Australia* (Sydney, Allen & Unwin, 1996). Some helpful recent book-length treatments include Tim Rowse,

*After Mabo: Interpreting Indigenous Traditions* (Melbourne, Melbourne University Press, 1993); H. C. Coombs, *Aboriginal Autonomy* (Melbourne, Cambridge University Press, 1994); Frank Brennan, *One land, one nation* (St Lucia, University of Queensland Press, 1995).

23  *Mabo*, p. 429.The claimant will have to show that at the time of settlement, and still today, they are not only an 'identifiable community' but that they have (according to their laws and customs) a 'traditional connection' with the land 'currently acknowledged and observed'; *Mabo*, pp. 430–431. For a discussion of the difficulties this presents, with reference to a particular claim, see Francesca Merlan, 'The Regimentation of Customary Practice: From Northern Territory Land Claims to Mabo', *The Australian Journal of Anthropology*, 6 (1995), 64–82.

24  Noel Pearson, 'The concept of native title at common law', in G.Yunupingu (ed.), *Our Land is Our Life: Land Rights – Past, Present and Future* (St. Lucia, Queensland University Press, 1997), pp. 150–162.

25  See the discussion in Levy, 'Three modes of incorporating indigenous law', passim; and Tully, 'Aboriginal property'.

26  *Mabo*, pp. 408, 432.

27  *The Racial Discrimination Act (Cth)* was passed in 1975, prior to which there was no legal provision for protection from racial discrimination (Australia does not have a Bill of Rights).The Act was basically intended to give effect to the International Convention on the Elimination of All Forms of Racial Discrimination. This turned out to be 'critical to the actions brought to assert native title at common law' by Eddie Mabo; see Richard Bartlett, *Native Title in Australia* (Sydney, Butterworths, 2000), p. 16.

28  These might include, grants in fee simple, long-term residential leases, or public roadways. Pastoral leases are a special case, because of their unique terms, to be discussed below. Similarly, Crown reserves such as national parks or Aboriginal reserves, would only extinguish native title if the use of the lands was inconsistent with the enjoyment of native title.This means that as of 31 October 1975, when the *Racial Discrimination Act* came into place, native title could only be extinguished if a process 'which accorded equality before the law'had been followed; i.e which involved consultation with the native title holders, including potential compensation. At least, that was the idea in theory. See Bartlett, *Native Title in Australia*, p. 31; and Noel Pearson, '204 Years of Invisible Title', in Stephenson and Ratnapala, *Mabo: A Judicial Revolution?*, pp. 83–87.

29  Bartlett, *Native Title in Australia*, p. 31. For examples of the kind of response referred to above, see pp. 38–39.

30  *Wik Peoples v Queensland* (1996) 187 *CLR* 1: 141.

31  Bartlett, *Native Title in Australia*, p. 46; see also pp. 185–186.

32  *Wik*, p. 250.Thus I demur at Levy's suggestion that in 'the native title law established by Mabo ... customary usage and customary relationships reign almost supreme'. (Levy, 'After Mabo', p. 44). As mentioned above, the *Native Title Act* back-validated grants that came into effect even after the *Racial Discrimination Act*, thereby legitimating dispossession and overriding customary relationships, not installing them as supreme. There are numerous other examples from the Act, to do, for example, with the limitation of rights to negotiate over water-based resources, that show a similar disregard for customary usage and relationships.

33  The right to negotiate survived only for mining and compulsory acquisition. States now merely had to give 'notice' before granting licenses and authorities affecting native title, although failure to notify has no effect on their validity. Bartlett provides a comprehensive summary of the legislative and political response to *Wik* in Chapters 3–5 of *Native Title in Australia*.

34  In David Marr, 'Mad about the buoy', Good Weekend Magazine, *Sydney Morning Herald*, 18 August, 2001 p. 19.

35  *Native Title Amendment Bill 1997, Explanatory Memorandum*, 1996–97–98, para 18.27, cited in Bartlett, *Native Title in Australia*, pp. 53, 353.

36  For this argument see Jacob Levy, 'After Mabo: Review of Mabo. The Native Title Legislation', *Policy* (Winter 1996), 41–44; and 'Three modes', especially pp. 320–325.

37  Jeremy Webber, 'Beyond Regret', in Duncan Ivison, Paul Patton and Will Sanders (eds), *Political Theory and the Rights of Indigenous Peoples* (Cambridge, Cambridge University Press, 2000) p. 61.

38  And there may be strategic reasons for focusing on land rights rather than sovereignty issues, as least in the short term. See Noel Pearson, 'To be or not to be – separate Aboriginal nationhood or Aboriginal self-determination and self-government within the Australian nation?', *Aboriginal Law Bulletin*, 3 (1993), p. 16.

39  As Kent McNeil points out, if the 'proprietary community title 'ascribed to the Meriam people could co-exist with 'individual non-proprietary [or proprietary] rights that are derived from the community's laws and customs and are dependent on the community title', then 'this presupposes the existence of community authority that must be governmental in nature ... While their communal title obviously has a proprietary aspect, it also has social, cultural and political dimensions that are beyond the scope of standard conceptions of private property'. See McNeil, 'Self-Government and the Inalienability of Aboriginal Title', unpublished paper. For a discussion of just these kinds of variations in specific Aboriginal communities in Australia, see Peter Sutton, 'The robustness of Aboriginal land tenure systems: underlying and proximate customary titles', *Oceania*, 67, 1 (1996), 7–29, especially at p. 11. On the difficulties Aboriginal groups face in exercising these internal powers, including challenges posed by the modes of incorporation available to them for doing so, see Patrick Sullivan, 'Dealing with native title conflicts by recognizing Aboriginal authority systems', in *Fighting Over Country: Anthropological Perspectives* (Canberra, Centre for Aboriginal Economic Policy Research , 1997), pp. 129–140.

40  Note that the High Court in *Mabo* did not challenge the sovereignty of Australia as a settled territory, but whether or not native title was part of the common law of a settled territory like Australia. In subsequent decisions the Court has backed even further away from the sovereignty issue. See *Dennis Walker vs NSW (1994)* 126 *ALR* 321 at 322–323. A summary discussion of the case can be found in the *Aboriginal Law Bulletin*, 3 (1995), 39–41; also *Coe v Commonwealth (1993)* 118 *ALR* 193 at 200; *Isabel Coe on Behalf of the Wiradjuri Tribe v The Commonwealth of Australia and the State of New South Wales (1993)* 118 *ALR*, 193.

41  Webber, 'Beyond Regret', pp. 70, 73–74.

42  See Patrick Macklem, *Indigenous Difference and the Constitution of Canada* (Toronto, University of Toronto Press, 2001) pp. 103–104; also McNeil,

'Self-Government and the Inalienability of Aboriginal Title'; and Webber, 'Beyond Regret', pp. 70–71.

43  See for example, *The Report of the Royal Commission on Aboriginal Peoples:Vol 2: Restructuring the Relationship*, (Ottowa, Ministry of Supply and Services, 1996) pp. 448–464; also Yunupingu (ed), *Our Land is Our Life*.

44  For an example of such an agreement, see the Cape York 'Heads of Agreement' on future land use on Cape York Peninsula, February 1996.

45  Rowse, 'Culturally appropriate indigenous accountability'; Sullivan, 'Dealing with native title conflicts'.

46  Webber, 'Beyond Regret', p. 66; Macklem, *Indigenous Difference*, pp. 198–199.

47  The phrase is adapted from Tully, 'Aboriginal property', though he should not be held responsible for how I use it here. A similar point is made by Slattery, 'Understanding Aboriginal Rights', pp. 700–703.

48  There are conflicting views over the extent to which the Crown actually recognized an equal Aboriginal sovereignty in the Royal Proclamation, however much it is clear that certain rights to land were recognized.Tully thinks the Crown was not exerting sovereignty over Indian territories and recognized Aboriginal nations as equals, though mainly for strategic reasons ('Aboriginal property', pp. 170–171, 174–175); compare Patrick Macklem (who argues the opposite) in 'First Nations Self-government and the Borders of the Canadian Legal Imagination', *McGill Law Journal*, 36 (1991), 414–415.

49  Stephen Cornell and Joseph P. Kalt, 'Sovereignty and Nation-Building:The Development Challenge in Indian Country Today', *Harvard Project on American Indian Economic Development, Project Report 98-25* (1998), p. 29.

50  'Sovereignty and Nation-Building', pp. 29–30.

51  Self-government mechanisms can help improve the representativeness of the overall political system, but the issue is complex. It might lead to representation on bodies that interpret or modify the division of powers, such as the Supreme Court or land claims courts.But it might also follow that representation in federal legislative bodies may be reduced, as more powers are gradually asserted by self-governing communities. But since there will be considerable numbers of indigenous people not living in self-governing communities – in urban areas for example – the ideal of complex mutual coexistence suggests some mixture of group representative and self-government measures will be required. For more discussion see Will Kymlicka, *Finding Our Way: Rethinking Ethnocultural Relations in Canada* (Don Mills, Oxford University Press, 1998), pp. 109–114; *Report of the Royal Commission on Aboriginal Peoples Vol 2: Restructuring the Relationship*, Chapter 3; Borrows, 'Landed Citizenship', in Kymlicka and Norman (eds), *Citizenship in Diverse Societies*, pp. 331–339.

52  *Bedard v. Isaac* [1972] 2 *O.R.* 391 (Ont. H.C.); *Isaac v. Bedard* [1974] *SCR*. 1349. See also: *Santa Clara Pueblo v Martinez*, 436 US 49 (1978); compare *Canada (AG) v Lavell* [1974] *SCR* 1349. See more generally, Sally Weaver, 'First Nations Women and Government Policy 1970–92: Discrimination and Conflict', in *Changing Patterns: Women in Canada*, 2nd edition, ed. Sandra Burt, Lorraine Code and Lindsay Dorney (Toronto, McClelland and Stewart, 1993).

53  See *Cape York Justice Report*; also *The Aboriginal and Torres Strait Islander Women's Task Force on Violence Report* (The State of Queensland, 1999).

54  See *The Indian Civil Rights Act*. The US Supreme Court has usually allowed tribal courts to enforce the Act, with some exceptions. The history of the emergence of this Act is instructive, however; see the discussion in Frank Pommersheim, 'The Crucible of Sovereignty: Analyzing Issues of Tribal Jurisprudence', *Arizona Law Review*, 31 (1989), p. 361. Tribes, of course, remain subject to the supreme plenary power of Congress.

55  Section 15 of the *Canadian Charter of Rights and Freedoms* provides for the equal protection before and under the law and equal protection and bene-fit of the law, thus expressing a commitment both to the equal worth and dignity of all persons, and to rectifying and preventing discrimination against particular groups suffering social, political and legal disadvantage. See Macklem, *Indigenous Difference*, pp. 210–211.

56  Sub-section 35 (4) also provides that 'Aboriginal and Treaty rights are guar-anteed equally to male and female persons'. Note also that section 25 of the Charter provides that the rights and freedoms therein 'shall not be con-strued so as to abrogate or derogate from any Aboriginal, treaty or other rights or freedoms that pertain to the Aboriginal peoples of Canada'. As one can see, these different normative emphases often pull claimants and the Court in different directions. But that is as it should be in a complex multi-national context.

57  Mary Ellen Turpel, 'Aboriginal Peoples and the Canadian Charter: Interpretive Monopolies, Cultural Differences', *Canadian Human Rights Yearbook*, 3 (1989–90), p. 30; Peter Hogg and Mary Ellen Turpel, 'Implementing Aboriginal Self-Government: Constitutional and Jurisdictional Issues, *The Canadian Bar Review*, 74 (1995), especially Section IX. For a summary of some of these issues see the *Report of the Royal Commission on Aboriginal Peoples vol 2: Restructuring the Relationship*, Chapter 3, section 2.3. Note also that the *Draft Declaration on the Rights of Indigenous Peoples*, Part IX, Article 42 states that 'all the rights and freedoms recognized herein are equally guaranteed to male and female indigenous individuals'. For a draft version of the declaration see the *United Nations Commission on Human Rights*, E/CN.4/Sub.2/1993/29Annex 1.

58  See John Borrows, 'Contemporary, Traditional Equality: The Effect of the Charter on First Nation Politics', in David Schneiderman and Kate Sutherland (eds), *Charting the Consequences: The Impact of Charter Rights on Canadian Law and Politics* (Toronto, University of Toronto Press, 1997), pp. 169–199; T. Issac and M. S. Maloughney, 'Dually Disadvantaged and Historically Forgotten? Aboriginal Women and the Inherent Right of Aboriginal Self-government', *Manitoba Law Journal*, 21 (1992), 453; com-pare M. E. Turpel, 'Patriarchy and Paternalism: The Legacy of the Canadian State for First Nations Women', *Canadian Journal of Women and the Law*, 6 (1993), 174; also *Report of the Royal Commission on Aboriginal Peoples vol 4: Perspectives and Realities*, Chapter 2.

59  See, for example, Macklem, *Indigenous Difference*, Chapter 7 passim.

60  For a discussion of the constitutional, legal and statutory position of indige-nous people in Australia since Federation, and the particular kinds of obsta-cles thrown up by the Australian Constitution, see John Chesterman and

Brian Galligan, *Citizens Without Rights: Aborigines and Australian Citizenship* (Cambridge, Cambridge University Press, 1997).

61  Macklem, *Indigenous Difference*, p. 231.

62  See the *Report of the Royal Commission on Aboriginal Peoples vol 4: Perspectives and Realities*, Chapter 2, sec 3.3, on the obstacles faced by indigenous women in Canada in receiving equitable treatment from both Band Councils and the Federal Government, in many cases to do with discriminatory elements of the *Indian Act*. The Royal Commission recommends that new membership criteria be developed which abandon the categories imposed by the *Indian Act*, and that foster 'inclusion' and 'nurture nation building'.

63  See the case-study presented by Deborah Bird Rose, *Dingo Makes us Human* (Cambridge: Cambridge University Press, 1992), pp. 153–164.

64  For more extensive consideration of this issue in the Canadian context see *Bridging the Cultural Divide: Report on Aboriginal People and Criminal Justice in Canada* (Ottawa, Ministry of Supply and Services, 1996). For Maori claims for a separate system in New Zealand, see Moana Jackson, *The Maori and the Criminal Justice System; A New Perspective/He Whaipaanga Hou* (2 parts, Wellington, 1987–1988); the most extensive discussion in Australia is still the Australian Law Reform Commission's 1986 study, *The Recognition of Aboriginal Customary Law* (Canberra, Australian Government Printing Service, 1986).

65  *Royal Commission into Aboriginal Deaths in Custody* (5 vols, Canberra, Australian Government Publishing Service, 1991).

66  Peter Sutton, 'The Politics of Suffering: Indigenous Policy in Australia since the Seventies', *Anthropological Forum*, 11, 2 (2001), 125–173; David Martin, 'Is welfare dependency "welfare poison"? An assessment of Noel Pearson's proposals for Aboriginal welfare reform', *Centre for Aboriginal Economic Policy Research, Discussion Paper No. 213* (Canberra, 2001).

67  *The Recognition of Aboriginal Customary Laws*, p. 287. See K. Maddock, 'Two Laws in One Community', in R. M. Berndt (ed.), *Aborigines and Change* (Canberra, AIAS, 1977); N. Williams, *Two Laws: managing disputes in a contemporary Aboriginal community* (Canberra, Australian Institute of Aboriginal Studies, 1987); *Three Years On* (Canberra: Commonwealth of Australia, 1995), pp. 148–178.

68  See *Royal Commission into Aboriginal Deaths in Custody*, vol. 4, p. 101; Jenny Blokland, 'Minor: Case and Comment', *Criminal Law Journal*, 16 (1992), 363–364.

69  *The Recognition of Aboriginal Customary Law*, pp. 364–368, 372–373; and detailed case-studies at pp. 351–359; see the interviews with Aboriginal Legal Aid lawyers in Jon Faine, *Lawyers in the Alice: Aboriginals and Whitefellas' Law* (Sydney, Federation Press, 1993); and the excellent discussion and detailed case-studies in Nanette Rogers, 'Aboriginal Law and Sentencing in the Northern Territory Supreme Court, Alice Spring 1986–1995', unpublished PhD thesis, Faculty of Law, University of Sydney, 1998.

70  See Rogers, *Aboriginal Law and Sentencing*, Chapter 4. The Law Reform Commission made specific recommendations to do with the submission and evaluation of evidence and sentencing guidelines, the bulk of which have never been systematically implemented.

71  See *Mamarika v The Queen (1982)* 42 *ALR* 94. The practice of Australian police and prosecution services has been to take into consideration the voluntary nature of these punishments when deciding whether prosecution is warranted – and prosecution has, in fact, been extremely rare; see *The Recognition of Aboriginal Customary Law*, p. 364.

72  See the discussion in the *Report of the Royal Commission on Aboriginal Peoples, vol 2: Restructuring the Relationship*, Chapter 3.

73  See the Yirrkala proposals, discussed in *The Recognition of Aboriginal Customary Law*, p. 377; Coombs, *Aboriginal Autonomy*, pp. 118–130; on the use of re–integrative shaming in contemporary criminology, see John Braithwaite, *Crime, Shame and Reintegration* (Cambridge, Cambridge University Press, 1989).

74  Noel Pearson, 'On the Human Right to Misery, Mass Incarceration and Early Death', *Dr Charles Perkins Memorial Oration*, delivered at the University of Sydney 25 October 2001; more generally *Our Right to Take Responsibility* (Cairns, Noel Pearson and Associates, 2000). See also Marcia Langton et al, 'Too Much Sorry Business – The Report of the Aboriginal Issues Unit of the Northern Territory', in *Towards Reconciliation, Royal Commission on Aboriginal Deaths in Custody*, vol 5, Appendix D (I) part G; Peter Sutton, 'The Politics of Suffering: Indigenous Policy in Australia since the Seventies'.

75  Noel Pearson, 'Passive welfare and the destruction of Indigenous society in Australia', in P. Saunders (ed.), *Reforming the Welfare State* (Melbourne, Australian Institute of Family Studies, 2000), pp. 136–155, especially at pp. 153–154.

76  See A. Daly and D. Smith, 'The role of welfare in the economy of two indigenous communities', *Australian Economic Review*, 33 (2000), 363–368; D. F. Martin, 'Is welfare dependency "welfare poison"?' For a general critique of the welfare dependency arguments that have become prevalent not just in Australia, but in the western liberal democratic world in general in recent years, see Robert Goodin, 'Social Welfare as a collective social responsibility', in D. Schmidtz and Robert E. Goodin, *Social Welfare and Individual Responsibility* (New York, Cambridge University Press, 1998), pp. 97–194.

77  See for example 'Laws are broken to make a future', *Sydney Morning Herald*, Monday 10 December, 2001, p. 9. The article describes how one Aboriginal community used and adapted aspects of their indigenous laws and customs to make them more relevant to helping discipline and treat young people addicted to petrol sniffing.

78  Martin, 'Is welfare dependency "welfare poison"?', p. 13; Sutton, 'The Politics of Suffering', passim.

79  See, for example, the discussion of the *Report of the Royal Commission on Aboriginal Peoples, vol 4: Perspective and Realities*, Chapter 7: 'Urban Perspectives'; and, in Australia, the *Commonwealth Grants Commission: Report on Indigenous Funding* (Canberra, CanPrint Communication, 2001), especially Chapter 4. Note that only 44 per cent of the indigenous population in Australia live in areas that are 'physically highly accessible' to government services (26 per cent live in remote or highly remote areas, the rest in urban or semi-urban areas, many of which are poorly serviced).

80  Consider the different models of Aboriginal government discussed in the *Report of the Royal Commission on Aboriginal Peoples, vol. 2: Restructuring the Relationship* Chapter 3, sec 3.1.

## Conclusion

1  John Borrows, 'Landed Citizenship', in Will Kymlicka and Wayne Norman (eds), *Citizenship in Diverse Societies* (Oxford, Oxford University Press, 1999), pp. 332–333.
2  See, for example, Brendan Edgeworth, 'Tenure, Allodialism, and Indigenous Rights at Common Law: English, United States and Australian Land Law Compared after Mabo v Queensland', *Anglo-American Law Review*, 23 (1994), 397–434.
3  On the 'common-law doctrine of Aboriginal rights', see *The Report of the Royal Commission on Aboriginal Peoples vol. 2: Reconstructing the Relationship*, sec. 2.3. On the history of rights discourse more generally see Richard Tuck, *Natural Rights Theories: Their Origin and Development* (Cambridge, Cambridge University Press, 1981); Raymond Geuss, *History and Illusion in Politics* (Cambridge, Cambridge University Press, 2001).
4  The establishment of the public government of Nunavut, in the eastern half of Northern Canada, is an exception to this.
5  Compare David Miller, 'Multicultural Justice', paper presented at the Morrell Conference, University of York, September 2001; Wayne Norman, 'The Ideology of Shared Values: A Myopic Vision of Unity in the Multi-Nation State', in Joseph Carens, *Is Quebec Nationalism Just? Perspectives from Anglophone Canada* (Montreal, McGill-Queens University Press, 1995), pp. 137–159.
6  This is not an original argument; it has been appealed to by Charles Taylor, Will Kymlicka, Jeremy Webber and James Tully, amongst others.
7  See Tully, 'Struggles over Recognition and Distribution', *Constellations* 7, 4 (2000), p. 480.

# Index

Aboriginal
  Charter of Rights, 154
  claims, 4, 59, 82, 90, 108
  communities, 66, 152, 155, 156, 159
  concepts, 163
  constitutional interests, 81
  criminal justice, 156
  culture, 67
  government, 153, 154
  groups, 68
  interests, 11, 112, 125, 133, 135–8,
    147, 151–2, 153, 155, 157–8
  land, 11, 15, 21, 22, 24, 25, 26, 95
  land rights, 15
  law, 1, 145–60
  nation, 4, 58, 128, 151, 196
  peoples, 2, 15, 34, 55, 56, 57, 58, 59,
    60, 62, 65, 67, 72, 82, 90, 112,
    113, 115, 116, 117, 120, 133,
    134, 136, 137, 138, 145, 151,
    163, 167, 196
  philosophies, 163
  practices, 44, 138, 158
  rights, 2, 3, 4, 10, 11, 12, 26–9, 34, 44,
    68, 69, 81, 92, 93, 112–39, 140,
    147, 153–60, 163, 165
  self-government, 22, 26, 27, 34, 112,
    113, 124, 125, 127, 135, 136, 138
  societies, 145, 154
  sovereignty, 113, 196
  title, 140, 149–50; see also Native Title
    treaties, 58; see also treaty
  women, 154, 155, 157–8, 194–5
  see also Indigenous
abstract rationalism
  and liberalism, 9, 47, 49, 54, 58
accommodation, 28, 38, 42, 67, 68, 69,
    70, 71, 72, 84, 93, 120, 128,
    151, 155, 157, 160–1, 166
  'transformative', 143, 157
  see also cultural accommodation
affect, 9, 21, 47, 73, 88–91
affective conditions, 47
affective frameworks, 47
  dimensions, 47, 89, 101, 103, 109
  relations with others, 90, 105, 108
  registers, 91
agency, 41, 52, 104
  collective, 29, 96, 104
  human, 96

  moral, 106
alcohol, 158, 159
  abuse, 153, 159, 160
  related violence, 153
Alfred, Taiaiake, 3, 4, 164
anthropology, 39, 175
anti-discrimination, 60
apology, for stolen generations, 188;
  for historical injustices, 189
Armitage, David, 34
assimilation, 15, 67, 98, 117, 125, 127, 136
association, 6, 16, 25, 27, 48, 50, 55, 56, 62,
    72, 79, 92, 100, 136, 140, 161, 164
  freedom of, 27, 45, 59, 60, 62, 66,
    72, 126
Australia, 1, 2, 57, 58, 60, 62, 93, 96, 100,
    107, 109, 113, 114, 127, 145, 146,
    147, 150, 151, 154, 158–9, 163,
    164, 165, 188, 194, 195
  colonialism, 58
  colonization, 15, 153
  constitution, 154, 203
  government, 148, 150, 159, 168, 188
  history, 15, 58, 150, 153
  history of treaty-making in, 150, 168,
    180
  law, 108, 109, 155–7
  sovereignty, 145, 151
authority, 21, 127, 143, 150, 154–6, 157,
    160, 161
autonomy, 6, 23, 32, 54, 57, 66, 119, 145
  Aboriginal, 3
  cultural, 114, 141
  individual, 119
  liberal, 23, 32


Barry, Brian, 60, 75, 87–8, 170, 173
bargaining, 57, 78–80, 91, 92, 93
becoming,
  politics of, 46–7, 89, 90, 110
belonging, 8, 13, 36, 41, 103–107, 109, 143
Bhabha, Homi, 37, 41–3
blood quantum, 183
Borrows, John, 136–7
boundaries, 21, 25, 42, 50, 55–7, 68, 97,
    137, 181
Britain, 42
British Empire, 34, 178
Butler, Judith, 46

Canada, 2, 4, 15, 57, 58, 82, 93, 96, 100, 109, 112, 145, 151, 153, 163, 164, 165, 183, 202, 203, 205
  constitution, 151, 153, 154
  First Nations, 167
  Supreme Court in, 202
capabilities, 11, 18, 69, 112, 120, 122, 123, 140, 141, 142, 143, 146, 152, 153, 154, 155, 157, 160, 161, 164
  approach to justice, 122, 123, 128–37, 138
capability set, 11, 129, 134
  Aboriginal rights understood as, 135
capacities, 6, 10, 11, 12, 29, 37, 45, 63, 70, 104, 108, 109, 119–24, 129, 131, 135, 137
  and rights, 130–1
  socialization of, 121, 126, 131–2
capitalism, 25
Carens, Joseph, 67, 117, 169
Chakrabarty, Dipesh, 40–1, 43
*Charter of Rights and Freedoms* (Canada), 153, 154, 202
churches, 59, 180
'circumstances of politics', *see* Waldron, Jeremy
citizens, 6, 7, 8, 11, 13, 15, 16, 18, 19, 20, 41, 43, 51, 57, 67, 69, 70, 75, 77–9, 80, 83, 86, 87, 88, 93, 96, 97, 101, 104, 105, 106, 109, 113, 114, 117, 118, 119, 121, 130, 132, 141, 142, 144, 143, 155, 165, 166
citizenship, 1, 27, 38, 41, 43, 69, 79, 92, 96, 97, 103–4, 106, 126, 142, 144, 146, 152, 163
  Aboriginal, 141
  differentiated, 67, 120
  indigenous, 164
  liberal, 41, 43, 79, 144
  rights, 23, 92, 98, 103, 138, 146
civic friendship: *see* Gauthier, David
civic equality: *see* equality
civil
  rights, 44, 51, 59, 60–1, 124
  society, 17, 28, 35, 43, 51, 70, 107
civilization, 19, 25, 34, 35
collective action, 86, 90, 103
collective responsibility: *see* responsibility
collective rights: *see* rights
colonial
  control, 43, 154
  domination, 10, 95, 98
  expansion, 34
  governmentality, 41, 45
  history, 5, 58
  states, 26, 100
colonialism, 5, 9, 22, 24, 26, 28, 34, 39, 40, 43, 44, 45, 48, 159, 172
  and liberalism, 30–48, 71
common law: *see* law
common law doctrine of Aboriginal rights: *see* Aboriginal rights

communitarian, 49, 53–4, 103
  political thought, 49
communitarianism, 9, 71, 84
community, 3, 9, 18, 24, 37, 40, 42–3, 44, 49, 59, 60, 62, 63, 86, 141, 152, 155, 157, 159, 160
  cultural, 42, 68, 106–7
  political, 15, 18, 28, 63, 85, 92, 96–109, 128
compensation, 27, 28, 64, 65, 99–101, 112, 147, 148, 155, 199
complex mutual coexistence,
  ideal of, 2, 113, 129, 138, 140, 150, 154, 164, 201
conflict, 8, 9, 10, 12, 15, 32, 43, 46, 61, 65, 72–3, 84, 92–4, 117, 119, 138, 140, 141, 145, 148, 152, 153, 154, 155, 187, 190
Connolly, William E., 21, 46–7, 86, 90, 91, 110, 171
consent, 18–20, 54–5, 61, 73, 82–3, 110, 115, 147, 196
consensus, 10, 23, 28, 86, 88, 92, 73–6, 77, 95, 96, 105, 151
  overlapping, 21, 77, 80, 87, 130, 185
constitution, 3, 7, 75, 77–8, 79
constitutional essentials, 21, 73, 75–6, 79, 81, 87, 93, 107, 138, 140; *see also* Rawls, John
constitutional structures,
  intersocietal character of, 151
context, 3, 9–10, 15, 21, 22, 23, 28, 32, 33, 37, 44, 47, 50, 53, 55, 57, 71, 73, 76, 82, 83, 85, 90, 98, 103, 107, 109, 110, 117, 124, 129, 131, 138, 152, 153, 161, 163
  for choice, 8, 64–6; *see also* Kymlicka, Will
contextual approach
  to political theory, 12, 68, 117, 169
  to public reason, 7
conventions, 50, 82, 83, 84, 186
  constitutional, 81–2
Copp, David
  on political division, 9, 56
cosmopolitanism, 5
courts, 49, 153, 156, 161, 201–2
Cover, Robert, 197
criminal justice, 155–6
cultural
  appropriateness, 136, 154, 161
  associations, 27, 68, 79
  belonging, 4, 8
  contexts, 7, 8, 11, 47, 50, 53–5, 98, 107
  difference, 15, 28, 36, 44, 60, 61, 75, 93, 114, 117, 136
  disadvantage, 101
  discrimination, 31, 33
  diversity, 2, 22, 28, 61, 62–4, 142
  exemptions, 140
  frameworks, 23, 27, 29, 36–7, 53, 57, 62, 63, 65, 67

cultural (*contd.*)
    groups, 26, 30, 38, 39, 61, 66, 68, 72,
        81, 120, 143, 145, 163
    identity, 10, 42, 86, 135, 172
    membership, 8, 38, 61–2, 64, 66, 67,
        68
    minorities, 9–10, 42, 57, 60, 81
    pluralism, 5, 61, 86
    practices, 16, 37, 39, 57, 116, 124,
        125, 127, 136, 138, 152, 157, 158,
        163, 166
    recognition, 44
    rights, 5, 39, 58, 59, 67, 68, 113
cultural accommodation,
    core-periphery model of, 12, 141–2,
        144, 153
    deliberative model of, 12, 141–2, 144,
        153
    institutional design model of, 12,
        143–4, 197
'culturalist' argument
    for Aboriginal rights, 124–5, 127
culture, 15, 20, 21–2, 25, 51, 52, 56, 59, 61,
        62, 63, 64, 67, 69, 81, 88, 96, 98, 101,
        103, 106, 108, 116, 124–5, 126, 127,
        131, 135, 138, 140, 145, 152, 153, 160,
        164, 166
    defined, 35–9
    Geertz's account of, 36–7
    as Janus-faced, 39
    societal, 64–8, 124
    right to, 44–5
    customary law, 64, 146; *see also*
        Aboriginal law

democracy, 1, 6, 11, 19, 69, 74, 75, 95, 118
    aggregative, 51
    deliberative, 5, 18, 21, 92, 144
    discursive, 184
    liberal, 58, 70–71
democratic
    citizenship, 69
    deliberation, 109, 163
    dialogue, 130
    freedom, 142
    institutions, 75, 96, 123
    liberal, 5, 30, 96, 133, 137, 141, 144,
        145, 150, 152, 204
    politics, 45–6
    procedures, 23, 124
    states, 11, 12, 15, 59, 137
    theory, 25, 74, 172
dialogue, 72, 75, 81, 83, 88, 89, 143, 163
    cross-cultural, 61, 63
difference, 8, 19, 30, 32, 35, 40, 41–2, 46,
        48, 52, 63, 64, 68, 69, 74, 83, 86, 88, 89,
        90, 109, 110, 136
    arguments for Aboriginal rights, 26,
        27–9
    between Australia and Canada, 58
    -blind arguments for equality, 119,
        120, 136, 196

cultural, 15, 28, 35, 44, 47, 61, 93,
        114, 119
    and identity, 69, 83, 86, 105
    recognition of, 61
disagreement, 3, 6, 10, 11, 18, 21, 23, 32,
        54, 71, 72–94, 95, 96, 99, 108, 109,
        110–111, 113, 118, 148, 165, 166, 180
    reasonable, 31–2, 113
discourse, 73, 85, 86, 89, 91, 93, 96, 97,
        164, 165
    constellations of, 85, 91, 111; *see also*
        Dryzek, John
discovery
    doctrine of, 24
discrimination, 27, 31, 33, 202
dispossession, 25–26, 28, 100, 112, 147, 159,
        199
diversity: *see cultural diversity*
diversity awareness, 83, 166, 196
diversity attachment, 166
domination, 11, 12, 23, 24, 38, 40, 44, 54,
        65, 66, 69, 70, 109, 113, 119, 147, 161
    colonial, 10, 34, 95, 98
    defined, 169
*Draft Declaration of the Rights of Indigenous
    Peoples* (UN), 2
drug abuse, 158, 159, 160
Dryzek, John, 91, 111, 144, 184, 196, 198
Dworkin, Ronald
    on equality of resources, 120–2, 124,
        126
economic
    base for Aboriginal communities, 159
    development, 148, 152
    disadvantage, 30, 81, 107, 120, 146,
        152
    inequality, 20, 148
    liberalism not the same as political, 31
    relations between indigenous peoples
        and European settlers, 25, 173
    rights, 69, 130
effective social freedom, 11, 135, 138, 152;
    *see also* freedom
egalitarian
    objections to Aboriginal peoples'
        claims, 115; *see also equality*
egalitarianism, 117, 125
equal citizenship: see *citizenship*
equal opportunity, 1, 55, 121
equal respect, 27, 28, 31, 32, 73, 77, 78, 85,
        87–8, 113, 114, 117–19
equal treatment, 60, 114, 119, 120, 196
equality, 6, 10, 16, 19, 26, 27, 28, 29, 30, 31,
        32, 52, 58, 75, 78, 79, 88, 89, 90, 95, 98,
        107, 114, 116, 117–38, 140, 141, 146,
        149, 160, 164, 165
    argument for Aboriginal rights, 26–9,
        112–39; *see also* Aboriginal rights
    before the law, 146, 199
    and the capabilities approach, 122–4,
        128–39
    civic, 117–8

liberal, 114, 119, 120, 124, 129, 135–6
  and postcolonial liberalism, 30, 58,
    89–90, 95, 120
  and the postcolonial state, 117–38
  in Rawls, 120, 128
  of resources, 120, 124–39
  of welfare, 125–6
ethnic
  conflict, 8, 15
  groups, 26, 30, 39, 117, 145
  minorities, 9–10
ethnicity, 8, 36, 81, 117
ethos
  of engagement, 110; *see also* Connolly,
    William E.
  community, 96
  universalizing, 43
European, 4, 14, 27, 30, 35, 40, 41, 43, 45,
    112, 135, 140, 145, 152, 156, 158
exemptions, 60–1, 70, 141–3, 181–2
exit
  freedom to, 60, 143–4, 162, 197
expensive tastes
  objection and equality of resources,
    125–8
extinguishment
  of native title, 147–8; *see also* Native Title

fairness, 4, 17, 75, 82, 98, 106, 110, 126,
    137, 185, 190
First Nations (Canada), 167
Fish, Stanley, 74–5
Foucault, Michel, 20, 33, 49, 52, 70, 72,
    116, 169–70
freedom, 6, 9, 10, 16, 19, 21, 27, 30, 31, 32,
    37, 43, 45, 52, 63, 64, 66, 70, 75, 79, 88,
    89, 94, 95, 96, 106, 113, 115, 116, 119,
    122, 127, 129, 130, 132, 137, 140, 141,
    152–3, 154, 155, 166, 164
  of association, 27, 45, 58–59, 60, 62, 126
  and culture, 37, 39, 64–5, 67, 124–5,
    152
  effective, 11, 22, 92, 135, 138, 152
  individual, 6, 32, 67, 75, 89
  practice-dependent conception of,
    132–3
  real, 123, 134, 136, 140, 160, 161
  'state' versus 'voluntarist' conception
    of, 179
functioning
  as compared with capability, 11,
    122–3, 129, 130, 131, 133, 134,
    137
  public, 135

Gauthier, David, 76–8, 85
gender, 1, 81, 141
Goodin, Robert E., 53, 179
government, 1, 16, 31, 60, 65, 72, 116, 130,
    136, 137, 144, 145, 146, 147, 148, 149,
    150, 205

minimal, 31, 51
  *see also* self-government
governmental
  interests, 140, 149, 152
  relations between indigenous peoples
    and the state, 150, 151
  relationship to land, 149, 150, 200
governmentality, 33, 45
governmentalisation of the state, 116
groups
  in political philosophy, 62
group membership, 32, 59, 61–2, 112, 127,
    140, 152, 154, 155, 157, 203
group representation, 201
group rights, 6, 27, 41, 59, 61, 63, 64, 65,
    66, 68, 69, 70, 103, 135, 153, 155
  and individual rights, 42, 59, 66, 68,
    69–70, 103, 135, 155, 164
  Kymlicka's theory of, 64–7, 124–6, 182
  and liberalism, 50, 66, 68, 69, 70, 95
guilt
  and moral responsibility, 101–2, 108

Habermas, Jurgen, 10, 88, 118, 197
Hegel, G. W. F.: *see* reconciliation.
Held, David, 116
historical
  character of philosophical argument,
    43
  circumstances, 3, 22, 85, 113, 153,
    162
  communities, 57, 62, 64, 97
  contexts, 7, 9, 50, 55, 71, 98, 107, 138
  dimensions of public reason, 97–8
  frameworks, 53, 55, 102
  injustice, 10, 15, 26, 27, 28, 29, 48,
    61, 64, 93, 95–111; argument for
    Aboriginal rights, 26–7, 28, 61, 64;
    and liberal theories of justice,
    98–107
  interpretation, 10, 12
  legacy of colonialism, 40, 107, 159
  time, conflicts over the meaning of, 10,
    93
history, 40, 96, 101, 102, 103, 106, 107, 108,
    111, 127, 166
  of indigenous–state relations, 10, 15,
    17, 25–7, 95–6, 107, 152
  of injustice, 5, 61
  of liberal political thought, 33, 34
  of nation-building, 15, 69, 106
  and public reason, 17, 21, 22, 96–8
human rights, 3, 56, 98, 110, 132, 140, 141,
    186; *see also* rights
hybridity, 8, 37–38, 41–2, 48, 177

identity, 41, 47, 50, 52, 53, 54, 62, 65, 69,
    77, 86–9, 94, 95, 102, 103, 104, 105,
    106, 142, 167, 168
  individual, 41, 62
  multinational, 166

identity (*contd.*)
  national, 15, 26, 65, 166, 172
  political, 41, 103, 108
  related differences, 67–8, 83, 93
  relations, 95–6, 108
identification
  complex, 9, 41, 48
Ignatieff, Michael, 167
immigrants, 83, 100, 190
incommensurability, 22, 32, 36
individual rights: *see* rights
individualism, 18, 31, 47, 71
  holistic, 51–2
  liberalism and, 9, 31, 47, 49, 53, 54,
    71
  mediated, 50–5
  methodological, 32, 41, 48
  moral, 47, 49, 51, 160
*Indian Act* (Canada), 183, 203
Indian Bill of Rights, 153
indigenous
  alterity, 44, 73–4
  claims, 1, 14, 15, 19, 20, 21, 24, 25,
    26, 27, 29, 59, 99, 100, 115, 120,173
  communities, 12, 48, 108, 150, 152,
    159, 161, 165
  difference, 125, 196
  groups, 38, 120, 127–128, 155
  institutions, 137, 150
  land use agreements, 149, 150
  law, 156, 140, 141, 144–54, 156, 157
  and non-indigenous relations, 1, 11,
    28, 101, 108
  normative orders, 144, 151, 160, 162
  norms, 137, 157
  peoples, 1, 2, 3, 4, 5, 9, 10, 11, 12, 13,
    14, 15, 17, 22, 25, 30, 33, 34, 36,
    39, 44, 45, 46, 59, 65, 68, 69, 73,
    74, 81, 91, 92, 95, 96, 97, 98, 99,
    100, 101, 103, 104, 107, 110, 112,
    113, 116, 124, 125, 126, 127, 128,
    130, 135, 140, 141, 145, 146, 147,
    149, 150, 151, 152, 153, 154, 157,
    159, 160, 161, 167, 194
  political theory, 163
  rights, 11, 107, 136; *see also* Aboriginal
    rights
  and settler relations, 25–6
  societies, 24, 36, 154
  sovereignty, 196
  and state relations, 10, 17, 95–6, 107
*Indigenous Land Corporation*, 147
inequality, 25, 48, 114, 120
institutional design, 12
  model of cultural accommodation, 12,
    143–4, 197
*International Convention on the Elimination of
  All Forms of Racial Discrimination*, 199
interests, 3, 18, 28, 32, 38, 50, 60, 62, 67,
  68, 69, 70, 73, 76, 80, 81, 85, 87, 93,
  115, 118, 125, 130, 133, 135, 137, 141,

  143, 145, 146, 147, 148, 149, 150, 152,
    153, 154, 155, 157, 158, 161, 163, 165,
    166
  Aboriginal, 112, 133, 135–8
  of Aboriginal women, 157
  collective, 47, 104, 126
  group, 32, 56
  indigenous, 11, 12, 13, 32, 38, 136,
    140, 150–3, 154
  and rights, 3, 12, 150–1
international law, 15, 28, 44, 45, 56, 123,
  140, 196

Jonas, William, 113
jurisdiction, 68, 10, 112, 127, 143, 146, 152,
  154
jurisdictional authority, 143
justice, 1, 3, 6, 7, 9, 10, 11, 13, 15, 17, 21,
  22, 23, 26, 29, 30, 43, 46–7, 49, 54, 57,
  60, 62, 64, 73, 75, 79, 80, 84, 87, 89, 90,
  91, 92, 93, 94, 101, 108, 109, 111, 113,
  116, 120, 126, 127, 140, 166
  as capabilities, 123
  backward-looking, 99, 100, 101
  capabilities approach to, 122, 123,
    128–37, 138
  corrective, 101
  criminal, 155, 156
  distributive, 8, 11, 46, 78, 100, 119,
    121, 122, 124, 128
  forward-looking, 99–101, 108
  as mutual advantage, 76–7, 85
  postcolonial conception of, 19, 78, 79
  registers of, 46–7, 81, 90, 100, 105
  theories of, 6, 17, 22, 27, 48, 49, 62,
    64, 66, 72, 75, 76, 119, 128, 129,
    130, 132
justification, 3, 5, 20, 22, 24, 28, 32, 34, 40,
  43, 73, 77, 82, 89, 93, 99, 115, 130, 156
  of Aboriginal rights, 125–30, 137
  mutual, 23, 77, 118
  public, 14, 18, 19, 73, 75–80
justificatory ideal of liberalism, 9, 10, 14–29,
  71

Kukathas, Chandran, 182
Kymlicka, Will, 64–7, 124–6, 182

Laden, Anthony, 193, 194, 197
land, 21, 26, 34, 38, 62, 66, 99, 100, 108,
  140, 146, 147, 148, 149, 150, 189
  Aboriginal, 15, 22, 100
  Aboriginal interests in, 62, 69, 125,
    135, 138
  claims, 64, 164
  indigenous, 24, 25, 26, 112, 127
  interests in, 11, 125, 149
  law, 155, 156
  rights, 27, 60, 114, 124, 145, 148,
    159, 160, 168
  traditional, 98, 163, 164, 166, 167

Land Councils (Australia), 136
language, 25, 39, 42, 44, 45, 48, 52, 62, 63,
    65, 67, 68, 81, 82, 83, 125, 166, 186
    of rights, 2, 164
law
    Aboriginal, 1, 134–5, 145, 155–6, 157,
        158
    Australian, 157
    common, 4, 28, 34, 72, 74, 78, 82, 83,
        91, 107, 140, 145, 146, 147, 150,
        154;
    common-law doctrine of
        Aboriginal rights, 2, 4, 20;
    common-law mode of incorporation,
        149–51
    customary, 64, 146
    exemptions from, 60, 65
    generally applicable, 140, 141–2
    imperial constitutional, 145
    indigenous: see indigenous law
    international: see international law
    property, 108
    rule of, 115, 118, 145
legal
    doctrines, 1, 114
    institutions, 60, 117, 119, 143, 144, 145
    norms, 126, 134
    order, 35, 149, 158, 162
    recognition of, 38, 43
    rights, 3
    systems, 3, 140, 145, 147, 152, 157,
        158, 161, 165
    traditions, 134, 136
    theories, 101, 149
legitimacy, 2, 3, 17–20, 22–23, 47, 57, 78–9,
    91, 92, 95, 97, 100, 101, 103, 107, 112,
    114, 116, 128, 132, 133, 142, 161, 185
Levy, Jacob T., 61, 145–6, 181–2, 199
liberal
    account of the relation between land, cul-
        ture and justice, 21–2
    democracies, 1, 5, 12, 14, 17, 41, 61,
        86, 87, 90, 103, 112, 123, 164, 166
    democracy, 58, 70–71
    egalitarianism, 31, 118, 128, 131
    equality, 114, 119, 120, 124, 129,
        135–6
    freedom, 106, 119
    group rights, 64, 66
    individualism: see individualism
    institutions, 2, 5, 12, 18, 35
    justice, 1, 29, 47, 99
    modalities of government, 136, 137
    multiculturalism, 44, 66, 74
    nationalism, 55
    norms, 33, 136, 137, 157, 160
    political theory/thought, 5, 6, 16, 21,
        22, 24, 26, 33, 34, 41, 42, 43, 49,
        51, 119, 163
    post-, 22
    postcolonial political order, 113, 133,
        135, 163, 166

respect, 44, 74
rights, 21, 51, 59, 62, 69, 91, 103,
    115, 138
societies, 13, 16, 41, 52, 133, 137, 165
states, 5, 10, 15, 16, 19, 25, 32, 44, 54,
    58–59, 60, 66, 67, 72, 74, 95, 96,
    135, 145, 151, 161
theories of justice, 10, 11, 22, 48, 49, 80
values, 5, 43
liberals and communitarians, 49, 53, 103
liberalism, 6, 14–16, 17, 19, 20, 21, 22, 25,
    28, 30, 31–2, 33, 34, 39, 43, 44, 45, 46,
    47, 48, 49, 50–1, 52, 53, 58, 59, 84, 118,
    126, 132, 139, 140, 163, 164
    and Aboriginal rights, 124
    and colonialism, 5, 17, 34, 39, 40, 43
    and culture, 33–4
    and cultural diversity: see cultural
        diversity
    and deep diversity, 22
    egalitarian, 10, 118
    going local, the idea of, 5, 11, 85
    and indigenous peoples, 22, 34–5
    inter-cultural, 39
    political, 2, 5, 80, 129
    postcolonial critique of, 39–48, 49,
        53–4, 55, 71
    poststructuralist critique of, 89–90
    and universalism, 45–7, 49
liberty, 27, 45, 52, 58, 98, 129
    and empire, 25
    see also freedom
liberties, 120, 135
    basic, 121, 130
Locke, John, 18, 20, 31, 45, 115

Mabo v Queensland (No. 2) (1992), 60,
    146–9, 167
Macedo, Stephen, 170
majority, 68
    culture, 1, 65, 124
    nation, 57–58, 65
    rule, 69
McNeil, Kent, 200
membership, 104–6, 152, 154, 155
    affective dimension of, 109–10
    cultural, 8, 38, 51, 62, 64–7
    group, 32, 59, 61, 62
    rules, 155, 157, 183, 203
Metis nation, 154, 167
Mill, John Stuart, 34, 45, 62
Mills, Charles
    and the racial contract, 24
minority
    cultures, 57
    groups, 15, 39, 44, 47, 62–3, 65, 66,
        68, 97, 125, 127, 128
    nationalism, 15, 65
    rights, 42–4, 67, 69, 70, 126
modus vivendi, 9, 21, 28, 73, 76, 80, 84–8,
    138, 186
    discursive, 10, 85, 95, 130, 186

*modus vivendi (contd.)*
    dynamic, 84–5, 86, 95
    static, 78, 84, 85, 186
    *see also* complex mutual coexistence
morality, 19, 21, 22, 46, 57, 76, 96, 98, 103,
    105
multiculturalism, 6, 12, 33, 44, 48, 57, 66,
    70, 76, 116, 119, 120, 182
    liberal critique of, 68
multinational, 24–25
    corporations, 116, 149, 150
    identity, 166
    rights, 69
    societies, 44, 166
    states, 70, 165, 166
multiple
    affiliations, 141, 142
    realizability of basic capabilities, 130,
    137

Nagel, Thomas, 32
nation, 33, 40, 50, 51, 56, 72, 113, 130
    Aboriginal, 4, 58, 135, 151
    -building, 15, 26, 41, 58, 69, 106
    civilized vs barbarous, 28
    European, 24, 140, 145, 151
    indigenous, 112, 151–2
    state, 26, 48, 56, 116, 136
    stateless, 15, 30, 56, 116
nationhood, 40
national
    cultures, 42, 65, 116
    groups, 12, 44, 50, 70, 163, 166
    identity, 15, 25, 26, 42, 166, 172
    minorities, 65, 66, 67, 177
    multi-, 69, 70
    unity, 92, 165
nationalism, 25, 55, 65, 128
Native Title, 108, 146–50
*Native Title Act 1993* (Australia), 147, 148,
    150
*Native Title Amendment Act 1998* (Australia),
    147
negotiations, 57, 97, 135, 140, 166, 192
neutrality, 16–7, 81
New Zealand, 4, 15, 26, 203
norms, 5, 6, 7, 8, 10, 11, 12, 14, 16, 17, 18,
    20, 22, 23, 33, 34, 37, 38, 39, 42, 43, 47,
    60, 69, 73, 74, 75, 76, 78, 82, 83, 84, 85,
    89, 90, 96, 97, 98, 101, 103, 107, 109,
    110, 111, 116, 117, 118, 123, 126, 129,
    133, 136, 137, 138, 140, 141, 142, 145,
    152, 155, 157, 160, 161, 166
Northern Territory, 148, 156
Nussbaum, Martha, 123, 128–34

O'Neill, Onora, 29
O'Neill, Shane, 57
opportunity, 10, 110, 129, 134, 150, 155,
    157, 165

and responsibility, 195
    *see also* equal opportunity

pastoral lease, 148, 199
Parekh, Bhikhu, 41, 63
Patton, Paul, 178
Pearson, Noel, 146, 158–9, 160
Pettit, Philip, 169
Pippin, Robert
    on conceptions of freedom, 179
pluralism, 5, 9, 22, 31, 32, 33, 48, 86, 89
    cultural, 5, 61, 89
    reasonable, 16, 23, 80, 86, 89, 90, 121,
    123, 124, 129, 131
Pocock, J. G. A., 93
political
    arrangements, 2, 4, 5, 14, 51, 71, 76,
    84, 85, 92, 166
    associations, 16, 62
    belonging, 13
    boundaries, 42
    communities, 2, 15, 18, 24, 52, 57, 58,
    63, 67, 97, 102–103, 104–5, 106,
    107, 108, 128
    conception of justice, 19, 78–9; *see also*
    Rawls, John
    contractarianism, 54, 75
    culture, 103, 160
    deliberation, 32, 80, 88, 144
    disadvantage, 30, 101
    discourse, 46, 90
    division, 9, 54, 55–58, 71
    identification, 32, 48, 49
    identities, 10, 42, 48, 86
    impartiality, 109
    institutions, 9, 15, 18, 23, 60, 76, 79,
    85, 105, 117, 150, 153, 166
    interaction, 17, 43, 74
    liberalism, 2, 6, 31, 80, 129; *see also*
    Rawls, John
    liberties, 59–60, 61
    morality, 98, 103
    norms, 5, 6, 16, 78, 80, 84, 85, 126,
    134
    order, 2, 20, 34, 35, 133, 164
    philosophy, 2, 7, 8, 34, 43, 62
    pluralism, 86, 89
    power, 18, 19, 32, 71, 73, 78, 79, 80,
    89, 95, 118, 142, 145
    rights, 59, 70, 130
    recognition, 38, 43
    societies, 45, 78, 118
    stability, 92
political theory/thought, 6, 12, 16, 21, 22,
    24, 25, 26, 29, 30, 33, 34, 39, 41, 42, 49,
    52, 91, 119, 120, 163
*Political Liberalism* (Rawls), 7, 80, 123, 126,
    167, 169
politics, 11, 50, 74, 89, 90, 91, 92, 93, 96,
    108, 109, 111, 114

of becoming, 47–8, 89, 90, 110; *see also* Connolly, William E.
circumstances of, 95; *see also* Waldron, Jeremy
of recognition, 10, 88
Poole, Ross, 14–15
postcolonial
    challenge to liberalism, 9, 30, 47
    critics of liberalism, 24, 42, 45, 47, 66, 119, 124
    critique of liberalism, 33, 39–47, 49, 53–5, 66
    liberal political order, 163, 166
    societies, 10, 44, 95
    state, 10, 11, 12, 17, 23, 26, 56, 72, 73, 96, 112–39, 113, 116, 119
    theorists, 39, 40–41, 43–4, 45, 46
    theory, 20, 34, 39, 40, 42, 119; as anti-foundational and anti-essentialist, 176
postcolonialism, 26, 120
poststructuralist
    critiques of liberalism, 88–90
Povinelli, Elizabeth, 44, 74, 184
power, 1, 9, 16, 21, 22, 36, 44, 52, 75, 76, 79, 80, 84, 90, 115–116, 121, 128, 137, 138, 142, 143, 144–5
    as a dimension of public reason, 9, 73, 74–5
    governmental, 116
    political, 7, 18, 19, 29, 32, 71, 73, 76, 78, 82, 89, 95, 118
    relations of, 3, 4, 6, 22, 24, 38, 40, 52, 54, 55, 67, 70, 91, 97, 108, 111, 112, 122, 132, 139
    social, 132–3, 135, 142, 162
Prakash, Gyan, 40–1, 45
property, 3, 45, 100, 108, 135, 136, 138, 143, 145, 146, 149, 200
public reason, 4, 7, 9, 10, 11, 16, 17, 18, 19, 21, 22, 28, 29, 47, 54, 72–94, 95, 96, 103, 106–107, 109, 111, 133, 136, 142, 153, 166, 198
    five dimensions of, 9, 73, 74–9
    and history, 96–8
    interpretive dimensions of, 97–8
    liberal, 1, 4, 48
    pluralization of, 73, 91
    Rawls's conception of, 7–8, 75, 77–80, 96
public reasoning, 54, 69, 74, 135, 164, 196
public sphere, 11, 23, 24, 26, 42, 60, 73, 75, 82, 83, 85, 87, 90, 91, 107, 133, 142, 164, 196
punishment, 102, 131, 154–8, 204
    Aboriginal conceptions of, 157
    indigenous conceptions of, 155–6

Quebec
    nationalism, 128

race, 8, 36, 62, 81, 104, 117

*Racial Discrimination Act* (1975) (Australia), 147, 199
racial contract, 24
rationality, 53, 71
Rawls, John, 2, 7–8, 16, 19, 31, 51, 75, 77, 78–80, 174, 198
reason, 7, 9, 20, 43–4, 78, 79, 80, 95, 133, 142, 163
    communicative, 142
    and community, 9, 49–55, 71
    and force, 78
    neutral, 16–17
    and power, 84
reasonable, 21, 27, 29, 32, 77, 79, 80, 85, 87–8, 107, 112
    and the unreasonable, 8, 21, 54, 87, 91
reasonableness, 17, 20, 24, 45, 47, 71, 72, 107, 138
recognition, 24, 27, 38, 42, 44, 48, 50, 54, 61, 62, 67, 68, 69, 83, 89, 93, 100, 106, 113, 118–119, 133, 136, 142, 144, 151, 154, 155, 156, 157, 159, 160, 166
    legal, 38, 43
    mutual, 82, 133, 134
    political, 38, 43
    politics of, 10, 88
    rule of, 153
reconciliation, 8, 46, 94, 99, 169
    Hegel's concept of, 7
    process in Australia, 188
    in Rawls, 7, 169
relativism, 32, 35–6, 117
resistance, 25, 82
resources: see *equality*
responsibility, 94, 96, 99, 101–8, 121, 134, 152, 156, 165
    collective, 90, 105, 108
    individual, 20, 90
Reynolds, Henry, 173, 180
rights, 2–3, 4, 27, 28, 33, 34, 38, 46, 47, 56, 58, 61, 65, 66, 67, 69, 70, 88, 90, 99, 100, 103, 136, 141, 142, 143, 145, 146, 148, 149, 150, 151, 160, 164, 165, 183
    basic, 12, 56, 141, 142, 143, 152, 154
    and belonging, 103–4, 106, 107
    citizenship, 27, 92, 98, 103, 138, 146
    collective, 11, 27, 33, 34, 58–60, 61, 64, 68, 135, 136
    cultural, 5, 39, 58, 59, 68, 113
    economic, 69, 130
    individual, 22, 27, 31, 32, 42, 48, 51, 59, 61, 62, 135, 136
    'inherent', 156
    land, 27, 60, 114, 124, 145, 148, 159, 160
    liberal, 12, 51, 59, 62, 69, 91, 103, 115, 138
    minority, 42–4, 67, 69, 70, 126
    native title, 148–50
    and norms, 103–4
    political, 50, 59, 70, 130

rights (*contd.*)
　property, 145
　self-government, 22, 27, 50, 70, 146,
　　152, 156, 166
　'special', 27, 91, 99
　treaty, 153
　*see also* Aboriginal rights; group rights;
　　human rights; indigenous rights
Rowse, Tim, 136
*Royal Commission on Aboriginal Peoples* (1996)
　(Canada), 58, 168, 201, 203, 204, 205
*Royal Proclamation* (1763), 151, 201

Said, Edward, 33–4
Sandel, Michael, 4
Scanlon, T. M.
　on moral responsibility, 195
Shachar, Ayelet, 143–4
　on transformative accommodation,
　　143–4, 158
self-
　determination, 30, 34, 44, 50, 52, 56,
　　114, 116, 128
　government, 11, 22, 26, 27, 34, 44, 50,
　　56, 57, 61, 62, 65, 67, 69, 70, 100,
　　107, 112, 113, 116, 124, 125, 127,
　　128, 132, 135, 136, 138, 141,
　　146–58, 164, 165, 166, 200
　interest, 76–8, 84, 85, 92
　ownership, 132
　respect, 66, 121, 133, 134
　understanding, 92, 103, 149, 161
settlement, 147, 151, 199
　negotiated, 72, 150
　political, 87, 88, 111
settlers, 4, 25, 26, 45, 58, 151
shame,
　compared with guilt, 102–3
　and moral responsibility, 102–3, 108,
　　189
sovereign, 3, 56, 115, 147
　interests, 135–6, 150
sovereignty, 43, 56, 68, 112, 116, 145, 148,
　149, 156, 164, 200
　Aboriginal, 201
　Australian, 151, 200
　Canadian, 151
　coordinate, 112, 151
　Crown, 145
　inherent, 149
　shared, 56
　state, 112, 116
Sreenivasan, Gopal, 97
state, 3, 5, 6, 8, 10, 14, 15, 16, 17, 18, 20,
　26, 28, 33, 34, 42, 43, 44, 45, 50, 51, 56,
　57, 58, 62, 63, 67, 68, 72, 73, 75, 81, 91,
　96, 97, 98, 104, 107, 109, 112, 115, 118,
　124, 127, 131, 136, 137, 140, 141, 142,
　143, 144, 146, 150, 153, 155, 157, 161,
　163, 164, 166
　colonial, 100, 107

concept of, 115–7
liberal-democratic, 5, 12, 15, 58–59,
　96, 145
multicultural, 70
multinational, 70, 165, 166
nation, 26, 48, 56, 116, 136
postcolonial, 10, 11, 12, 17, 23, 26,
　56, 72, 73, 96, 112–39
settler, 58, 98, 112
state of nature, 85, 115
stateless nations, 15, 30, 56, 116
stolen generations, 188
Supreme Court, 201
　Canadian, 202
　United States, 202

Tamir, Yael, 105
Taylor, Charles, 7, 52, 145, 189
title, 148
　Native, 108, 146–50, 165
traditions, 3, 22, 28, 30, 57, 69, 136, 163,
　192, 196
treaty, 78, 80, 114
　making, 58, 150, 180
　negotiations, 168, 192
　rights, 153, 202
Tully, James, 81–3, 112, 173, 177, 182, 197,
　201, 205
Turner, Dale, 4

United Nations
　Charter of Rights, 44
　*Draft Declaration on the Rights of*
　　*Indigenous Peoples*, 2, 202
United States, 2, 15, 151, 152
universal, 10, 40, 45, 47
　norms, 123
　principles, 45, 54
　values, 45
universalism, 24, 33, 46, 49

value pluralism, 32
vulnerable
　members of groups, 38, 67, 70–1, 138,
　　141, 143, 144, 146, 154, 157, 159,
　　161

Walzer, Michael, 54, 55, 56–7, 58, 66, 97
Waldron, Jeremy, 21, 37–8, 99–101, 109, 172
Webber, Jeremy, 151, 190
Weber, Max, 115
White, Richard, 25, 173
Williams, Bernard, 102–3, 168, 189
Williams, Robert, 24
*Wik Peoples v Queensland* (1996), 148
women, 62, 66, 68, 83, 91, 134, 140
　Aboriginal, 157, 154, 194–5

Yanner, Murrandoo, 148
Young, Iris Marion, 169, 173